# 11 Years

## CBSE Class 10

# SOCIAL SCIENCE

## Previous Year-wise

Solved Papers (2013 - 2024) with Value Added Notes

**DISHA™**
Publication Inc

# DISHA Publications Inc.

45, 2nd Floor, Maharishi Dayanand Marg,
Corner Market, Malviya Nagar, new Delhi -110017
Tel: 49842349/ 49842350



## Typeset By

DISHA DTP Team

**Buying books from DISHA**

# Just Got A Lot More Rewarding!!!

We at DISHA Publication, value your feedback immensely and to show our apperciation of our reviewers, we have launched a review contest.

To participate in this reward scheme, just follow these quick and simple steps:
- Write a review of the product you purchase on Amazon/Flipkart.
- Take a screenshot/photo of your review.
- Mail it to *disha-rewards@aiets.co.in*, along with all your details.

Each month, selected reviewers will win exciting gifts from DISHA Publication. Note that the rewards for each month will be declared in the first week of next month on our website.

**https://bit.ly/review-reward-disha.**

## Write To
## Us At
feedback_disha@aiets.co.in

# Contents

# CBSE Social Science Class-X
# 2023-2024 Syllabus

| History: India and the Contemporary World - II | |
|---|---|
| **Chapter No. and Name** | **Specific Learning Objectives** |
| I. The Rise of Nationalism in Europe | • Examine the impact of the French Revolution on the European countries in the making of the Nation state.<br>• Explore the nature of the diverse social movements of the time. (1830-1848)<br>• Examine the ways by which the idea of nationalism emerged and led to the formation of nation states.<br>• Comprehend how the World War I was triggered by the scramble for colonies in the Balkan states |
| II. Nationalism in India | • Explore various facets of Nationalistic movements that ushered in the sense of Collective Belonging<br>• Discuss the impact of the first world war on triggering two defining movements (Khilafat & Non-cooperation Movement) in India.<br>• Assess/ appraise the role of Mahatma Gandhi and other leaders in the two movements (NCM & CDM) |
| III. The Making of a Global World<br>**Sub topic 1**<br>The pre modern world<br>**Sub topic 2**<br>19th century<br>1815 -1914<br>**Sub topic 3**<br>The inter- war economy<br>**Sub topic 4**<br>Rebuilding of world economy: the post war era. | • Explore various aspects of how the world changed profoundly in the 19th century in terms of Economic, Political, Social, Cultural and technological areas.<br>• Analyse the destructive impact of colonialism on the economy and the livelihoods of colonised people.<br>• Inter disciplinary Project with chapter 7 of Geography: Life lines of National Economy and chapter 4 of Economics:<br>• Globalization and the Indian Economy |
| IV. The Age of Industrialisation | • Examine economic, political, social features of Pre and Post Industrialization.<br>• Analyse the impact of Industrialisation in the colonies with specific focus on India. |
| V. Print culture and the Modern World. | • Examine the development of Print from its beginnings in East Asia to its expansion in Europe and India<br>• Analyse the impact of the spread of technology and consider how social life and culture changed with coming of print |

| Political Science: Democratic Politics - II | |
|---|---|
| I. Power - sharing | • Examines and comprehendshow democracies handle demands and need for power sharing.<br>• Analyse the Challenges faced by countries like Belgium and Sri Lanka ensuring effective powersharing |
| II. Federalism | • Comprehend the theory andPractice of Federalism in India.<br>• Analyse the policies and politics that has strengthened federalism in practice. |
| III. Gender, Religion and Caste | • Examines the role and differences of Gender, religion and Caste in practicing Democracy inIndia.<br>• Analyses the different expressions based on these  differences are healthy or<br>• otherwise in a democracy |
| IV. Political Parties | • Examine the role, purpose and no. of Political Parties in Democracy<br>• Evaluates the contributions made by national and regional political parties in making or otherwise of Indian democracy. |
| V. Outcomes of Democracy | • Comprehends the expected and actual outcomes of democracy in view of quality of government, economic wellbeing, in equality, social differences, conflict, freedom and dignity.<br>• Analyses the reasons behind gap that occurs in conversion of expected outcomes into actual outcomes of democracy in various respects: quality of government, economic well- being, inequality, social differences and conflict and finally freedom and dignity |

| Geography: Contemporary India - II | |
|---|---|
| I. Resources and Development | • Examine the significance, interdependence, utilizationdevelopment need of Planning of resources in India.<br>• Summarise the rationale fordevelopment of resources<br>• Comprehends the reasons for non-optimal utilization ofland in India.<br>• Analyse the need to conserve all the resources<br>• Examine the significant rolefor resource planning in thelight of the present requirements in India |

| | |
|---|---|
| II. Forest and Wildlife Resources | • Examine the importance of conserving forests and wild life and their interdependencyin maintaining the ecology forthe sustainable development of India.<br>• Analyse the role of grazingand wood cutting in the development and degradation<br>• Comprehends the reasons for conservation of biodiversity in India under sustainable development. |
| III. Water Resources | • Examine the reasons forconservation of water resource in India.<br>• Analyse and infer how the Multipurpose projects are supporting the requirementof water in India. |
| IV. Agriculture | • Examine the crucial role played by agriculture in oureconomy and society.<br>• Analyses the challengesfaced by the farming community in India.<br>• Comprehends the various aspects of agriculture, including crop production, types of farming, modern agricultural practices, and the impact of agriculture on the environment. |
| V. Minerals and Energy Resources | • Comprehends the formation of different types of minerals, location, their uses, importance for human life and the economy.<br>• Analyses the importance of minerals and natural resources for economic development of the country their distribution, and sustainable use.<br>• Distinguishes between the conventional and non- conventional sources of energy . |
| VI. Manufacturing Industries | • Distinguishes between various types of manufacturing industries based on their input materials, processes, and end products, and analysetheir significance in the Indian economy.<br>• Examines the impact of manufacturing industries on the environment, and develop strategies for sustainable development ofthe manufacturing sector.<br>• Analyses the relation between the availability of raw material and location ofthe Industry |
| VII. Life Lines of National Economy | • Inter disciplinary project with chapter 3 of History: The making of a Global world and chapter 4 of Economics: Globalization and the Indian Economy |



| | |
|---|---|
| I. Development | • Examine the significance of designing suitable developmental goals in shaping the nation.<br>• Examine the importance of per capita income and compare the per capita income of various countries to infer about reasons for the variance<br>• Analyse the HDI in relation to PCI.<br>• Examine the need for Sustainable development |
| II. Sectors of the Indian Economy | • Analyse and evaluate the economic activities in different sectors and how they contribute to the overall growth and development of the Indian economy.<br>• Identify problems in different sectors and propose solutions based on their understanding of the sectors.<br>• Analyse the major employment generating sectors and observe the challenges faced in an effort to provide employment to all.<br>• Examines the role of Unorganised sector in impacting PCI currently and proposes suggestive steps to reduce the unorganised sector for more productive contributions to GDP |
| III. Money and Credit | • Examine money as a medium of exchange in all transactions of goods and services since ancient times to the present times.<br>• Analyse the different sources of credit<br>• Identify the significance and role of self-help groups in the betterment of the economic condition of rural people/women. |
| IV. Globalization and the Indian Economy<br>**Sub topics:**<br>What is Globalization?<br>Factors that have enabled Globalisation<br>**Sub topics:**<br>Production across the countries Chinese toys in India World Trade Organisation The Struggle For A Fair Globalisation | • Examine the concept of globalization and its definition, evolution, and impact on the global economy.<br>• Explore the details of the key drivers of globalization and their role in shaping the<br>• global economic landscape in various countries<br>• Examines the significance of role of G20 and its significance in the light of India's present role<br>• **Inter disciplinary Project** with chapter 3 of History: "The making of a Global World" and chapter 7 of Geography: "Lifelines of National Economy" |
| V. Consumer Rights<br>**OR**<br>Social Issues<br>**OR**<br>Sustainable Development | Project work |

| Subject | Name of the Chapter | List of areas to be pointed on the Map |
|---|---|---|
| History | Nationalism in India | **I. Congress sessions:**<br>• 1920 Calcutta<br>• 1920 Nagpur.<br>• 1927 Madras session,<br>**II. 3 Satyagraha movements:**<br>• Kheda<br>• Champaran.<br>• Ahmedabad mill workers<br>**III. Jallianwala Bagh**<br>**IV. Dandi March** |
| Geography | Resources and Development Water Resources | **Locating and Labelling:**<br>• Salal<br>• Bhakra Nangal<br>• Tehri<br>• Rana Pratap Sagar |
| | Agriculture | **Identify:**<br>• Major areas of Rice and Wheat<br>• Largest/ Major producer states of Sugarcane, Tea, Coffee, Rubber, Cotton and Jute |
| | Minerals and Energy Resources | **Identify:**<br>**a. Iron Ore mines**<br>• Mayurbhanj<br>• Durg<br>• Bailadila<br>• Bellary<br>• Kudremukh<br>**b. Oil Fields**<br>• Digboi<br>• Naharkatia<br>• Mumbai High<br>• Bassien<br>• Kalol<br>• Ankaleshwar<br>**Locate & label: Power Plants**<br>**a. Nuclear**<br>• Narora<br>• Kakrapara<br>• Tarapur<br>• Kalpakkam |
| | Manufacturing Industries | **I. Manufacturing Industries (Locating and Labelling only)**<br>**Iron and Steel Plants:**<br>a. Durgapur b. Bokaro c. Jamshedpur d. Bhilai e. Vijayanagar f. Salem |
| | Lifelines of National Economy | **Locating and Labelling:**<br>**a. Major sea ports**<br>• Kandla<br>• Mumbai<br>• Marmagao<br>• New Mangalore<br>• Kochi<br>**b. International Airports:**<br>• Amritsar (Raja Sansi - Sri Guru Ram Dass jee)<br>• Delhi (Indira Gandhi)<br>• Mumbai (Chhatrapati Shivaji) |

# All India 2023

# CBSE Board Solved Paper

## SECTION - A

**(Multiple Choice Questions)**

(20 × 1 = 20)

1. In which one of the following regions is the participation of women in public life the highest? **1**

   (a) Nordic countries   (b) Arab states

   (c) European countries   (d) Asian countries

2. Match Column I with Column II and choose the correct option. **1**

   | Column I | | Column II | |
   |---|---|---|---|
   | i. | Union List | 1. | Agriculture |
   | ii. | State List | 2. | Computer Software |
   | iii. | Concurrent List | 3. | Banking |
   | iv. | Residuary Subjects | 4. | Education |

   **Options:**

   (a) i - 3, ii - 1, iii - 4, iv - 2

   (b) i - 4, ii - 3, iii - 2, iv - 1

   (c) i - 2, ii - 4, iii - 3, iv - 1

   (d) i - 1, ii - 2, iii - 3, iv - 4

3. Which one of the following is an example of 'coming together federation'? **1**

   (a) India   (b) USA

   (c) Belgium   (d) Spain

4. There are two statements given as Assertion (A) and **Reason (R):** Read both the statements and choose the correct option. **1**

   **Assertion (A):** Belgium amended their constitution four times.

   **Reason (R):** Amendments were to enable everyone to live together in the same country.

   (a) Both Assertion (A) and Reason (R) are true and Reason (R) is the correct explanation of the Assertion (A).

   (b) Both Assertion (A) and Reason (R) are true, but Reason (R) is not the correct explanation of the Assertion (A).

   (c) Assertion (A) is true, but Reason (R) is false.

   (d) Assertion (A) is false, but Reason (R) is true.

5. Match Column I with Column II and choose the correct option. **1**

   | Column I | | Column II | |
   |---|---|---|---|
   | **(Port)** | | **(Type)** | |
   | i. | Kandla | 1. | Riverine port |
   | ii. | Mumbai | 2. | Deepest landlocked port |
   | iii. | Visakhapatnam | 3. | Biggest port |
   | iv. | Kolkata | 4. | Port developed after independence |

   Options:

   (a) i - 4, ii - 3, iii - 2, iv - 1

   (b) i - 2, ii - 1, iii - 3, iv - 4

   (c) i - 2, ii - 4, iii - 1, iv - 3

   (d) i - 1, ii - 2, iii - 4, iv - 3

6. There are two statements given as Assertion (A) and Reason (R). Read both the statements and choose the correct option. **1**

   **Assertion (A):** Agriculture and industry move hand in hand.

   **Reason (R):** Industrial development is a precondition for eradication of unemployment and poverty from the country.

   (a) Both Assertion (A) and Reason (R) are true and Reason (R) is the correct explanation of the Assertion (A).

(b) Both Assertion (A) and Reason (R) are true, but Reason (R) is not the correct explanation of the Assertion (A).

(c) Assertion (A) is true, but Reason (R) is false.

(d) Assertion (A) is false, but Reason (R) is true.

7. Which one of the following soils develops in an area with high temperature and heavy rainfall?                    1

(a) Red and Yellow        (b) Black

(c) Alluvial              (d) Laterite

8. Look at the picture given below. Identify the name of the senior littérateur shown in the image and choose the correct option.                    1

(a) Ram Mohan Roy

(b) Raja Ravi Varma

(c) Lakshminath Bezbaruah

(d) Gangadhar Bhattacharya

**Note:** The following question is for the **Visually Impaired Candidates** only, in lieu of Q. No. 8.

Who among the following is the writer of 'Gulamgiri'?

(a) Dr. B.R. Ambedkar       (b) E.V. Periyar

(c) Jyotiba Phule           (d) Ram Mohan Roy

9. In which one of the following countries was 'mass production' an important feature in the 1920s?        1

(a) United States of America

(b) Poland

(c) France

(d) Japan

10. Choose the correct option from the following regarding Central Powers in the First World War:        1

(a) Germany, Austria-Hungary and Ottoman Turkey

(b) Britain, France and Russia

(c) Italy, Japan and Russia

(d) France, Austria-Hungary and China

11. Which one of the following ideologies were the European Governments driven by after the defeat of Napoleon in 1815?        1

(a) Socialism          (b) Conservation

(c) Liberalism         (d) Romanticism

12. Which one of the following is a challenge of Globalisation?

(a) Access to New Markets        1

(b) Access to New Talent

(c) International Recruitment

(d) Disproportionate Growth

13. Which one of the following categories of urban households take the highest percentage of loan from the formal sector?        1

(a) Poor households

(b) Households with few assets

(c) Well-off households

(d) Rich households

14. Which one of the following is the modern form of currency?        1

(a) Paper notes          (b) Gold coins

(c) Silver coins         (d) Copper coins

15. Which one of the following is a feature of the unorganized sector?        1

(a) Terms of employment are regular.

(b) People have assured work.

(c) They have some formal processes and procedures.

(d) There are rules and regulations but not followed.

16. Natural products being changed into other forms is known as:        1

(a) Primary product

(b) Secondary product

(c) Tertiary product

(d) Quaternary product

17. Which of the following States is ruled by a regional party?        1

(a) Haryana          (b) Madhya Pradesh

(c) Odisha           (d) Rajasthan

**18.** Which one of the following countries adopted multi-party system? **1**

(a) USA

(b) India

(c) China

(d) United Kingdom

**19.** Choose the correct option to fill in the blank. **1**

For comparing countries, their ________ is considered to be one of the most important attributes by the World Bank.

(a) Education

(b) Income

(c) Health Status

(d) Living Standard

**20.** Study the given table and answer the question that follow: **1**

Some data regarding India and its Neighbours for 2019

| Country | Gross National Income (GNI) per capita (2011 PPP $) | Life Expectancy at birth | Mean Years of Schooling of People aged 25 and above | HDI Rank in the world (2018) |
|---|---|---|---|---|
| Sri Lanka | 12,707 | 77 | 10.6 | 73 |
| India | 6,681 | 69.7 | 6.5 | 130 |
| Myanmar | 4,961 | 67.1 | 5.0 | 148 |
| Pakistan | 5,005 | 67.3 | 5.2 | 154 |
| Nepal | 3,457 | 70.8 | 5.0 | 143 |
| Bangladesh | 4,976 | 72.6 | 6.2 | 134 |

Which of the following countries has the highest level of 'Human Development Index (HDI)'?

(a) India      (b) Bangladesh      (c) Sri Lanka      (d) Nepal

# SECTION - B

### (Very Short Answer Type Questions)

**(4 × 2 = 8)**

**21.** Why did the feeling of alienation increase among the Sri Lankan Tamils in 1956? Explain. **2**

**22.** Explain any two causes of depletion of forests during the colonial period in India. **2**

**23.** (a) Analyse the role of Chief Minister Cavour who led the movement to unite the regions of Italy. **2**

**OR**

(b) Examine the ideas of liberal nationalism in Europe during the nineteenth century.

**24.** Differentiate between formal and informal sources of loans. **2**

# SECTION - C

### (Short Answer Type Questions)

**(5 × 3 = 15)**

**25.** Examine the rising importance of the tertiary sector in India. **3**

**26.** Analyse any three ways to conserve energy resources. **3**

**27.** Suggest any three ways to enhance political participation of women in India. **3**

**28.** Differentiate between secondary and tertiary sectors with examples. **3**

**29.** (a) How did print come into existence in Europe? Explain. **3**

**OR**

(b) How did access to books create a new culture of reading? Explain. **3**

# SECTION - D

### (Long Answer Type Questions)

**(4 × 5 = 20)**

**30.** (a) Why did Gandhiji decide to launch a nationwide Satyagraha against the proposed Rowlatt Act, 1919. Explain. **5**

**OR**

(b) Why did the Non-Cooperation Movement spread to the countryside from the cities? Explain.   **5**

31. (a) How do Multinational Corporations (MNCs) interlink production across countries? Explain with examples.   **5**

**OR**

(b) Explain any five steps taken by the Central and State Governments to attract foreign investments.   **5**

32. (a) 'Democracy is a better form of government' Support this statement.   **5**

**OR**

(b) 'Democracy is an accountable and legitimate government' Support this statement.   **5**

33. (a) Explain the features of primitive subsistence and commercial farming in India.   **5**

**OR**

(b) Explain the features of intensive subsistence and plantation farming in India.   **5**

## SECTION - E

### (Case-Based Questions)

**(3 × 4 = 12)**

34. Read the given source and answer the questions that follow:

The rise of political parties is directly linked to the emergence of representative democracies. As we have seen, large societies need representative democracy. As societies became large and complex, they also needed some agency togather different views on various issues and to present these to the government. They needed some ways, to bring various representatives together so that a responsible government could be formed. They needed a mechanism to support or restrain the government, make policies, justify or oppose them. Political parties fulfil these needs that every representative government has. We can say that parties are a necessary condition for a democracy.

(I) Explain the meaning of a 'political party'.   **1**

(II) "The rise of political parties is directly linked to the emergence of representative democracies." Support this statement.   **1**

(III) Why are political parties a necessary condition for a democracy? Explain.   **2**

35. Read the given source and answer the questions that follow:

Yet, till the First World War, industrial growth was slow. The war created a dramatically new situation. With British mills busy with war production to meet the needs of the army. Manchester imports into India declined. Suddenly, Indian mills had a vast home marked to supply. As the war prolonged, Indian. factories were called upon to supply war needs: jute bags, cloth for army uniforms, tents and leather boots, horse and mule saddles and a host of other items. New factories were set up and old ones ran multiple shifts. Many new workers were employed and everyone was made to work longer hours. Over the war years industrial production boomed.

After the war, Manchester could never recapture its old position in the Indian market. Unable to modernise and compete with the US, Germany and Japan, the economy of Britain crumbled after the war. Cotton production collapsed and exports of cotton cloth from Britain fell dramatically. Within the colonies, local industrialists gradually consolidated their position, substituting foreign manufactures and capturing the home market.

(I) Why did Manchester imports decline in India?   **1**

(II) Why could Manchester never recapture its old position in the Indian market after the First World War?   **1**

(III) Analysis any two benefits of the First World War to India.   **2**

36. Read the given source and answer the questions that follow:

Most of the objections to the projects arose due to their failure to achieve the purposes for which they were built. Ironically, the dams that were constructed to control the floods have triggered floods due to sedimentation in the reservoir. Moreover, the big dams have mostly been unsuccessful in controlling floods at the time of excessive rainfall. You may have seen or read how the release of water from the dams during heavy rains aggravated the flood situation in Maharashtra and Gujarat in 2006. The floods have not only devastated life and property but also caused extensive soil erosion. Sedimentation also meant that the flood plains were deprived of silt, a natural fertiliser, further adding on the problem of land degradation. It was also observed that the multi-purpose projects induced earthquakes, caused water-bor-ne diseases and pests and pollution resulting from excessive use of water.

(I) Name the movement against the river project in Gujarat. **1**

(II) How have the big dams mostly been unsuccessful in controlling floods at the time of excessive rainfall? **1**

(III)Analyse any two merits of multi-purpose river projects. **2**

# SECTION - F

### (Map Based Question)

**(2 + 3= 5)**

37. (a) Two places A and B have been marked on the given political outline map of India (on page 23). Identify them with the help of the following information and write their correct names on the lines drawn near them:

(i) The place where the session of the Indian National Congress was held in December, 1920. **1**

(ii) The place where Jallianwala Bagh incident occurred.

**1**

(b) On the same political outline map of India, locate and label any three of the following with suitable symbols: **3**

(i) Noida – Software Technology Park

(ii) Bailadila – Iron-ore mines

(iii)Tarapur – Nuclear Power Plant

(iv)Haldia – Sea port

**Note:** The following questions are for the Visually Impaired Candidates only, in lieu of Q. No. 37.

Answer any five questions. **(5 × 1 = 5)**

(I) Name the place where Indian National Congress session took place in December, 1920.

(II) Name the place where the Jallianwala Bagh incident occurred.

(III)Name any one major coffee producing state of India.

(IV) Name the state where Bailadila iron ore mines are located.

(V) Name the state where Tarapur nuclear power plant is located.

(VI) Name the state where Haldia sea port is located.

## Solutions

**1.** **(a)** Nordic countries like **Denmark**, Finland.

**2.** **(a)** i-3, ii - 1, iii - 4, iv - 2.

**3.** **(b)** USA - one of the **oldest democracy** has coming together federation.

**4.** **(a)** Belgium presented a good model of power sharing successfully.

**5.** **(a)** i - 4, ii - 3, iii - 2, iv - 1.

**6.** **(b)** Agriculture and Industry are interdependent and are **backbone** of a **country's development**.

**7.** **(d)** Laterite soil develops in **high temperature** with **heavy rainfall**.

*Note*

*Laterite soil is main ly found in Eastern Ghats and the western Ghats.*

**8.** **(c)** Laxminath Besbaruah- was a great **Assamese poet** and **novelites**.

**9.** **(a)** USA - A well-known pioneer of mass production was the car manufacturer **Henry Ford**.

**10.** **(a)** The central powers **Germany - Austria - Hungry** and **Ottoman Turkey** fought against Great Britain, France, Russia, *thay known* as **Allied** Power.

**11.** **(b)** Conservation was a political philosophy that strengthened the importance of tradition, customs and established institution.

**12.** **(c)** Difficult to find international candidates ready for a relocation to fulfill the requirements of a profile.

**13.** **(d)** Rich households have all the documents and fulfill all the conditions for loan from the formal sector.

**14.** **(a)** Paper notes and coins are the modern form of money authorised by **The Reserve Bank of India (RBI)**

*Note*

*Traditional form of money consists of gold, copper coins, grain etc. which are not authorised by ary universal authority. Wheareas modern form of money are in the form of currency notes and coins.*

**15.** **(d)** In the unorganised sector no rules and regulation are followed, it works in its own interest.

**16.** **(b)** The primary or natural products are converted into more useful products under the secondary sector for eg. **cotton cloth from cotton plant**.

**17.** **(c)** Odisha - Ruled by **'Indian People's Party' (State Unit of BJP)**

**18.** **(b)** India has a multi-party system where many parties contest elections and after people a lot of choice to vote for.

**19.** **(b)** **Income** - The world Bank Publishes its report regarding different countries on the basis of their per capita Income.

**20.** **(c)** Sri Lanka has the highest HDI which includes, Literacy Rate, Per Capita Income, Life Expectancy etc.

**21.** **(1)** Due to the act passed in **1956** to make Sinhala the **official language** of Sri Lanka disregarding Tamil.

**(2)** The govt. followed preferential policies in govt. jobs favouring Sinhala applicants.

**22.** **(1)** British cleared out forests to make way for **tea plantation**.

**(2)** They needed **timber** to build railway sleepers and railway lines.

**23.** **(a)** The Chief Minister of Sardinia - Piedomont Cavour played a very important role in

**(a)** Unifying Italy

He could speak French very well so through a diplomatic alliance with France Sardinia - Piedmont succeeded in defeating the Austrian Forces in **1859**.

**OR**

**(b)** 'Liberalism' derives from **Latin** word **'Liber'** which mean **free**

**(1)** For the new middle classes it stood for freedom and equality for all.

**(2)** It also emphasised the concept of govt. by consent.

**24.** Formal sources of credit follows laws and regulations and supervised by RBI (Reserve Bank of India. For eg. Banker Cooperation. Informal Sources of Credit is not supervised by any organisation. It does not follow any laws and the main aim is to earn profit by charging high rate of interest for eg. money tenders, relatives etc.

**25.** In the past 100 years there has been shift to tertiary sector in India from primary and secondary sectors because of the following reasons.

(1) Rise in the income level and more demand for services like **hotels, tourism, shopping** malls etc.

(2) Coming of **I.T sector**.

(3) Need for **hospitals/banks**, schools etc.

(4) More development in agriculture, **transportation**, is storage, etc. in demand.

**26.** Energy Resources are very important so we should conserve them-

(1) Instead of cars and bikes, **a bicycle** should be used to **conserve** fuel.

(2) We can do **car pooling** too with our colleages.

(3) Using renewable resources like **solar energy** instead of electricity whenever possible.

(4) Clean or replace **air filters** when required.

**27.** (1) More seats for women should be reserved in political bodies. For eg. in local govt. bodies **1/3 seats** are reserved for women.

(2) Membership of women should be increased in political parties.

(3) Women should be encouraged to contest election.

**28. Secondary Sector:-**

(1) It is known as manufacturing sector as natural products are converted into more useful goods.

(2) It is organised, gives a **employment** to of lot a people. Use latest machines and technology.

**Tertiary Sector**

(1) Also known as service sector, provides various service like banking, transport, etc.

(2) Its employment share and importance has increased in recent years.

Both the sectors contribute in the development of economy along-with the primary sector.

**29. (a)**

(1) In 1295 Marco Polo a great explorer returned to Italy after many years of exploration in China.

(2) He brought the knowledge of **wood block printing** from China.

(3) Italians began producing books with wood blocks and soon it spread to the other parts of Europe.

**OR**

**(b)**

(1) Earlier the books were expensive as they were handwritten, it was difficult to afford books.

(2) After printing books became cheaper, now they could reach a large section of people.

So, 'Reading, Public' became, common instead of 'Hearing Public' earlier.

**30. (a)**

**Satyagrah against the proposed Rowlatt Act 1919:**

(i) The Rowlatt Act was hurriedly passed through the Imperial Legislative Council.

(ii) Indian members unitedly opposed it.

(iii) It gave government enormous powers to repress political activities.

(iv) It allowed detention of political prisoners without trials for two years.

**Organization of Satyagrah:**

(i) Mahatma Gandhi wanted non-violent civil discbedience against such unjust laws.

(ii) It was started with a 'Hartal' on 6th April.

(iii) Rallies were organized in various cities.

(iv) Workers went on strike in railway workshops.

(v) Shops closed down.

> **Note**
>
> *The British passed the Rowlats Act, which in Grandhi's words was the 'Black Act.' This act gave the police way more power than appropriate.*

**OR**

**(b)** Non-Cooperation Movement spread in the countryside:

(i) In Awadh, peasants were led by Baba Ramchandra. Here the movement was against talukdars and landlords who demanded exorbitantly high rents from peasants and a variety of other cesses.

(ii) Peasants had to do begar and work at landlords farms without any payments. As tenants they had no security of tenure and were regularly evicted so that they have no right over the leased land.

(iii) The peasant movement demanded reduction of revenue, abolition of begar and social boycott of oppressive landlords. In the meantime, Jawaharlal Nehru began going around the villages in Awadh.

(iv) The Awadh Kisan Sabha was set up in the villages. The peasant movement, however, developed in forms that the Congress leadership was unhappy with.

(v) As the movement spread, the houses of talukdars and merchants were attacked, bazaars were looted and grain hoards were taken over.

**31. (a)**

1. MNCs usually set up production units across the globe in places where the market is nearby, there is the availability of skilled and unskilled labour at low costs and other factors essential to the growth of production.

2. The setting up of production in various countries leads to the development of products globally. Sometimes, the MNCs might also set up production with the local companies of a country as a joint responsibility, thus bringing in the latest technology and foreign investment.

3. The MNCs also link and control the production of goods. Large MNCs in developed countries often place orders for production with small producers all around the world which are then sold by the MNCs under their brand name.

4. The power of control and influence of such corporations has contributed to the interlinking of such widely dispersed locations across the globe. This process, in turn, has contributed to the growth of globalization process.

**Note**

*MNCs are increasingly entering the local markets of various countries and playing the role of integration of these markets with the world economy and thus contributing immensely to the process of globalization. MNCs, in rapid course of time, have not only resulted in the global expansion of their brand names but have also made the process of production and selling of goods and services, a complex and interdependent process.*

**OR**

**(b)** The Central and the State governments Eire taking special steps to attract foreign companies to invest in India.

1. Special Economic Zones are being set up.

2. Special Economic Zones are to have world class facilities in the field of electricity, water, roads, transport, storage recreational and educational facilities.

• Companies which set up production units in the SEZs, do not have to pay taxes for an initial period of five years.

• Government has allowed flexibility in the labour laws. In recent years, the government has allowed companies to ignore many of rules and regulations.

• Companies can hire workers for short periods when there is intense pressure of work. This is done to reduce the cost of labour for the company.

**32. (a)** Following are the reasons :-

1. Democracies give people a chance to become personally involved with their government.

2. The structure of a democracy works to reduce issues with exploitation.

3. A democracy encourages equality in a positive way.

4. There is more consistency available in democracy than other government structures.

5. Countries who use democracy are less likely to enter into armed conflicts.

**OR**

**(b) Democracy Produces an Accountable Government:** Democracy produces an accountable governments, as the people has the right in choose their representatives through the electoral process. These elected representatives form the government and participate in the decision making process on behalf of the people. If these elected representatives (In not work in a proper way, people have a chance to not elect them in next election.

**Democracy Produces Responsive Government:** Democratic governments are elected by the people and are responsible towards the people and Parliament. These governments promote the formation of public opinion and take care of the needs and expectations of the people.

**Democracy Produces Legitimate Government :** Democratic government is a legitimate government because regular elections are its key feature. After five years, elections are held for the legislature and people elect then government on the basis of their right to vote (universal adult franchise) The party which secures the majority forms the government. In the next election, if it loses the majority, it has to resign from office. Beside elections, the decisions in a democratic government are taken in a transparent manner.

**33. (a)** Some of the characteristics of primitive subsistence farming are as follows:

(1) This type of farming is practised on small patches of land with the help of primitive tools like hoe, dao and digging sticks and family labour.

(2) This type of farming depends upon Monsoons, natural fertility of soil and environmental suitability.

(3) It is a 'slash and burn' agriculture. Farmers clear a patch of land and produce crops for their sustenance.

(4) When the soil fertility decreases, farmers shift to new area, clear forest by burning and again sow crops. This type of farming is practised on small patches of land with the help of primitive tools like hoe, dao and digging sticks and family labour.

**Commercial farming :** Major characteristics of commercialfarming in India are given below

(i) Commercial farming is crop selective and aim for industrial inputs or export oriented.

(ii) Intensive application of modern technologies.

(iii) Intensive use of modern inputs like High Yielding Variety (HYV) seeds, chemical fertilizers, insecticides, pesticides etc to increase productivity.

(iv) Commercial farming induces development activities in transport, connectivity and processing industries.

**OR**

**(b) Intensive farming :** It is a type of farming in which the agricultural production is increased by using scientific methods and better agricultural inputs.

**Features :**

(i) HYV seeds and modern inputs are used to increase the production.

(ii) More than one crop is cultivated during a year.

(iii) It is practised in thickly populated areas.

(iv) The per hectare yield is very high.

**Plantation farming:**

This is a type of agriculture which involves growing and processing of a single cash crop purely meant for sale. Rubber, tea, coffee, spices, coconut and fruits are some of the  important crops which come under the category of plantation agriculture.

**Features :**

(i) It is a single crop farming.

(ii) It is a capital intensive farming, i.e., a huge amount of capital is required.

(iii) It needs vast estates, managerial ability, technical know-how, sophisticated machinery, fertilisers, good transport facilities and a factory for processing.

(iv) This type of agriculture has developed in areas of north-eastern India, Sub-Himalayan region, West Bengal and Nilgiri.

*The intensive subsistence farming has to be seen from the perspective of a family or a small unit deriving their basic needs from it. Commercial farming, on the other hand, has to be seen from the perspective of a market or an industry, to garner profits.*

**34. (I)** A politacal. party is a group of people who come together to contets election and hold power in govt.

**(II)** It helps in formulation of public opinion contest election, form govt or play role of opposition.

**(III)** (i) Political parties present the representation of people  who take decision on their behalf by sitting in the govt. bodies.

(ii) As societies become large, they need some agency to gatter wicues and present to the governemnt. Political parties paly a major role in it.

**35. (1)** After the 1st World War Factories and mills were burry in producing goods to fulfill the need of **British Army** The supply to India became limited.

(2) During the war the Industries boomed in India and new industries were set up.

(3) (1) Indian industries flourished.

(2) Local industrialisations  gradually consolidated their position, substituting foreign instance.

**36.** (1) **'Narmada Bachao Andolan'** [Save **Narmada Movement**]

    (2) Due to **sedimentation** in the **reservoir**.

    (3) (1) Produce **Hydro-electricity**.

       (2) Help in **irrigation**.

**37.** **(a)** (i) Nagpur          (ii) Amritsar

# CBSE Board Solved Paper

## SECTION - A

### (Multiple Choice Questions)

(20 × 1 = 20)

1. Read the following statements about Human Development and choose the correct option:　　1

   (I) It is the composite Index prepared by United Nations Development Programme (UNDP).

   (II) Parameters to measure it are Longevity, Literacy and Per Capita Income.

   (III) Countries are ranked according to Developed and Low Developing countries.

   (IV) World Bank also prepares report of Human Development on the basis of Quality of Life.

   (a) I and II

   (b) II and III

   (c) I and III

   (d) II and IV

2. Why did the Indian government liberalize trade regulations in 1991?　　1

   (a) Government wanted foreign exchange equivalent to Indian Currency.

   (b) Government wanted to maintain good relations with Western Countries.

   (c) Government wanted Indian producers to compete in the World Market.

   (d) Government wanted to provide socio-economic justice to all.

3. Which one of the following sectors contribute highest in the GDP of India?　　1

   (a) Primary

   (b) Secondary

   (c) Tertiary

   (d) Quaternary

4. Which of the following countries has better rank in Human Development Index?　　1

   (a) Afghanistan　　(b) Myanmar

   (c) India　　(d) Nepal

5. Which of the following is correctly matched?　　1

   (a) Alluvial Soil　-　Consist of sand and silt

   (b) Black Soil　-　Salt content is high

   (c) Arid Soil　-　Diffusion of iron in crystalline

   (d) Laterite Soil　-　Made up of lava flows

6. Match the column - 1 with column - 2 and choose the correct option:　　1

   | Column - 1 (Resources) | Column - 2 (Example) |
   |---|---|
   | (I) Biological | 1. Coal |
   | (II) Renewable | 2. Wildlife |
   | (III) Non-renewable | 3. Solar Energy |

   **Options:**

   |  | I | II | III |
   |---|---|---|---|
   | (a) | 1 | 3 | 2 |
   | (b) | 3 | 2 | 1 |
   | (c) | 2 | 3 | 1 |
   | (d) | 1 | 2 | 3 |

7. Which one of the following is an example of the Ferrous Metal?　　1

   (a) Copper　　(b) Tin

   (c) Bauxite　　(d) Nickel

8. Who among the following improved the steam engine? 1

   (a) James Watt

   (b) Thomas Edison

   (c) Benjamin Franklin

   (d) Alexander Fleming

9. There were three important developments that greatly shrank the pre-modern world. Identify the incorrect one from the following options:　　1

   (a) The flow of trade

   (b) The flow of labour

   (c) The flow of capital

   (d) The flow of technology

**10.** Which one of the following aspects was common among the writings of Kailashbashini Debi, Tarabai Shinde and Pandita Ramabai? **1**

(a) Demanded economic equality for masses.

(b) Highlighted the experiences of women.

(c) Raised awareness about cultural heritage.

(d) Motivated Indians for their national freedom.

**11.** Arrange the following in chronological order and choose the correct option: **1**

(I) Napoleonic wars

(II) The Treaty of Vienna

(III) Greek Struggle for Independence

(IV) Slav Nationalism in Ottoman Empire

(a) III, II, I and IV

(b) I, II, III and IV

(c) IV, III, II and I

(d) IV, II, III and I

**12.** Which one of the following countries has two party system? **1**

(a) China

(b) Russia

(c) America

(d) India

**13.** Identify the administrative level of Indian Government with the help of the information given in the box and choose the correct option: **1**

| |
|---|
| 1. Power shared between Central to Local Government. |
| 2. The State Governments are required to share some powers and revenue with them. |
| 3. It is called a three tier government. |

(a) Dictatorial System (b) Unitary Federal System

(c) Decentralized System (d) Imperialistic System

**14.** Match column - A with column - B and choose the correct option: **1**

| Column - 1 | Column - 2 |
|---|---|
| **(Subjects)** | **(List)** |
| (I) Banks | 1. Concurrent List |
| (II) Agriculture | 2. Union List |
| (III) Education | 3. State List |
| (IV) Computer | 4. Residuary Subjects |

| | I | II | III | IV |
|---|---|---|---|---|
| (a) | 4 | 3 | 1 | 2 |
| (b) | 3 | 4 | 1 | 2 |
| (c) | 2 | 3 | 1 | 4 |
| (d) | 4 | 2 | 1 | 3 |

**15.** Two statements are given below as Assertion (A) and Reason (R). **1**

Read the statements and choose the correct option:

**Assertion (A):** Sri Lanka adopted 'Tamil' as the official language of the State.

**Reason (R):** The Govt. of Sri Lanka adopted a series of majoritarian measures.

(a) Both (A) and (R) are true and (R) is the correct explanation of (A).

(b) Both (A) and (R) are true but (R) is not the correct explanation of (A).

(c) (A) is true but (R) is false.

(d) (A) is false but (R) is true.

**16.** Consider the following statements on Power Sharing and choose the correct option: **1**

(I) Majoritarianism is the real spirit of democracy.

(II) It creates balance and harmony in different groups.

(III) It reduces the possibility of conflict among social groups.

(IV) Power sharing is the essence of democracy.

**Options:**

(a) I, II and III

(b) II, III and IV

(c) I, III and IV

(d) I, II and IV

**17.** Which one of the following pairs is correctly matched? **1**

(a) Primary Sector - Flower Cultivator

(b) Secondary Sector - Milk Vendor

(c) Tertiary Sector - Fisherman

(d) Manufacturing Sector - Gardener

**18.** Which one of the following is a development goal of the factory workers? **1**

(a) Better wages

(b) Better technology

(c) More hours of work

(d) More labour work

**19.** Read the following data and answer the question that follow:    **1**

| Some comparative Data on Haryana, Kerala and Bihar | | | |
|---|---|---|---|
| **State** | **Infant Mortality Rate (per thousand person)** | **Literacy Rate %** | **Net Attendance Ratio (per 100 person)** |
| Haryana | 30 | 82 | 61 |
| Kerala | 7 | 94 | 83 |
| Bihar | 32 | 62 | 43 |

How much is the Net Absence Ratio of Haryana? Choose the appropriate option from the following:

(a) 39      (b) 27      (c) 38      (d) 18

**20.** Which type of government is likely to be more acceptable to the people in the world?    **1**

(a) Democratic      (b) Military

(c) Dictatorship      (d) Theocratic

## SECTION - B

**(Very Short Answer Questions)**

**(4 × 2 = 8)**

**21.** (A) Mention any two changes that occurred in West Punjab in the 19$^{th}$ Century.    **2**

**OR**

(B) Mention any two advantages of the Silk route in the pre-modern trade.    **2**

**22.** "Industrialisation and Urbanisation go hand in hand." Explain.    **2**

**23.** "Women face discrimination in various ways in our society." Explain any two ways.    **2**

**24.** "Different persons can have different developmental goals." Support the statement with an example.    **2**

## SECTION - C

**(Short Answer Questions)**

**(5 × 3 = 15)**

**25.** Describe any three measures that were introduced by the French revolutionaries to create a sense of collective identity amongst the French people.    **3**

**26.** How is information technology connected with globalization?    **3**

**27.** Explain any three institutional reforms taken for the development of Indian agriculture.    **3**

**28.** Explain the role of Regional Parties in Indian democracy.    **3**

**29.** (A) Examine the benefits that are enjoyed by the people working in the organized sector.    **3**

**OR**

(B) Examine how 'Public Sector' contributes in the economic development of the nation?    **3**

## SECTION - D

**(Long Answer Questions)**

**(4 × 5 = 20)**

**30.** (A) "Gandhiji felt the Khilafat issue as an opportunity to bring Hindus and Muslims under the umbrella of a unified national movement." Explain the statement. **5**

**OR**

(B) Explain the participation of women in the 'Civil Disobedience Movement'.    **5**

**31.** (A) Analyse the problems of Road Transport in India.    **5**

**OR**

(B) 'Railways in India promotes the socio-economic life of the country.' Examine the statement.    **5**

**32.** (A) Justify the role of 'Self Help Groups' in the rural economy.    **5**

**OR**

(B) "Cheap and affordable credit is crucial for the country's development." Justify the statement.    **5**

**33.** (A) "Democracy stands much superior to any other forms of governments in promoting dignity and freedom of the individual." Support the statement with arguments.    **5**

**OR**

(B) "Democracy produces an accountable, responsive and legitimate government." Support the statement with arguments.    **5**

## SECTION - E

### (Case-Based Source Based Questions)

(3 × 4 = 12)

**34.** Read the given source and answer the questions that follow:

#### Language Diversity of India

How many languages do we have in India? The answer depends on how one counts it. The latest information that we have is from the Census of India held in 2011. This census recorded more than 1300 distinct languages which people mentioned as their mother tongues. These languages were grouped together under some major languages. For example languages like Bhojpuri, Magadhi, Bundelkhandi, Chhattisgarhi, Rajasthani and many others were grouped together under 'Hindi'. Even after this grouping, the Census found 121 major languages. Of these 22 languages are now included in the Eighth Schedule of the Indian Constitution and are therefore called 'Scheduled Languages'. Others are called 'Non-Scheduled Languages'. In terms of languages, India is perhaps the most diverse country in the world.

(I) Explain the importance of language diversity in India. **1**

(III) Differentiate between Scheduled and Non-Scheduled Languages. **1**

(III) 'The fusion of languages has united the country into one cultural entity.' Explain the statement with an example. **2**

**35.** Read the given source and answer the questions that follow:

#### WHY NEWSPAPERS?

'Krishnaji Trimbuck Ranade inhabitant of Poona intends to publish a Newspaper in the Marathi Language with a view of affording useful information on every topic of local interest. It will be open for free discussion on subjects of general utility, scientific investigation and the speculations connected with the antiquities, statistics, curiosities, history and geography of the country and of the Deccan especially.... the patronage and support of all interested in the diffusion of knowledge and Welfare of the People is earnestly solicited.'

Bombay Telegraph and Courier, 6 January, 1849

'The task of the native newspapers and political associations is identical to the role of the Opposition in the House of Commons in Parliament in England: That is of critically examining government policy to suggest improvements, by removing those parts that will not be to the benefit of the people, and also by ensuring speedy implementation.

These associations ought to carefully study the particular issues, gather diverse relevant information on the nation as well as on what are the possible and desirable improvements, and this will surely earn is considerable influence.'

Native Opinion, 3 April, 1870

(I) Explain the main reason of publishing newspaper by Krishnaji? **1**

(II) How was the task of native newspaper and political association seen identical to the role of opposition? **1**

(III) Analyze the reasons of popularity of newspapers during 19th century. **2**

**36.** Read the given source and answer the questions that follow:

#### RAIN WATER HARVESTING

Many thought that given the disadvantages and rising resistance against the multi purpose projects, water harvesting system was a viable alternative, both socio-economically and environmentally. In ancient India, along with the sophisticated hydraulic structures, there existed an extraordinary tradition of water harvesting system. People had in-depth knowledge of rainfall regimes and soil types and developed wide ranging techniques to harvest rainwater, groundwater, river water and flood water in keeping with the local ecological conditions and their water needs. In hill and mountainous regions, people built diversion channels like the 'guls' or 'kuls' of the Western Himalayas for agriculture. 'Rooftop rainwater harvesting' was commonly practised to store drinking water, particularly in Rajasthan. In the flood plains of Bengal, people developed inundation channels to irrigate their fields. In arid and semi-arid regions, agricultural fields were converted into rain fed storage structures that allowed the water to stand and moisten the soil like the 'khadins' in Jaisalmer and 'Johads' in other parts of Rajasthan.

(I) Why is water harvesting system a viable alternative? **1**

(II) Describe the process of 'rooftop rainwater harvesting?

**1**

(III) Mention any two methods adopted by ancient India for water conservation. **2**

## SECTION - F

### (Map Based Questions)

**(2 + 3 = 5)**

**37.** (i) Two places A and B have been marked on the given political outline map of India. Identify them with the help of given information and write their correct names on the lines drawn near them.

(a) The place where Mahatma Gandhi started Satyagraha for Indigo peasants. **1**

(b) The place where the session of Indian National Congress held in December, 1920. **1**

(ii) On the same outline map of India locate and label any three of the following with suitable symbols: **3**

(a) Tehri Dam **1**

(b) Naraura Atomic Power Station **1**

(c) Pune Software Technology Park **1**

(d) Haldia Sea port **1**

**Note:** The following questions are only for the **Visually Impaired Candidates** in lieu of Q. No. 37.

**ATTEMPT ANY FIVE:** **5 × 1 = 5**

(i) Name the place where the session of Indian National Congress was held in December, 1920. **1**

(ii) Name the place where Mahatma Gandhi started Satyagraha for Indigo peasants. **1**

(iii) Name the State where Naraura Nuclear Plant is located. **1**

(iv) Name the state where Tehri Dam is located. **1**

(v) Name the State where Mumbai Software Technology Park is located. **1**

(vi) Name the State where Haldia Sea Port is located. **1**

## Solutions

1. **(a)** The Human Development Index (HDI) measures each country's social and economic development by focusing on the following four factors: mean years of schooling, expected years of schooling, life expectancy at birth, and gross national income (GNI) per capita.

**Note**

*India ranks 132 out of 191 countries in the Human Development Report by the United Nations Development Programme.*

2. **(c)** The Government wanted Indian producers to compete in the which world market was the reason that the Indian government liberalised trade regulations in 1991.

**Note**

*India made LPG reforms in 1991. LPG reforms are also known as liberalisation, privatisation, and globalisation reforms. Liberalisation of the economy means freedom from direct or physical controls imposed by the government and privatisation is the general process of involving the private sector in the ownership or operation of a state-owned enterprise.*

3. **(c)** The services sector accounts for 53.89% of total India's Gross Value Added of 179.15 lakh crore Indian rupees.

4. **(c)** In accordance with the 2023 Human Development Report, India, Nepal, Mayanmar, and Afghanistan ranked 132nd, 143rd, 149th, and 180th, respectively.

5. **(a)** Alluvial soil is one of the best soils, requiring the least water due to its high porosity. The consistency of alluvial soil ranges from drift sand and rich, loamy soil to silt clay.

6. **(c)** A renewable resource can replenish itself at the rate it is used, while a non-renewable resource has a limited supply. Biological resources refer to the plants, animals, and other aspects of nature that occur on farmland, forests, and other natural lands.

**Note**

*Bhadla Solar Park is the world's largest solar park located in India which is spread over a total area of 14,000 acres in Bhadla, Phalodi tehsil, Jodhpur district, Rajasthan, India.*

7. **(d)** Ferrous metals refer to any metal that contains iron. They are favoured for their tensile strength and durability, so they are often used in housing construction, large-scale piping, and industrial containers.

8. **(a)** James Watt was an 18th-century inventor and instrument maker. He is best remembered for his improvements to the steam engine.

9. **(d)** After European sailors discovered a sea route to Asia and successfully sailed across the western ocean to America in the sixteenth century, the pre-modern globe significantly diminished. The Indian Ocean had formerly seen a thriving trade.

10. **(b)** Tarabai Shinde, Kailashbashini Debi, and Pandita Ramabai wrote with passionate anger about the miserable lives of upper-caste Hindu women, especially widows.

11. **(b)** Napoleonic wars- 1803-1815

    The Treaty of Vienna- 1815

    Greek Struggle for Independence- 1821

    Slav Nationalism in Ottoman Empire- 1905

12. **(c)** The modern political party system in the United States is a two-party system, with the parties being the Democratic Party and the Republican Party.

13. **(c)** Decentralisation is when power is taken away from central and state governments and given to local governments. The basic idea behind decentralisation is that there are a large number of problems and issues that are best settled at the local level.

14. **(c)** Article 246 deals with the 7th Schedule of the Indian Constitution, which mentions three lists named Union List, State List,and Concurrent List,which specify the divisions of power between the Union and States.

15. **(d)** The Sri Lankan government declared Sinhala the official language of Sri Lanka in 1956.

16. **(b)** Power sharing means the distribution of power among the organs of the government such as the legislature, executive, and judiciary. Power sharing is essential to avoid violent conflicts, tyranny of the majority and ensure political stability.

17. **(a)** Primary sector comprises activities related to the extraction and production of natural resources. Agriculture, forestry, animal husbandry, fishing, poultry farming, mining and quarrying.

18. **(a)** It is crucial for the overall development of factory workers, as it directly impacts their standard of living, job satisfaction, and productivity. It allows workers to meet their basic needs and improve their socio-economic conditions.

19. **(a)** 39 is the Net Absence Ratio of Haryana.

    The net attendance ratio is the total number of children in the age group of 6–10 attending school as a percentage of the total number of children in the same age group.

20. **(a)** More than a hundred countries in the world have a democratic setup of government. The word democracy comes from the Greek words "demos", meaning people, and "kratos" meaning power; so democracy can be thought of as "power of the people": a way of governing which depends on the will of the people.

*Note*

*A theocracy is a type of government that is ruled by a divine being or religious texts. In this form of government, religious doctrines are used to rule the country.*

21. **(A)** The changes occurred in west Punjab in the 19th century are as follows:

    (i) The British Indian government built a network of irrigation canals in order to transform semi-desert wastes into fertile agricultural lands that could grow wheat and cotton for export.

    (ii) Peasants from various parts of Punjab settled in the canal colonies, which were watered by the new canals.

**OR**

**(B)**

    (i) The Silk Route facilitated the exchange of goods and ideas between different regions, which led to an expansion of trade.

    (ii) It also facilitated the exchange of ideas, beliefs, and culture between different regions. It also led to the introduction of new technologies, such as paper-making, which transformed the social and economic landscape of the regions.

    (iii) Merchants from China, India, and Persia traded goods like tea, spices, silk, and precious stones, leading to economic growth and prosperity in the region.

*Note*

*The Silk Road was a network of paths connecting civilizations in the East and West that was well travelled for approximately 1,400 years. Merchants on the Silk Road transported goods and traded at bazaars or caravanserai along the way.*

22. Industrialization is the transformation from an agricultural-based economy to one based on mechanised manufacturing. Urbanisation is basically the shifting of a population from rural areas to urban areas, which leads to the formation and increase in size of towns and cities.

    As industries and businesses grow, so do the number of workers needed to support them. This increases the number of jobs available to people. People from rural areas begin migrating to these towns where the industries have developed to fill those jobs. Hence, it leads to the formation of towns and cities, or it increases the size of the already existing ones.

23. In rural areas, the literacy rate of men is 82.14%, while the female literacy rate is 65.46%. The following are the ways in which women face discrimination in our society:

    (i) Daughters are seen as burdens, while sons are assets, so investing in their education is not prioritised. The role of women in society is only to look after the house and children, which does not require any schooling.

    (ii) The structure of Indian society is patriarchal, in which everything revolves around males and women are reduced to a negligible role.

*Note*

*The International Day for the Elimination of Violence against Women is celebrated on November 25 to raise public awareness about the issues surrounding gender-based violence.*

24. Different people can have different developmental goals based on their age, gender, socio-economic status, location, and other factors.

    (i) A girl expects as much freedom and opportunity as her brother, and he also shares in household work. Her brother may not like this. Industrialists may want more dams for power generation. But this may submerge the land and displace the people living around it.

    (ii) The farmer may be more concerned with access to clean water, agricultural infrastructure, and affordable healthcare, while the businessman may be more concerned with access to finance, technology, and skilled labour.

**25.** Some of the measures that were introduced by the French revolutionaries to create a sense of collective identity and unity among the French were as follows:

(i) The French revolutionaries introduced the ideas of the fatherland and the citizen. This emphasises the idea of a community that has a sense of unity having a constitution and enjoying equal rights under it.

(ii) The French revolutionaries installed a centralised administrative system and formulated uniform laws for all French citizens.

(iii) The French revolutionaries had made French the common language and discouraged speaking regional dialects of the different regions of France.

**26.** Information technology has accelerated the pace of globalisation in the following ways:

(i) Information technology has facilitated the introduction of various satellite communication devices through which people can get connected to anyone in every corner of the world instantly.

(ii) With information technology, there has been coordination across the different geographic locations in situations where a product is developed in one part of the world, assembled in another country, and sold in yet another country.

(iii) Without information technology, globalisation would have taken many more years to spread since it would have taken longer for the necessary information to be conveyed, which would have slowed down the rate of country-to-country integration.

**27.** Institutional reforms are the term used to describe the government's efforts to alter the agricultural industry. These are as follows:

(i) The government introduced various land reforms, such as collectivization, holding consolidation, cooperation, and zamindari abolition.

(ii) Land development programmes such as the construction of Grameen banks, cooperative societies, and banks to offer farmers lending opportunities at cheaper interest rates

(iii) Providing crop insurance to protect farmers from damages brought on by natural calamities like fires, cyclones, fires, and droughts

(iv) Specific radio and radio weather reports, as well as agricultural programmes, have been introduced.

**28.** (i) At the regional level, they offer better governance and a stable government.

(ii) They make politics more competitive and popular participation in the political process more extensive at the grass-roots level.

(iii) They widen the choice for voters in both the parliamentary and assembly elections.

(iv) They bring into focus local issues, which immediately attract the attention of the masses.

(v) They pose a challenge to the dominant one-party system in the country.

(vi) They oppose the ruling party at the centre on certain issues and force the dominant party to be more reasonable in its approach to the process of conflict resolution.

**29.** **(A)** The organised sector covers those enterprises that are registered by the government and follow the rules and regulations of the Factory Act, Minimum Wages Act, Payment of Gratuity Act, etc. The benefits are:

(i) The organised sector offers its employees job security. They are typically employed on a permanent basis and are entitled to various benefits, such as notice periods, etc., in the event of termination.

(ii) They only need to work a specific number of hours and are entitled to paid leave, including sick leave, annual leave, and maternity leave.

(iii) This sector also provides training and development opportunities for its employees to enhance their skills and knowledge.

(iv) They receive overtime pay, money for holidays, provident fund contributions, gratuities, etc.

**OR**

**(B)** The public sector contributes in the economic development of the nation in the following ways:

(i) The public sector plays an important role in contributing to the Human Development Index through its functioning in health and education services.

(ii) It encourages the development of small medium and cottage industries.

(iii) It ensures easy availability of goods at reasonable rates.

(iv) It promotes fast economic development through infrastructure creation and generates financial resources for further development.

(v)   It creates employment opportunities.

(vi)  It ensures equality of income and wealth and, thus, balanced regional development.

**30.  (A)**

(i)   The Khilafat issue was a political crisis that arose in India in the aftermath of World War I, following the defeat of the Ottoman Empire. And there were rumours that a harsh peace treaty was going to be imposed on the Ottoman emperor, the spiritual head of the Islamic world (the Khalifa).

(ii)  To defend the Khalifa's temporal powers, a Khilafat Committee was formed in Bombay in March 1919. Muslim leaders, like the brothers Muhammad Ali and Shaukat Ali, began discussing with Mahatma Gandhi the possibility of a united mass action on the issue.

(iii) Gandhiji saw this as an opportunity to bring Muslims under the umbrella of a unified national movement. He believed that the issue was not just about the fate of the Caliphate but was also a broader issue about the rights of Muslims in India and their place in Indian society.

(iv)  At the Calcutta session of the Congress in September 1920, he convinced other leaders of the need to start a non-cooperation movement in support of Khilafat as well as Swaraj.

(v)   As the movement gathered momentum and millions of Muslims and Hindus came together to protest the British government's policies, it quickly emerged as a significant political force in India.

**OR**

**(B)** The participation of women in the 'Civil Disobedience Movement' as follows:

(i)   Women from different parts of the nation participated in protest marches, manufactured salt, and picketed foreign cloth and liquor shops.

(ii)  Women were arrested and sent to jail for participating in these activities.

(iii) In urban regions, women from high-caste families participated, while in rural areas, they were from rich peasant families.

(iv)  They started organizing prabhat pheris, or morning processions, on the streets of Bombay and Ahmedabad, where they sang songs about the bounty of the motherland.

(v)   Being the hub of female education in India, Bengal, enhanced the involvement of women in nationalism. In support of the cause, women demonstrated in front of Bethune College in Calcutta in 1930.

(vi)  They were moved by Gandhiji's call and started to believe that women had a divine duty to serve their nation.

**31.  (A)** The problems of road transport in India as follows:

(i)   The road network is insufficient for the volume of traffic and passengers.

(ii)  In the rainy season, the un-metalled roads—about half of them—get damaged.

(iii) The number of National highways is inadequate and is poorly maintained. Even, most of the bridges are old and narrow.

(iv)  The roads are congested in cities and lack safety measures. Many roadways lack adequate equipment, have poor sidewalks, have endless crossings, and have inadequate sidewalk capacity.

(v)   There are many checkpoints on motorways and octroi that slow down speeds, waste time, and irritate travellers.

**OR**

**(B)** The Indian railways promote socio-economic life of the country in the following ways:

(i)   The nation's economic life is tied together by the transportation of various goods by Indian railways, including agricultural products, iron and steel, fertilisers, and mineral ores.

(ii)  It facilitates the movement of goods and provides affordable connectivity for people at lower cost.

(iii) It also makes it possible for people to conduct multifarious activities like business, sightseeing, pilgrimage, etc.

(iv)  Railways help industrial and agricultural development proceeds more quickly, which boosts the nation's economy.

(v)   Perishable foods, agricultural implements, and other items can be transported quickly over long distances.

(vi)  Railways help in facing man-made calamities like social, political, and religious disturbances, insurgencies, etc. It facilitates the easy movement of police, troops, defence equipment, etc. during times of emergency.

*Dibrugarh – Kanniyakumari Vivek Express is the longest train of Indian Railways which runs from Dibrugarh in India's North-eastern state Assam to Kanniyakumari in Tamil Nadu the southernmost state of India. The train covers a distance of 4189 kilometres and traverses through nine states in India.*

**32.  (A)** Self-help groups are informal groups of people who come together to address their common problems. There role in rural economy are follows:

(i) Self help groups are a crucial supplier of microfinance services to the underprivileged. They serve as an intermediary for official banking services to the underprivileged, particularly in rural areas.

(ii) Additionally, they urge the impoverished to develop saving habits.

(iii) In the area of employment and income-generating activities, they work to increase the functional ability of the underprivileged and marginalised groups in society.

(iv) They provide collateral-free loans to groups of people who typically struggle to obtain loans from banks.

(v) SHGs help people earn their livelihood by providing vocational training and also by improving their existing source of livelihood by offering tools, etc. They also help ease the dependence on agriculture.

**OR**

**(B)**

• Increased lending would increase earnings and encourage more people to start small businesses, invest in agriculture, and operate small enterprises.

• Cheap credit indicates that the borrower will have more money available to invest rather than pay back as interest. The result is an increase in economic activity.

• Additionally, accessible credit would free up underprivileged groups from the exploitation of unregulated moneylenders and enable them to participate in the legal lending market. As a result, it might help the poor and landless with their economic situation.

• They will be shielded from debt traps by accessible financing, and they will be able to support national economic growth.

• As more people take advantage of the low-cost credit, they will invest more in small businesses, agriculture, and other industries, raising the GDP of the nation.

**33.  (A)**

(i) Democracy upholds a person's freedom and dignity. Everyone likes to be respected by other people. In many nations, democracies have succeeded in achieving this to some extent.

(ii) Women have fought for respect and equality for a very long time. For a very long time, women were denied the right to vote in many countries, but they now have it. Women can now fight against what is already morally and legally wrong. Women would not have a legal foundation to strive for equality under a non-democratic system.

(iii) The castes that are underprivileged and are subject to discrimination now have stronger arguments for equal opportunity and status.

(iv) The work of the powerful, wealthy, and in positions of authority is now scrutinised by the public. They complain loudly about their displeasure. It demonstrates that they are now citizens of a democracy rather than being treated as subjects.

(v) Our fundamental rights are protected by the constitution in a democratic nation like India.

**OR**

**(B)**

"Democracy is the government of the people, by the people, for the people." by Abraham Lincoln. It is an accountable, responsive, and legitimate government due to the following reasons:

(i) It is a legitimate government, as it is elected by citizens and enjoys the confidence and trust of the citizens.

(ii) People have the right to choose their rulers and they have control over their rulers. Citizens can participate in decision making.

(iii) People have the power to compel the government to act by organising protests, campaigns, and rallies.

(iv) Citizens can take part in decision-making whenever the government takes feedback regarding some laws or policies.

(v) A democratic government is the people's own government, and it is run by the people. People are ruled by representatives elected by them.

**34.** **(I)** Language diversity helps preserve the unique identities and cultures of different communities. It has also contributed to the development of various art forms, literature, and music.

**(II)** Scheduled languages are those languages that are listed in the Eighth Schedule of the Indian Constitution. These languages have been given official recognition and support by the government.

Non-Scheduled Languages are all other languages that are spoken in India, but have not been given official recognition by the government.

**(III)** It indicates that India's many different linguistic and cultural traditions have converged to forge a strong feeling of national identity. Bollywood films are one example of this combination.

*Assamese, Bengali, Gujarati, Hindi, Kannada, Kashmiri, Konkani, Malayalam, Manipuri, Marathi, Nepali, Odia, Punjabi, Sanskrit, Sindhi, Tamil, Telugu, Urdu, Bodo, Santhali, Maithili and Dogri are the 22 languages presently in the eighth schedule to the Constitution.*

**35.** **(I)** The main reason to publish a newspaper is to spread useful information on every topic of local interest at an affordable price.

**(II)** Both critically examine the government policy to suggest improvements by removing those parts that will not benefit the people and ensuring speedy implementation.

**(III)** Newspapers were popular during the 19th century as they served as "mouthpieces" for the independence struggle both nationally and locally.

*James Augustus Hicky published the first Indian Newspaper in India named The Bengal Gazette in 1780. The first English-language newspaper published on the Indian subcontinent.*

**36.** **(I)** A water harvesting system does not displace local people and does not cause environmental problems like a decrease in flora and fauna.

**(II)** Rooftop rainwater harvesting is a technique used for the conservation of water. In this method, rainfall that has accumulated on houses or other structures' roofs is gathered via pipelines and stored in underground storage tanks.

**(III)** In hill and mountain regions, people built channels like guls or kuls in the western Himalayas for agriculture. In arid and semi-arid regions, agriculture fields were converted into fed storage to allow water to stand and moisten the soil, like khadins in Jaisalmer and johads in other parts of Rajasthan.

**37. (i)**

(a)  Champaran district of Bihar

(b)  Nagpur district in Maharashtra.

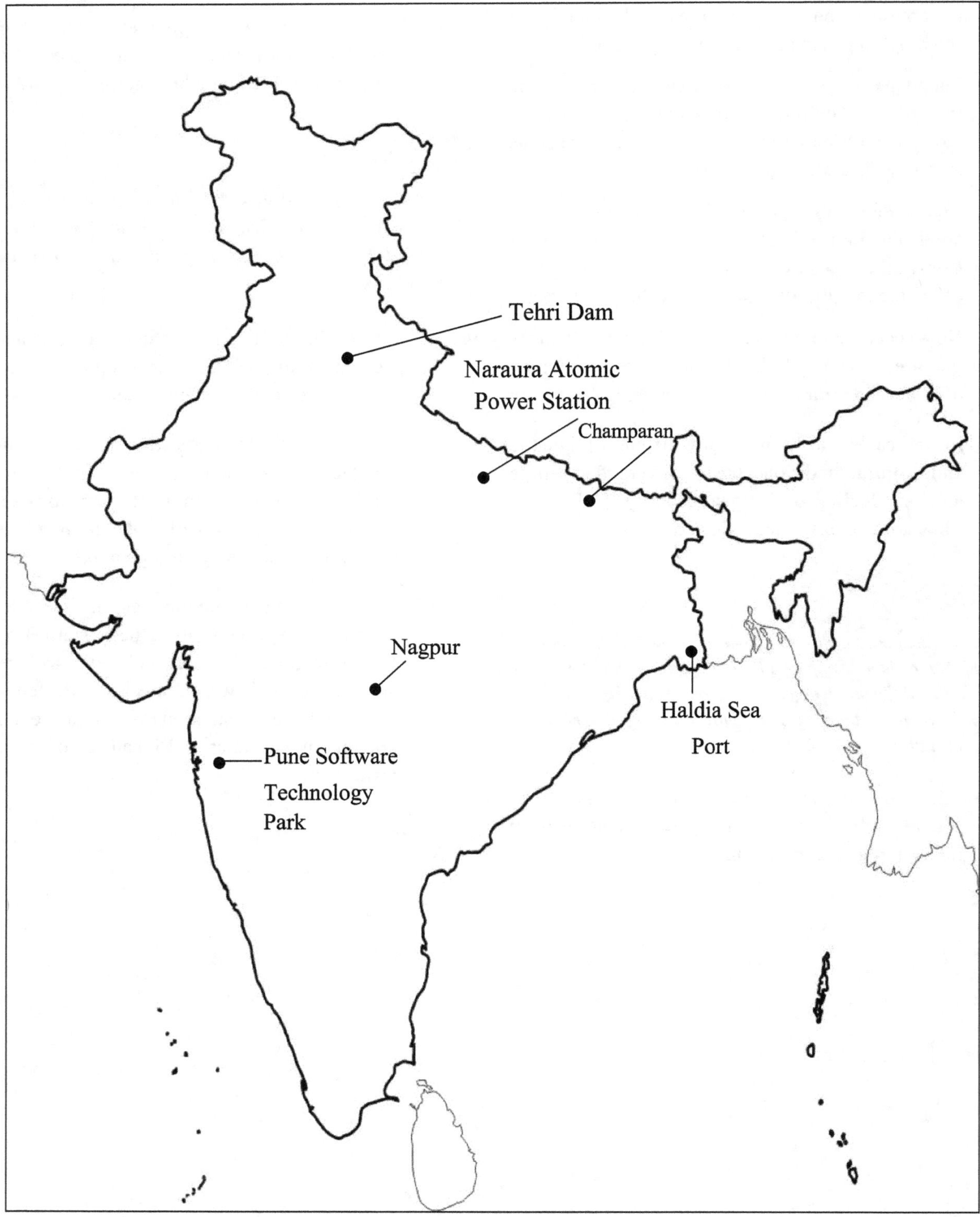

# CBSE Board Solved Paper Term-II

## SECTION - A

**(Very Short Answer Questions)**

$(2 \times 5 = 10)$

1. Why did Mahatma Gandhiji travel to Champaran in Bihar in 1917? Explain. **2**
2. Explain the importance of National Highways in India **2**
3. Classify industries on the basis of source of raw materials. **2**
4. How is one-party system different from two-party system? Explain with examples. **2**
5. How do double coincidence of wants arise? **2**

## SECTION - B

**(Short Answer Type Questions)**

$(3 \times 3 = 9)$

6. Why did Mahatma Gandhi decide to withdraw the Non-Cooperation Movement in February 1922? Explain. **3**

**OR**

How did the First World War create a new economic situation in India? Explain.

7. Analyse the outcomes of democracies in terms of economic growth and development. **3**
8. Explain the three important terms of Credit. **3**

## SECTION - C

**(Long Answer Questions)**

$(5 \times 2 = 10)$

9. (a) Examine any five major challenges faced by the political parties in India. **5**

**OR**

(b) "Political parties play an important role in democratic countries." Justify the statement. **5**

10. (a) How are our markets transformed in recent years? Explain with examples. **5**

**OR**

(b) How do Multi National Corporations (MNCs) interlink production across countries? Explain with examples. **5**

## SECTION - D

**(Case Based Questions)**

$(4 \times 2 = 8)$

11. Read the given case and answer the questions that follow:

Mahtma Gandhi's thoughts on Satyagraha

'It is said of "passive resistance" that it is the weapon of the weak, but the power which is the subject of this article can be used only by the strong. This power is not passive resistance; indeed it calls for intense activity. The movement in South Africa was not passive but active...,

'Satyagraha is not physical force. A satyagrahi does not inflict pain on the adversary; he does not seek his destruction.. In the use of satyagraha, there is no ill-will whatever.'

'Satyagraha is pure soul-force. Truth is the very substance of the soul. That is why this force is called satyagraha. The soul is informed with knowledge. In it burns the flame of love.... Non-violence is the supreme dharma....

'It is certain that India cannot rival Britain or Europe in force of arms. The British worship the war-god and they can all of them become, as they are becoming, bearers of arms. They hundreds of millions in India can never carry arms. They have made the religion of non-violence their own...'

(i) What type of movement Gandhiji organised in South Africa? **1**

(ii) Why is satyagraha considered as pure soul-force? **1**

(iii) How has Gandhiji described passive resistance? **2**

12. Read the given case and answer the questions that follow:

Challenges faced by the Jute industry include stiff competition in the international market from synthetic substitutes and from other competitions like Bangladesh, Brazil, Philippines, Egypt and Thaliland. However, the internal demand has been on the increase due to the Government policy of mandatory use of jute packaging. To stimulate demand, the products need to be diversified. In 2005, National Jute policy was formulated with the objective of in creasing productivity, improving quality, ensuring good prices to the jute farmers and enhancing the yield per hectare. The main markets U.S.A., Canada, United Arab Republic, U.K. and Australia. The growing global concern for environment friendly, biodegradable materials, has once again opened the opportunity for jute products.

(i) Mention any two challenges faced by 'jute industry' in India.                                                                                    **1**

(ii) What was the main objective of National Jute Policy formulated in 2005?                                                                **1**

(iii) How has Jute industry once again opened the new opportunities for its products?                                                    **2**

13.  (1)  On the given outline political Map of India, identify the place marked as (A) with the help of following information and write its correct name on the line marked near it.

(A) The place where National Congress Section was held in September 1920.

(2)  On the same given Map of India, located and label the following with appropriate symbols.

(i)  (a) Tarapur – Nuclear Power Plant

**OR**

(b) Kalpakkam – Nuclear Power Plant

(ii) Hyderabad – Rajiv Gandhi International Airport

## Solutions

**1.** (a) The Champaran Satyagraha in Bihar in 1917 was the first Satyagraha movement led by Mahatma Gandhi in India.

(b) In 1917, Gandhiji travelled to Champaran in Bihar to inspire the peasants to struggle against the oppressive planation system.

(c) He fought for farmers' freedom to grow the crops they desired as well as for the protection of the peasants

***Note***

*Buddhist Stupa: Located in Kesariya near Motihari in the Champaran district of Bihar, it is known to be the largest Buddha Stupa in the world. Kesariya Stupa has a circumference of almost 400 feet and rises to a height of about 104 feet.*

**2.** (a) The National Highways are the arterial roads of the country for inter-state movement for all.

(b) National Highways link the extreme parts and important states and cities of the country.

(c) These are primary road systems for smoother and faster movement of goods and people.

***Note***

*The National Highways Authority of India (NHAI) works under the administrative control of the Ministry of Road Transport and Highways. It is the central authority to develop, maintain, and manage the national highways entrusted to it by the Government of India.*

**3.** (a) **Agro based industries:** These industries use agricultural products as their raw materials are called agro based raw materials are called agro based industries. E.g., jute industry, cotton textile industry, sugar industry, etc.

(b) **Mineral based industries:** These industries get their raw material from mineral ores are called mineral based industries. E.g., iron and steel industry, copper setting industry, cement industry, etc.

**4.** Difference between one-party and two-party systems:

|  | One-party system | Two-party system |
|---|---|---|
| (a) | When only one party is allowed to control and run the government. | When only two main parties have serious chance of winning a majority of seats to form a government. |
| (b) | It is non-democratic system | It is democratic system. |
| (c) | For example, in China, only the Communist Party is allowed to rule. | The United States of America and the United Kingdom are example of a two-party system. |

**5.** It arises when a person desires to sell is exactly what the other wishes to buy goods are directly exchanges without the use of maney.

For example, one person has potatoes but is in need of wheat, and another has wheat but is in need of potatoes. Then they will exchange their goods. This exchange is known as a "double coincidence of wants".

**6.** Mahatma Gandhiji decided to withdraw the Non-Cooperation Movement because:

(a) In 1922, at Chauri-Chaura in Gorakphur, a peaceful mob turned violent and clashed with the police setting the police station on fire which results in the death of several policemen.

(b) Gandhiji felt that the movement was turning violent and satyagrahis needed more tolerance before they and preparation before they were ready for a mass struggle.

**OR**

The First Word War created a new economic and political situation in India because:

(a) The British government increase the deference expenditure.

(b) Taxe and custom duties were raised and also income tax was introduced.

(c) Through the war years, prices increased doubling between 1913 and 1918 leading to hardship for common people.

(d) Food shortage had created due to the failure of crops in many parts of India.

(e) The First World War created a situation where there was higher demand for goods like rails, cloth, and jute bags, and imports from other countries were reduced.

(f) The Nationalist Movement grew stronger during the war years.

**7.** Economic outcomes of democracy:

**(a) Economic development and growth:** Democracy is considered a better government than other forms of government. So, we can expect better economic growth and development. But, if we look at the years between 1950 and 2000, dictatorships had a slightly higher rate of economic development than democracies because of the speed of their decision-making process. Here, the ruler does not follow any rules or procedures to make policies.

**(b) Decrease in poverty:** Democracies do not appear to be very successful in reducing economic inequalities. In most of the democracies, a small number of ultra rich enjoy a highly disproportionate wealth and income. Their share in the total income of the country has been increasing. Those at the bottom have little to depend upon.

**(c) Decrease of Inequality:** As democracy is the government of the people, one expects democracies to reduce economic disparities by giving equal right to votes to every citizen, protecting rights without discrimination.

**8.** Credit means a loan, an agreement in which the lender supplies the borrower with money, goods or services which is to be returned in future.

Three important terms of credits are:

(a) **Interest Rate:** The extra money on the principal amount the borrower has to pay.

(b) **Collateral:** It is the security that the borrower has to deport to the leder. It can be house documents, gold, etc.

(c) **Mode of payment:** This is the duration for which the loan is to be repaid. Long-term loans can be repaid in 12 months, 6 months, or monthly instalments.

**9.** (a) The challenges faced by political parties are as under:

(i) **Lack of internal democracy:** All over the world, there is a tendency in political parties towards the concentration of power in few hands at the top. Most of the parties do not have accountability, they do not hold its routine organisational meetings, fail to conduct their internal elections regularly.

(ii) **No integrity:** Personal loyalty to the leader becomes more important than the loyalty to party policies and principles.

(iii) **Dynastic succession:** The top leaders, are in a position of unfair advantage to favour people close to them or their family members. In many parties, the top positions are always controlled by members of one family.

(iv) **Muscle power:** Parties use shortcuts to win elections. They tend to nominate those candidates who have or can raise lots of money. Rich people and companies who provide funds to the parties tend to have an influence on the policies and decisions of the party.

(v) **Lack of meaningful choice to the voters:** Across the world, parties do not seem to offer a meaningful choice to the voters. Due to decline in the ideological differences among parties thereby reducing choice to voters in most parties of the world. For example, the difference between the Labour Party and the Conservative Party in Britain is very little.

**OR**

(b) They play an important role in democratic countries: A political party is a group of people who follow an ideology and come together to contest elections and run the government.

(i) Each political party has a local leader who interacts with people, hears their demands, and promises to carry them out. Thus, they play an important role in building a relationship between the people and the government.

(ii) **Contesting elections:** In democracies, elections are fought mainly among the candidates put up by political parties.

(iii) **To form and run the government:** The governments are formed and run by political parties. The representatives of the government are the members of different political parties.

(iv) **Unstable government:** The government may be formed, but its life will remain ever uncertain. Elected representatives will be accountable to their constituencies for what they did to the locality.

(v) **Formation of policies:** Political parties play an important role by making important decisions, such as forming much-needed laws and policies, after participating in legislative debates on the subject.

*India had its first general election in 1951, which was won by the Indian National Congress, a political party that went on to dominate subsequent elections until 1977.*

**10.** (a) The markets have been transformed in the following ways:

(i) The markets of the entire world are interlinked. For example, we can buy any goods & services from other countries by just clicking on our devices.

(ii) Perishable products of other countries are available in local markets in no time due to faster and better transportation network.

(iii) Market has grown multifold and the transactions are happening more on virtual mode.

(iv) We now have a wide variety of products to choose in the market.

(v) MNCs organise the production, distribution process globally in a complex way. For example, Tata Motors, Coca Cola or Tesla have unique styles of investment plans for different countries.

**OR**

(b) Multinational Corporations are expanding their production in the following ways:

(i) The global brands outsource the manufacturing keeping in mind the low-cost factor. They placed orders with local companies. Eg: Garments, footwear, sports items etc.

(ii) By setting up partnership with local companies. For example, Maruti and Suzuki has a partnership in automobile industry. Here, Suzuki is a Japanese company which had a tie up with an Indian company, Maruti.

(iii) Due to the availability of, cheap labour and other resources, MNCs set up offices and factories in different regions

(iv) By buying local companies. Eg. Cargill Foods is a MNC which has bought Parakh foods in India.

*Maruti Suzuki India Limited is the Indian subsidiary of Japanese automaker Suzuki Motor Corporation. As of September 2022, the company had a leading market share of 42 percent in the Indian passenger car market.*

**11.** (i) Gandhiji organised satyagraha to fought against the racist regime.

(ii) Satyagraha is considered as a pure soul-force because the idea of satyagraha emphasised the power of truth and the need to search for truth. Truth is the very substance of the soul. A satyagrahi doesnot inflict pain on the adversary. There is no ill-will whatever.

(iii) The term Passive Resistance as used by Gandhi was not really passive, it was passive only in the sense of absence of violence or active armed action. It was really active in the sense of offering resistance to the alien ruling power with the help of 'Love Force' or 'Soul Force'. Without seeking vengeance or being aggressive, a satyagrahi could win the battle through non-violence. This could be done by appealing to the conscience of the oppressor.

**12.** (i) The two challenges of jute industry are:

(a) Stiff competition in the international market from synthetic substitutes.

(b) Competition from other jute supplier countries like Bangladesh, Brazil, Philippines, Egypt and Thailand.

(ii) The main objective of National Jute Policy (2005) was to increase productivity improve, quality and to ensure good price and enhance yield to the jute farmers.

(iii) Due to the visible harmful impacts of artificial fibre and the biodegradability of jute to control the environment pollution, the demand the jute industry has revived again.

*Jute fibers accounted for 37 billion Indian rupees in the Indian economy in fiscal year 2020. This variety of fibers made up nearly five percent of the sector that year. Fibers, overall, contributed about 810 billion rupees to the Gross Value Added of crops that same year.*

**13.**

# CBSE Board Solved Paper

## SECTION - A

**(Very Short Answer Questions)**

**(2×5 = 10)**

1. Mention any two causes that led to the Civil Disobedience Movement. **2**

2. How is chemical industry in India diversified? Explain. **2**

3. Differentiate between ruling and opposition parties. **2**

4. Classify industries on the basis of raw materials. **2**

5. Read the following source and answer the questions that follow: **2**

### A House Loan

Megha has taken a loan of 5 lakhs from the bank to purchase a house. The annual interest rate on the loan is 12 percent and the loan is to be repaid in 10 years in monthly installments. Megha had to submit to the bank, documents showing her employment records and salary before the bank agreed to give her the loan. The bank retained as collateral the papers of the new house, which will be returned to Megha only when she repays the entire loan with interest.

(i) From which house of credit Megha has taken loan? **1**

(ii) Explain the terms of credit given in the source. **1**

## SECTION - B

**(Short Answer Type Questions)**

**(3×3 = 9)**

6. (a) Explain, why the banks do not lend credit to certain borrowers? **3**

   **OR**

   (b) Explain the functions of "Self Help Group". **3**

7. "The effect of Non-Cooperation Movement on the economic front were more dramatic." Support the statement with examples. **3**

8. Explain, how the rise of political parties are directly linked to the emergence of representative democracies. **3**

## SECTION - C

**(Long Answer Type Questions)**

**(5 × 2 = 10)**

9. (a) "Democracy is attentive to the needs and demands of the people." Justify the statement. **5**

   **OR**

   (b) "Democracies accommodate social diversities and provide dignity and freedom to the citizens." Justify the statement. **5**

10. (a) "Technology is the vital force in the modern form of globalisation." Explain the statement with suitable examples. **5**

    **OR**

    (b) "The impact of globalisation has not been uniform." Explain the statement with suitable examples. **5**

## SECTION - D

**(Case Based Questions)**

**(4 × 2 = 8)**

11. Read the following case carefully and answer the questions that follow: **4**

### Nationalism in India

Modern nationalism is Europe came to be associated with the formation of nation-states. If also meant a change in people's understanding of who they were, and what defined their identity and sense of belonging. New symbols and icons, new songs and ideas forged new links and redefined the boundaries of communities. In most countries the making of this new national identity was a long process. How did this consciousness emerge in India?

In India and as in many other colonies, the growth of modern nationalism is intimately connected to the anti-colonial movement. People began discovering their unity in the process of their struggle with colonialism. The sense of being oppressed under colonialism provided a shared bond that tied many different groups together. But each class and group felt the effects of colonialism differently, their experiences were varied, and their nations of freedom were not always the same. The Congress under Mahatma Gandhi tried to forge these groups together within one movement. But the unity did not emerge without conflict.

(i) What was people's understanding of nation? **1**

(ii) How was the growth of modern nationalism intimately connected to the anti-colonial movement? **1**

(iii) How did people in India develop a sense of collective belonging? Explain. **2**

12. Read the following case and answer the questions that follows: **4**

**Tourism**

Tourism in India has grown substantially over the last three decades. More than 15 million people are directly engaged in the tourism industry. Tourism also promotes national integration, provides support to local handicrafts and cultural pursuits. It also helps in the development of international understanding about our culture and heritage. Foreign tourists visit India for heritage tourism, eco tourism, adventure tourism, cultural tourism, medical tourism and business tourism.

There is a vast potential for development of tourism in all parts of the country. Efforts are being made to promote different types of tourism for this upcoming industry.

(i) Explain the importance of tourism. **1**

(ii) Give an example of 'Heritage tourism'. **1**

(iii) Assess the benefits of improving tourism in India. **2**

## SECTION - E
### (Map Based Questions)

(1 +2= 3)

13. **(i)** On the given outline Political Map of India, identify the place marked as 'A' with the help of following information and write its correct name on the line marked near it:

(A) The place where India National Congress Session was help in September, 1920. **1**

**(ii)** On the same given map of India, locate and label the following:

I. (a) Ramagundam Thermal Plant **1**

**OR**

(b) Pune Software Technology Park **1**

II. Chennai (Meenambakkam) International Airport. **1**

## Solutions

1.  Following were the two causes that led to the Civil Disobedience Movement:

    (a) **Failure of the Simon Commission:** The Simon Commission was constituted in 1927 in response to the nationalist movement. But the Commission failed to satisfy the Indian people and the leaders. However, no Indian was nominated as a member of the commission, which sparked outrage in India because the British government's decision to exclude Indians from the Simon Commission implied that Indians were unfit to decide the next course of constitutional reforms. All the parties, including the Congress and the Muslim League, participated in the demonstrations.

    (b) **Rejection of Gandhi's Eleven Demands:** Mahatma Gandhi, on 31$^{st}$ January, 1930, put forward eleven demands to correct the wrongs done to the Indians and assured the Viceroy that he would withdraw the Civil Disobedience on the British Government's acceptance of these demands. However, viceroy refused to accept Gandhi's demands.

2.  (a) It consists of both large and small scale manufacturing units.

    (b) Rapid growth has been recorded in both inorganic and organic sectors.

**Note**

*Small-scale industries have a smaller production capacity compared to large-scale industries. Also, small-scale industries require less capital to start and operate compared to large-scale industries.*

3.  Differences between ruling and opposition parties:

| Ruling Political Party | | Opposition Political Party | |
|---|---|---|---|
| (a) | The party which wins the majority of seats in the election is known as ruling party | (a) | The party which is not able to get the majority seats is known as the opposition party. |
| (b) | This political party has power and forms the government. | (b) | This is party or parties fails to form the government. It conduct the most important function of criticism of the working of ruling party. |
| (c) | It is responsible for governance and administration of the country. | (c) | It checks the government from assuming dictatorial power. |

4.  Classification of industries on the basis of source of raw material used are:

    (a) **Agro based industries:** The industries which obtain raw materials from agriculture products are called agro based industries. For example, cotton, woollen, jute, silk textile, rubber and sugar, tea, coffee, edible oil, etc.

    (b) **Mineral based industries:** The industries which uses minerals as their raw materials are called mineral based industries. For example, iron and steel, cement, aluminium, machine tools, petrochemicals, etc.

5.  (i) Megha has taken loan from bank which is the formal sector of credit.

    (ii) The following terms of credit are mentioned in the given passage:

    (a) Interest Rate (12%)

    (b) Repayment duration (10 years).

    (c) Repayment mode (Monthly installments).

    (d) Collateral (Documents of house).

    (e) Documents required (Employment records and salary slips).

6.  (a) The banks do not lend credit to certain borrowers because of the following reasons:

    (i) Banks require proper documents to raise the loans. Some people fail to meet this requirement.

    (ii) Banks require collateral to be submitted against the loan amount. Those who do not have any collateral to submit, fail to get loan from the bank.

    (iii) The borrowers who have bad credit history, the banks might not be willing to lend them further.

    **OR**

    (b) Self-help groups are informal groups of people who come together to address their common problems.

   (i) They build the functional capacity of poor and marginalised sections of society in the areas of employment and income-generating activities.

   (ii) They offers collateral-free loans to the sections of people that generally find it hard to get loans from banks.

   (iii) They resolve conflicts through mutual discussions and collective leadership.

   (iv) They also the platform for rural women to discuss their social issues.

**Note**

*Self-help groups (SHGs) are informal associations of people who choose to come together to find ways to improve their living conditions. The origin of SHGs in India can be traced back to the establishment of the Self-Employed Women's Association (SEWA) in 1972.*

**7.** The effects of Non-Cooperation Movement on the economic front are:

   (a) The import value of foreign cloth dropped from ₹102 crore to ₹57 crore between 1921 and 1922.

   (b) Merchants and traders refused to trade in foreign goods or finance foreign trade.

   (c) Foreign goods were boycotted, liquor shops picketed, and foreign cloth burnt in huge bonfires.

   (d) People discarded imported clothes and wearing only Indian ones.

   (e) The domestic textile mills and handlooms industry got a shot in the arm since people had begun to prefer Indian clothes over imported ones.

**8.** The rise of parties is directly linked to the emergence of representative democracies due to the following reasons:

   (a) Due to the large territory and large population, it is not possible for people to assemble together and make policies for themselves; therefore, representatives from parties are to be chosen.

   (b) Societies need some agency to gather different views on various issues and to present these in front of the government.

   (c) Societies needed some ways, to bring various representatives together so that a responsible government could be formed.

   (d) Society needed a mechanism to support or restrain the government, make policies, and justify or oppose them.

   (e) These political parties act as the voices of the masses.

**9.**   (a) Democracy is a form of government in which the supreme power is vested in the people and is exercised by them directly or indirectly.

   (i) It is a more accountable form of government, and it enables the peaceful transfer of power through free and fair elections.

   (ii) It is responsive to the needs and expectations of the people. It also provides subsides and welfare policies for their citizens.

   (iii) Democracy provides a method to deal with differences and conflicts.

   (iv) Democracy is attentive to the needs and demands of the people and it responds to the grievances of people faster.

   (v) Democracies provide practices and institutions like- Election Commission for regular, free and fair elections and open public debate.

   (vi) Citizens have right to information about the government and its function.

   (vii) Democracy gives protection from arbitrary interference on the part of the authorities; it is the primary safeguard against arbitrary arrest and prosecution.

   (viii) Democracy provides a system to deal with differences and disagreements and allows us to correct our own mistakes.

**Note**

*More than a hundred countries in the world have a democratic system of government. India is the largest democratic country in the world.*

**OR**

   (b) Democracies accommodate social diversities and provide dignity and freedom to the citizens because:

   (i) In a democracy, minority and majority opinions are not permanent. To make sure that the government functions to represent general views, minority and majority must work together.

   (ii) Democracies develop a procedure to conduct their competition. This reduces the possibility of these tensions becoming explosive or violent. Ability to handle social differences, divisions and conflicts thus a definite plus point of democratic regimes.

   (iii) Democracy stands much superior to any other form of government in promoting dignity and freedom of the individual.

(iv) The passion for respect and freedom are the basis of democracy.

(v) Democracies provide equal status and equal opportunity to the depressed class people. Democracy has strengthened the claims of the disadvantaged and discriminated castes for equal status and equal opportunity.

(vi) The passion for respect and freedom is the basis of democracy. This principle is universally recognised.

**10.** (a) (i) Technology has led to the emergence of the global village. For example, the world wide web has reduced the barriers of time and place in business dealings.

(ii) Technology has made much faster delivery of goods and services across long distances possible at lower costs.

(iii) Technology in the areas of telecommunications, computers and Internet is used to contact one another around the world, to access information and to communicate from remote areas.

(iv) Communication between different countries has been revolutionised because of technology.

(v) Satellite communication devices are used very rapidly.

(vi) Buyers and sellers can now make transactions at any time and in any part of the globe.

**OR**

(b) (i) Due to the ushering in of new technologies, output increases, but employment opportunities are limited, especially in rural areas, where over 60% of the population lives. This has a negative impact on employment and real wages.

(ii) Globalisation is mainly beneficial to large capitalists, industries and large companies.

(iii) The small-scale industries are not able to compete with large players such as multinational corporations.

(iv) Globalisation mainly allows developing and underdeveloped economies to supply raw material to developed countries.

(v) On the one hand, it has increased the GDP, investment, and volume of trade, which in turn gives employment to millions and facilitates the expansion of companies like Tata Motors, etc. However, on the other hand, it has increased income inequality, increased the contractualization of labour, and shifted hazardous industries to developing countries. This shows the uneven impact of globalisation.

**11.** (i) People understand that a nation is associated with who they were and what defined their identity and sense of belonging.

(ii) The sense of oppression and exploitation under colonialism provided a shared bond that tried many different groups together and connected to the anti-colonial movement.

(iii) Through the experience of united struggles against the British rule and colonialism people in India, developed a sense of collective belonging.

*The key exponent of the modern idea of the nation-state was the German G. W. Friedrich Hegel. He introduced the concept of nationalism in Europe.*

**12.** (i) Tourism generates employment opportunities, promotes national integration, and it provides support to local handicrafts and cultural pursuits.

(ii) Visiting the Mahabalipuram in Tamil Nadu is an example of Heritage tourism.

(iii) Foreign Travellers help India in getting Foreign Exchange

(i) It will open the new ventures of employment in India,

(ii) It boost new infrastructural development in the nation.

(iii) A large number of businesses engaged in the service sector, such as airlines, hotels, surface transportation, etc., grow with the growth of the tourism industry.

*'Dekho Apna Desh', 'Swadesh Darshan Scheme' and Vibrant Villages Programme" have been launched to promote domestic tourism. The "Dekho Apna Desh' scheme focuses on encouraging the middle class to choose domestic travel over international.*

 SOCIAL SCIENCE-10

13.

# 2021

# CBSE Board Solved Paper Term-I

## General Instructions:

(i) This question paper contains 60 questions out of which 50 questios are to be attempted. All questions carry equal marks.

(ii) This question paper consists of four sections- Section A, B, C and D.

(iii) Section A contains 24 questions. Attempt any 20 questions from Q. No. 1 to 24.

(iv) Section B contains 22 questions. Attempt ant 18 questions from Q. No 25 to 46.

(v) Sections C contains 12 questions (Case-Based Study Questions). Attempt any 10 questions from Q. No. 47 to 58.

(vi) Section D contains 2 Map-based questions. Attempot both the questions.

(vii) The first 20 questions in Section A, 18 questions in Section B and 10 questions in Section C attempted by a candidate will be evaluated.

(viii) There is only one correct option for every multiple choice question (MCQ). Marks will not be awarded for answering more than one option.

(ix) There is no negative marking.

## SECTION - A

### (Multiple Choice Questions)

(20 × 1 = 20)

1. Industrialisation began in which one of the following European countries in the second half of the eighteenth century? 1

   (a) Germany     (b) France

   (c) Italy     (d) England

2. Which type of governments were mainly driven in Europe after the defeat of Napoleon in 1815? 1

   (a) Conservation     (b) Liberal

   (c) Federal     (d) Feudal

3. Which one of the following group of countries collectively defeated Napoleon in 1815? 1

   (a) Britain, Russia, Prussia and Austria

   (b) Britain, Russia, Prussia and Australia

   (c) Britain, Russia, Netherlands and Germany

   (d) Britain, Luxembourg, Germany and Italy

4. In which one of the following countries did the first liberalist-nationalist upheaval take place in July 1830? 1

   (a) France     (b) Germany

   (c) England     (d) Italy

5. Who among the following remarked "When France sneezes, the rest of Europe catches cold"? 1

   (a) Lord Byron     (b) Metternich

   (c) Johann Herder     (d) Napoleon

6. Who among the following was the architect for the unification of Germany? 1

   (a) Otto Von Bismarck     (b) William I

   (c) Frederick III     (d) William II

7. Who among the following had sought to put together a coherent programme for a unitary Italian Republic during 1830s? 1

   (a) Victor Emmanuel I

   (b) Victor Emmanuel II

   (c) Giuseppe Mazzini

   (d) Count Cavour

**8.** In which one of the following states is overgrazing the main reason for land degradation? **1**

   (a) Maharashtra      (b) Punjab

   (c) Haryana         (d) Uttar Pradesh

**9.** Identify the soil which ranges from red to brown in colour and saline in nature: **1**

   (a) Red soil        (b) Laterite soil

   (c) Arid soil        (d) Alluvial soil

**10.** Which one of the following forces leads to maximum soil erosion in plains? **1**

   (a) Wind           (b) Glacier

   (c) Running water   (d) Earthquake

**11.** Deforestation due to mining has caused severe land degradation in which one of the following states? **1**

   (a) Odisha        (b) Tamil Nadu

   (c) Kerala        (d) Gujarat

**12.** Who among the following was proclaimed King of united Italy in 1861? **1**

   (a) Charles I      (b) Victor Emmanuel II

   (c) Giuseppe Garibaldi   (d) Nero

**13** Which one of the following subjects is included in the Union List? **1**

   (a) Communication   (b) Trade

   (c) Commerce     (d) Irrigation

**14.** Which one of the following elements is *not* included in the Belgium model? **1**

   (a) Dutch and French speaking ministers shall be equal in the government.

   (b) Many powers of the central government have been given to state governments.

   (c) Brussels has a separate government in which both the communities have equal representation.

   (d) There is a community government which has special powers of administration.

**15.** Which one of the following countries is the example of 'Holding together federation'? **1**

   (a) Australia      (b) India

   (c) U.S.A.        (d) Switzerland

**16.** Which one of the following ethnic communities is in majority in Sri Lanka? **1**

   (a) Sri Lankan Tamils   (b) Indian Tamils

   (c) Muslims       (d) Sinhalese

**17.** Which one of the following subjects is included in the State List? **1**

   (a) Banking      (b) Business

   (c) Currency     (d) Communication

**18.** Activities that help in the development of Primary and Secondary sectors come under which one of the following sectors? **1**

   (a) Primary      (b) Secondary

   (c) Tertiary      (d) Quaternary

**19.** Identify the correct feature of Unitary form of government from the following options: **1**

   (a) There are two or more levels of government.

   (b) Different tiers of government govern the same citizens.

   (c) Each tier of government has its own jurisdiction.

   (d) The sub-units are subordinate to the central government.

**20.** At the initial stages of development, which one of the following sectors was the most important of economic activity? **1**

   (a) Primary

   (b) Secondary

   (c) Tertiary

   (d) Quaternary

**21.** Activities in which natural products are changed into other forms come under which one of the following sectors? **1**

   (a) Primary      (b) Secondary

   (c) Tertiary      (d) Quaternary

**22.** The products received by exploiting natural resources come under which one of the following sectors? **1**

   (a) Quaternary    (b) Tertiary

   (c) Secondary     (d) Primary

**23.** Which one of the following factors is mainly responsible for declining water level in India? **1**

   (a) Irrigation

   (b) Industrialisation

   (c) Urbanisation

   (d) Over-utilization

**24.** Which one of the following subjects is included in the Concurrent List? **1**

   (a) Trade       (b) Commerce

   (c) Agriculture    (d) Marriage

# SECTION - B

### (Multiple Choice Questions)

(18 × 1 = 18)

**25.** Two statements are given below as Assertion (A) and Reasoning (R). Read the statement and choose the most appropriate option. **1**

**Assertion (A):** After Russian occupation in Poland, the Russian language was imposed on its people.

**Reason (R):** The use of Polish soon come to be a symbol of struggle against Russian dominance.

(a) Both Assertion (A) and Reason (R) are true and Reason (R) is the correct explanation of Assertion (A).

(b) Both Assertion (A) and Reason (R) are true, but Reason (R) is *not* the correct explanation of Assertion (A).

(c) Assertion (A) is true but Reason (R) is false.

(d) Assertion (A) is false but Reason (R) is true.

**26.** Read the facts regarding the Revolution of the Liberals in Europe during 1848 and choose the correct option: **1**

1. Abdication of the monarch

2. Universal male suffrage had been proclaimed

3. Political Rights to women were given

4. Freedom of the press had been asked for

(a) Only 1 and 2 are correct

(b) Only 1, 2 and 3 are correct

(c) Only 1 and 4 are correct

(d) Only 1, 2 and 4 are correct.

**27.** Two statements are given below as Assertion (A) and Reasoning (R). Read the statement and choose the most appropriate option. **1**

**Assertion (A):** Weavers in Silesia had led a revolt against contractors in 1845.

**Reason (R):** Contractors had drastically reduced their payments.

(a) Both Assertion (A) and Reason (R) are true and Reason (R) is the correct explanation of Assertion (A).

(b) Both Assertion (A) and Reason (R) are true, but Reason (R) is *not* the correct explanation of Assertion (A).

(c) Assertion (A) is true but Reason (R) is false.

(d) Assertion (A) is false but Reason (R) is true.

**28.** On which of the following modern aspects did the new Germany place a strong emphasis? **1**

1. Currency

2. Banking

3. Legal system

4. Demography

(a) Only 1 and 2 are correct

(b) Only 2 and 3 are correct

(c) Only 3 and 4 are correct

(d) Only 1, 2 and 3 are correct.

**29.** Which one of the following Italian states was ruled by an Italian princely house? **1**

(a) Papal State          (b) Lombardy

(c) Venetia          (d) Sardinia-Piedmont

**30.** Identify the characteristics of Cavour among the following and choose the correct option: **1**

1. He was an Italian statesman.

2. He spoke French much better than Italian.

3. He was a tactful diplomat.

4. He belonged to a Royal family.

(a) Only 1 and 2 are correct.

(b) Only 1, 2 and 3 are correct.

(c) Only 2, 3 and 4 are correct.

(d) Only 1, 2 and 4 are correct.

**31.** Two statements are given below as Assertion (A) and Reasoning (R). Read the statement and choose the most appropriate option. **1**

**Assertion (A):** In Britain, the formation of the nation-state was not result of a sudden upheaval.

**Reason (R):** Ethnic groups of Britain extended its influence.

(a) Both Assertion (A) and Reason (R) are true and Reason (R) is the correct explanation of Assertion (A).

(b) Both Assertion (A) and Reason (R) are true, but Reason (R) is *not* the correct explanation of Assertion (A).

(c) Assertion (A) is true but Reason (R) is false.

(d) Assertion (A) is false but Reason (R) is true.

**32.** Which among the following is *not* a problem of resource development? **1**

(a) Depletion of resources for satisfying the greed of few individuals.

(b) Accumulation of resources in few hands.

(c) Indiscriminate exploitation of resources.

(d) An equitable distribution of resources.

**33.** Which one of the following human activities has contributed most in land degradation? **1**

(a) Deforestation       (b) Overgrazing

(c) Mining       (d) Over-irrigation

**34.** Two statements are given below as Assertion (A) and Reasoning (R). Read the statement and choose the most appropriate option. **1**

**Assertion (A):** Indian farmers should diversify their cropping pattern from cereals to high value crops.

**Reason (R):** This will increase income and reduce environmental degradation simultaneously.

(a) Both Assertion (A) and Reason (R) are true and Reason (R) is the correct explanation of Assertion (A).

(b) Both Assertion (A) and Reason (R) are true, but Reason (R) is *not* the correct explanation of Assertion (A).

(c) Assertion (A) is true but Reason (R) is false.

(d) Assertion (A) is false but Reason (R) is true.

**35.** Two statements are given below as Assertion (A) and Reasoning (R). Read the statement and choose the most appropriate option. **1**

**Assertion (A):** Majority community is dominant in a few democratic states.

**Reason (R):** Dominance can undermine the unity of the country.

(a) Both Assertion (A) and Reason (R) are true and Reason (R) is the correct explanation of Assertion (A).

(b) Both Assertion (A) and Reason (R) are true, but Reason (R) is *not* the correct explanation of Assertion (A).

(c) Assertion (A) is true but Reason (R) is false.

(d) Assertion (A) is false but Reason (R) is true.

**36.** Two statements are given below as Assertion (A) and Reasoning (R). Read the statement and choose the most appropriate option. **1**

**Assertion (A):** Power sharing is good.

**Reason (R):** It helps to reduce the possibility of conflicts between social groups.

(a) Both Assertion (A) and Reason (R) are true and Reason (R) is the correct explanation of Assertion (A).

(b) Both Assertion (A) and Reason (R) are true, but Reason (R) is *not* the correct explanation of Assertion (A).

(c) Assertion (A) is true but Reason (R) is false.

(d) Assertion (A) is false but Reason (R) is true.

**37.** Choose the correct pair among the following: **1**

(a) Russia – Unitary       (b) China – Federal

(c) Canada – Unitary       (d) Argentina – Federal

**38.** Two statements are given below as Assertion (A) and Reasoning (R). Read the statement and choose the most appropriate option. **1**

**Assertion (A):** The distrust between Sinhalese and Tamil communities turned into widespread conflict in Sri Lanka.

**Reason (R):** 1956 Act recognized Sinhala as the only official language.

(a) Both Assertion (A) and Reason (R) are true and Reason (R) is the correct explanation of Assertion (A).

(b) Both Assertion (A) and Reason (R) are true, but Reason (R) is *not* the correct explanation of Assertion (A).

(c) Assertion (A) is true but Reason (R) is false.

(d) Assertion (A) is false but Reason (R) is true.

**39.** Identify 'Horizontal power sharing' arrangements among the following in modern democracies: **1**

(a) Different organs of government

(b) Governments at different levels

(c) Different social groups

(d) Different parties, pressure groups and movements

**40.** Match Column I with Column II and choose the correct option: **1**

|     | Column I          |    | Column II                |
| --- | ----------------- | -- | ------------------------ |
| I   | Union List        | A. | Computer-related matter  |
| II  | State List        | B. | Forest                   |
| III | Concurrent List   | C. | Police                   |
| IV  | Subsidiary Matters | D. | Defence                  |

(a) I-D, II-C, III-B, IV-A

(b) I-A, II-B, III-C, IV-D

(c) I-D, II-C, III-B, IV-A

(d) I-B, II-A, III-C, IV-D

**41.** Which of the following countries is an example of 'coming together' federation?   **1**

(a) United States of America

(b) India

(c) Spain

(d) Belgium

**42.** What is *not* an integral part of the government?   **1**

(a) Office of the Prime Minister

(b) Legislature

(c) Executive

(d) Judiciary

**43.** Two statements are given below as Assertion (A) and Reasoning (R). Read the statement and choose the most appropriate option.   **1**

**Assertion (A):** Kerala has low Infant Mortality Rate.

**Reason (R):** Kerala has adequate provision of basic health and education facilities.

(a) Both Assertion (A) and Reason (R) are true and Reason (R) is the correct explanation of Assertion (A).

(b) Both Assertion (A) and Reason (R) are true, but Reason (R) is *not* the correct explanation of Assertion (A).

(c) Assertion (A) is true but Reason (R) is false.

(d) Assertion (A) is false but Reason (R) is true.

**44.** Suppose there are four families in your locality, the average per capita income of whom is ₹10,000. If the income of three families is ₹6,000, ₹8,000 and ₹14,000 respectively, what would be the income of the fourth family?   **1**

(a) ₹5,000        (b) ₹10,000

(c) ₹12,000       (d) ₹15,000

**45.** Which one of the following sectors shows the highest share in Gross Domestic Product (GDP) in India?   **1**

(a) Primary        (b) Secondary

(c) Tertiary        (d) Quaternary

**46.** Which one of the following sectors shows the highest share in employment in 2017-18, in India?   **1**

(a) Primary        (b) Secondary

(c) Tertiary        (d) Quaternary

## SECTION - C

### (Case Based Questions)

**(5 × 2 = 10)**

*Case A : Read the source given below. Attempt any 5 questions out of 6 (Q. No. 47-52) questions.*

**Jhumming:** The 'slash and burn' agriculture is known as 'Milpa' in Central America, 'Conuco' in Venzuela, 'Roca' in Brazil, 'Masola' in Central Africa, 'Ladang' in Indonesia, 'Roy' in Vietnam.

In India, this primitive form of cultivation is called 'Bewar' or 'Dahiya' in Madhya Pradesh, 'Podu' or 'Penda' in Andhra Pradesh, 'Pama Dabi' or 'Koman' or 'Bringa' in Odisha, 'Kumari' in Western Ghats, 'Valre' or 'Waltre' in South-eastern Rajasthan, 'Khil' in the Himalayan belt, 'Kuruwa' in Jharkhand, and 'Jhumming' in the North-eastern region.

**47.** How is Primitive Subsistence Agriculture related with Jhumming?   **2**

(a) It is based on shifting cultivation.

(b) It is intensive in nature.

(c) It is based on plantation cultivation.

(d) It depends upon cash crop.

**48.** The 'slash and burn' agriculture is known as 'Conuco' in which one of the following countries?   **2**

(a) Venezuela       (b) Brazil

(c) Indonesia       (d) Mexico

**49.** The 'slash and burn' agriculture is known as 'Roca' in which one of the following countries?

(a) Mexico        (b) Indonesia

(c) Brazil         (d) Venezuela

**50.** Identify the major problem of Jhumming cultivation.   **2**

(a) Single crop dominance

(b) Modern inputs

(c) High cost

(d) Low production

**51.** In India 'slash and burn' agriculture is known as 'Bewar', in which one of the following states?   **2**

(a) Andhra Pradesh

(b) Madhya Pradesh

(c) Rajasthan

(d) Jharkhand

**52.** Match Column I with Column II and choose the correct option: **2**

| | Column I | | Column II |
|---|---|---|---|
| I | Andhra Pradesh | A. | Kuruwa |
| II | Odisha | B. | Valre |
| III | Rajasthan | C. | Penda |
| IV | Jharkhand | D. | Pama Dabi |

(a) I-C, II-D, III-B, IV-A

(b) I-A, II-B, III-C, IV-D

(c) I-B, II-A, III-D, IV-C

(d) I-D, II-C, III-A, IV-B

**Case B: Read the source given below. Attempt any 5 questions out of 6 (Q. No. 53-58) question.**

Take the case of Laxmi with her two-hectare plot of unirrigated land. The government can spend some money or banks can provide a loan, to construct a well for her family to irrigate the land. Laxmi will then be able to irrigate her land and take a second crop, wheat, during the *rabi* season. Let us suppose that one hectare of wheat can provide employment to two people for 50 days (including sowing, watering, fertiliser application and harvesting). So two more members of the family can be employed in her own field. Now suppose a new dam is constructed and canals are dug to irrigate many such farms. This could lead to a lot employment generation within the agriculture sector itself reducing the problem of underemployment.

**53.** Which one of the following economic sectors is Laxmi related to? **2**

(a) Primary      (b) Secondary

(c) Tertiary      (d) Quaternary

**54.** Which one of the following categories of farmers is Laxmi related to? **2**

(a) Big      (b) Medium

(c) Marginal      (d) Agricultural labourer

**55.** In which one of the following sectors is underemployment seen at the maximum? **2**

(a) Industry      (b) Agriculture

(c) Trade      (d) Commerce

**56.** How does construction of dams and canals create employment in large numbers in rural areas? **2**

(a) Large number of engineers are needed.

(b) Large number of technicians are also required.

(c) Adjustment of large number of unskilled labourers.

(d) Executives and administrators can easily be adjusted.

**57.** Which one of the following is the main result of increasing irrigation facilities in the field of agriculture? **2**

(a) Increase in production

(b) Increase in productivity

(c) Change in cropping pattern

(d) Promote high yielding of crops

**58.** Which one of the following means of irrigation generally comes under the Public Sector? **2**

(a) Well      (b) Tube well

(c) Tank      (d) Canal

## SECTION - D

**(Map-Based Questions)**

(2 × 1 = 2)

**59.** On the outline political map of India 'A' is marked as Dam. Identify it from the following options: **1**

(a) Tehri      (b) Sardar Sarovar

(c) Hirakud      (d) Nagarjuna Sagar

**60.** On the same map 'B' is also marked as the largest 'Jute' producer state. Identify if from the following options. **1**

(a) West Bengal      (b) Bihar

(c) Assam      (d) Odisha

## Solutions

1. **(d)** In the second half of the eighteenth century, England began to industrialise. Rapid industrialization began in Britain in the 1780s with mechanised spinning, followed by rapid expansion in steam power and Iron manufacturing around 1800.

2. **(a)** Conservative regimes were set up in 1815 after the defeat of Napoleon.

3. **(a)** At the battle of Waterloo in 1815, Napoleon was defeated by four major powers: Britain, Russia, Austria and Prussia.

4. **(a)** France was the first country where the first liberal-nationalist upheaval took place in July 1830. Before the French Revolution, France was under a monarchical regime.

5. **(b)** Metternich, the Austrian chancellor, believed that the political developments in France were intriguing for other European nations. Similar to the French Revolution and democratic, egalitarian, and fraternal beliefs.

6. **(a)** Otto von Bismarck is considered the chief architect of German unification. He carried out the nation-building process with the army and the bureaucracy.

7. **(c)** During the 1830s, Giuseppe Mazzini had sought to put together a coherent programme for a unitary Italian Republic.

8. **(a)** In Maharastra, overgrazing is the main cause of land degradation. It reduces plant cover by eliminating the most desirable forage species first. This opens up the land to undesirable weeds, brush, and trees and leads to increased soil erosion and lower soil fertility.

> **Note**
>
> *Over 29% (96.4 million hectares) of India's total geographical area (328.7 million hectares) is degraded. In 2003–05, 94.53 mha (28.76% of the TGA) underwent land degradation. The number increased to 96.40 mha (29.32% of the TGA) in 2011–13.*

9. **(c)** Arid soils are the soils of desert or semi-desert regions, and their colours vary from red to brown. It has a sandy texture and high salinity. As precipitation is very low, the temperature is high, and evaporation is faster, making it deficient in moisture and humus.

10. **(c)** Soil erosion is the natural process by which the topsoil of a field is carried away by physical sources such as wind and water. Various agents, like wind, water, deforestation, overgrazing by cattle, etc., cause soil erosion.

11. **(a)** Deforestation due to mining has caused severe land degradation in states like Jharkhand, Chhattisgarh, Madhya Pradesh, etc. A mining operation needs big machines, labour, roads, railways, etc. All these lead to deforestation.

12. **(b)** Victor Emmanuel II (1820-1878) First king (1861-1878) of united Italy and last king of Piedmont-Sardinia (1849-1861).

13. **(a)** The Union List includes subjects of national importance such as defence of the country, foreign affairs, banking, communications and currency.

14. **(d)** The constitution created by the Belgian government after taking into account regional and cultural diversity is known as the Belgian model. The number of French and Dutch ministers in the central government is equal.

15. **(b)** A large country that chooses to split its power between the constituent states and the central government is known as a "holding-together" federation. India, Spain, and Belgium are examples of this kind of federation.

16. **(d)** Sri Lanka has two major social groups, Sinhalese and Sri Lankan Tamils. The Sinhalese comprise 74 per cent of the total population in Sri Lanka while Tamils make up 18 per cent of the total population in Sri Lanka.

17. **(b)** The state list specifies jurisdiction over subjects like public order, prisons, public health, manufacture, transport, purchase, and sale of intoxicating liquors, agricultural education and research, fisheries, state public services, etc.

> **Note**
>
> *The 7th Schedule of the Indian Constitution deals with the division of powers between the Union government and state governments. It consists of three lists: the union list consists of 100 subjects, the state list consists of 59, and the concurrent list consists of 52 subjects.*

18. **(c)** Tertiary sector activities help in the development of the primary and secondary sectors. These activities do not produce a good on their own, but they are an aid or a support for the primary and secondary sector.

19. **(a)** A unitary government is one in which all the powers of administration are vested in a single centre. The centre is omnipotent.

20. **(a)** The primary sector serves as the foundation for all of our other sectors. Agriculture, dairy, fishing, and forestry provide the majority of natural goods; this sector is sometimes known as agriculture and allied.

21. **(b)** The secondary sector covers all those activities consisting of varying degrees of processing of raw materials, such as manufacturing, construction industries.

22. **(d)** The primary sector includes all those activities whose end purpose is to exploit natural resources, such as agriculture, fishing, forestry, mining, and deposits.

23. **(a)** The reasons for the depletion of the water table are deforestation, overpumping of groundwater, unscientific methods of agriculture, chemical effluents from industries, and a lack of sanitation.

24. **(d)** Some of the important subjects on the concurrent list are: education, forests, trade unions, marriage, adoption, succession, etc.

25. **(a)** After the Russian occupation, the Polish language was banned from schools and replaced with Russian. In Poland, a large number of clergy members started using language as a tool of national resistance.

26. **(d)** The multiple national revolutions in Europe that were started by educated middle class people alongside uprisings by the underprivileged, jobless, and starving peasants and workers are together referred to as the liberals' 1848 revolution.

27. **(a)** In 1845, weavers in Silesia led a revolt against contractors who supplied them raw material and gave them orders for finished textiles but drastically reduced their payments.

28. **(d)** Improvement in Banking system, Modernization of currency and Legal and judicial system in Germany are the objective of the new state of German.

29. **(d)** Italy was divided into seven republics by the middle of the nineteenth century, but only one of them, Sardinia-Piedmont, was controlled by an Italian princely house.

30. **(b)** Count Camillo de Cavour was Chief Minister of Sardinia-Piedmont State. He spoke French much better than he did Italian. He engineered a careful diplomatic alliance with France, which helped Sardinia-Piedmont defeat the Austrian forces in 1859 and thereby free the northern part of Italy from the Austrian Habsburgs.

31. **(c)** As the English nation progressively increased in power, money, and importance, it was able to exert more influence over the other nations of the island. So it's the English nation who extended influence but not the ethnic groups.

32. **(d)** The major problems in the development of resources are that most of the resources are limited in supply and are unevenly distributed across the country. Also, the over-utilisation of the resources may lead to pollution of the environment.

33. **(a)** Over irrigation, deforestation due to mining activities, overgrazing and mineral processing are the factors that have lead to land degradation in India.

34. **(a)** Crop diversification reduces the chance of losing a crop to unfavourable weather. By significantly lowering the need for pesticides, chemical fertilisers, and supplementary water sources, multi-cropping and intercropping lower the overall cost to the farmer.

35. **(a)** The nation's unity suffers in the long run when the majority community imposes its will on others, even though this may seem like an appealing alternative in the short term. The tyranny of the majority is not just oppressive for the minority; it often brings ruin to the majority as well.

36. **(a)** The possibility of conflict between different ethnic groups is lowered through power sharing. Since all communities can govern a nation without giving priority to any majority community, political stability is ensured.

37. **(d)** Russia- Federal

China- Unitary

Canada- Federal

*Note*

*In federal forms of government, power is shared between the central and state governments. In a unitary form of government, there is only one level of government, or if subunits exist, they will be subordinate to the central government.*

38. **(a)** The 1956 Act was passed to make Sinhala the official language. The government followed preferential policies favouring Sinhala applicants for university positions and government jobs, and the Constitution provided for state protection for Buddhism.

39. **(a)** Horizontal power sharing refers to different organs of the state such as legislature, judiciary and executive . It means that every organ of the state has equal powers.

40. **(a)** Union List- Defence

State List- Police

Concurrent List- Forest

Subsidiary Matters- Computer- related matter

### Note

*Residuary powers include all matters not mentioned in any of the lists, such as cyber laws. The Union legislature alone has the power to legislate on such matters.*

41. **(a)** USA, Switzerland and Australia are countries which combined different states together to form a country and hence an example for 'Coming Together' federation.

42. **(a)** The Legislature, Executive, and Judiciary are integral parts of the Government. The office of the Prime Minister is not an integral part of the Government.

43. **(a)** Kerala's focus primarily on human resource development is the reason for its low infant mortality rate. It has also made many provisions on developing the quality of education and medical facilities.

### Note

*Madhya Pradesh had the highest rural infant mortality rate in India in 2018, with 52 baby deaths per 1,000 live births. Uttar Pradesh and Assam were two other states with high death rates.*

44. **(c)** Average = Sum of all incomes/ Number of families
$6,000 + 8,000 + 14,000 + x / 4 = 10,000$

$x = 12,000$

45. **(c)** The services sector accounts for 53.89% of India's total gross value added (GVA). The industry sector contributes 25.92%, while agriculture and allied sectors share 20.19%.

46. **(a)** In the Indian economy, the highest employment is found in agriculture and related fields. In India, 50% to 60% of the workforce is employed in agriculture.

47. **(a)** Primitive subsistence agriculture is also known as shifting cultivation or slash and burn cultivation.

A patch of land is cleared and then set on fire. This patch of land is used to sow seeds and grow crops.

48. **(a)** The 'slash and burn' agriculture is known as 'Conuco' in Venezuela.

49. **(c)** The 'slash and burn' agriculture is known as 'Roca' in Brazil.

50. **(d)** Low production is the major problem of Jhumming cultivation.

51. **(b)** The 'slash and burn' agriculture is known as 'Bewar' in Madhya Pradesh.

52. **(a)** Andhra Pradesh- Penda

Odhisa- Pama Dabi

Rajasthan- Valre

Jharkhand- Kuruwa

53. **(a)** Laxmi is related to the primary sector.

54. **(c)** Laxmi is related to the marginal farmer category.

55. **(b)** In agriculture, underemployment is at its maximum.

56. **(c)** Construction of dams and canals creates employment in large numbers in rural areas by adjusting the number of unskilled labourers.

57. **(a)** Increase in production is the main result of increasing irrigation facilities in the field of agriculture.

58. **(d)** Canals are the means of irrigation and fall under the public sector.

### Note

*According to Reserve Bank of India,*
- *A "marginal farmer" cultivates up to 1 hectare of agricultural land (as an owner, renter, or sharecropper).*
- *A farmer farming agricultural land of more than 1 hectare and up to 2 hectares (as owner, renter, or sharecropper) is referred to as a "small farmer".*

59.  **(c)** Hirakud

60.  **(a)** West Bengal

# All India 2020

# CBSE Board Solved Paper

## SECTION - A

**(Multiple Choice Questions)**

**(20 × 1 = 20)**

1. Name the Civil Code of 1804 which established equality before law and secured the right to property in France. **1**

2. Who among the following wrote the Vande Mataram? **1**

   (a) Rabindranath Tagore

   (b) Bankim Chandra Chattopadhyay

   (c) Abanindranath Tagore

   (d) Dwarkanath Tagore

3. Which one of the following was NOT the reason for the popularity of scientific ideas among the common people in eighteenth century Europe? **1**

   (a) Printing of idea of Isaac Newton

   (b) Development of printing press

   (c) Interest of people in science and reason

   (d) Traditional aristocratic groups supported it.

4. Name the two hostile group of Second World War. **1**

**OR**

Name the two industrialists of Bombay who built huge industrial empires during nineteenth century.

5. Which among the following best signifies the idea of liberal nationalism of nineteenth century Europe? **1**

   (a) Emphasis on social justice

   (b) State planned socio-economic system

   (c) Freedom for individual and equality before law

   (d) Supremacy of State oriented nationalism.

6. "When France sneezes, the rest of Europe catches cold". Who among the following said this popular line? **1**

   (a) Giuseppe Mazzini

   (b) Matternich

   (c) Otto Von Bismarck

   (d) Guiseppe Garibaldi

7. Certain events are given below. Choose the appropriate chronological order: **1**

   1. Coming of Simon Commission to India

   2. Demand of Purna Swaraj in Lahore Session of INC.

   3. Government of India Act, 1919

   4. Champaran Satyagraha

   Choose the correct option:

   (a) 3 – 2 – 4 – 1   (b) 1 – 2 – 4 – 3

   (c) 2 – 3 – 1 – 4   (d) 4 – 3 – 1 – 2

8. Complete the following table with appropriate terms in places of A and B. **1**

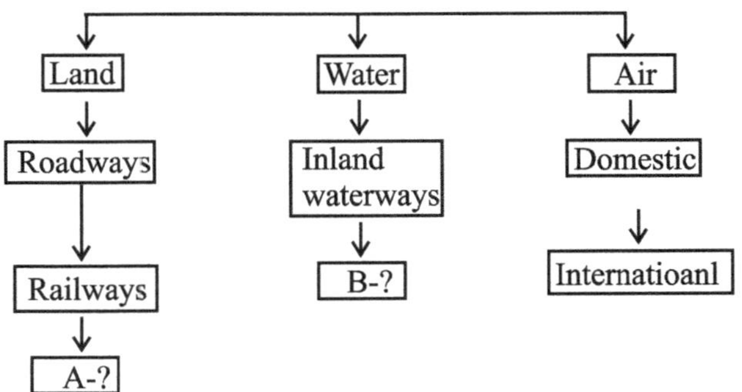


9. India has emerged as a software giant at the International level. Suggest any one way to enhance the export of information technology. **1**

10. Business processes Outsourcing (BPO) is an example of _____ industry in India. **1**

**OR**

Lime stone, silica, alumina and gypsum are the raw materials of _____ industry.

*Note: (**) Marked questions are out of syllabus so these are not explained or answered.*

**OR**

Limestone, Silica, Alumina and Gypsum are used as raw materials in the manufacture of cement.

**11.** Read the following features of a soil and name the related soil: 1

> (a) Develops in high rainfall area
> (b) Intense leaching process takes place.
> (c) Humus content is low.

**12.** Write the temperature requirement of Maize crop. 1

**OR**

Write the amount of annual rainfall required for the cultivation of Wheat.

**13.** Read the following information and write a single term for it. 1

> The Constitution of India provides freedom to profess and practice any religion to all its citizens. The Constitution of India prohibits discrimination on religious grounds.

**14.** Consider the following statements regarding language policy of Indian Federation. 1

1. Hindi was identified as the official language.

2. Besides Hindi, there are 21 other languages recognised as scheduled languages.

3. English can be used along with Hindi for official purpose.

Choose the right option from the following:

(a) 1 and 3      (b) 1 and 2

(c) only 1      (d) 1, 2 and 3

**15.** In the question given below, there are two statements marked as Assertion (A) and Reason (R). Read the statements and choose the correct option: 1

**Assertion (A):** Democracy is a legitimate government.

**Reason (R):** Regular, free and fair elections are the spirit of democracy.

(a) Both (A) and (R) are true and (R) is the correct explanation of (A).

(b) Both (A) and (R) are incorrect.

(c) (A) is correct, but (R) is incorrect.

(d) (A) is incorrect, but (R) is correct.

**16.** Suggest any one way to make political parties more responsive to the people's need and demand. 1

**OR**

Suggest any one way to promote the public participation in the Political Parties for enhancing the quality of democracy.

**17.** Correct the following statement and rewrite it.

Removing barriers or restrictions by the government is known as Globalisation. 1

**OR**

International Monetary Fund (IMF) is an organisation whose aim is to liberalise international trade.

**18.** Which among the following issues currency notes on behalf of the Central Government? 1

(a) State Bank of India

(b) Reserve Bank of India

(c) Commercial Bank of India

(d) Union Bank of India

**19.** Choose the incorrect option from the following: 1

| List I | List II |
|---|---|
| (a) Courier | (1) Tertiary Sector |
| (b) Fisherman | (2) Primary Sector |
| (c) Carpenter | (3) Primary Sector |
| (d) Banker | (4) Tertiary Sector |

**20.** Define the term Per Capita income. 1

**OR**

Define the term Literacy rate.

## SECTION - B

### (Short Answer Questions)

$(7 \times 3 = 21)$

$(1 \times 5 = 5)$

**21.** Describe the implications of First World War on the economic and political situation of India. 3

**OR**

Describe the role of poor peasantry in the 'Civil Disobedience Movement.'

**22.** How had Indian trade been beneficial for the British during seventeenth century? Explain. 1

**OR**

Why did the elite of Britain prefer hand made goods in the mid-nineteenth century? Explain.

**23.** "A concerted effort has to be made in order to use mineral resources in a planned and sustainable manner." Suggest and explain any three measures. **3**

**24.** "The pace of change in the communication sector has been rapid in modern times." Support the statement with examples. **5**

**OR**

"Roadways have an edge over Railways." Support the statement with examples.

**25.** Describe the rationale behind the implementation of Decentralisation in India. **3**

**26.** Read the sources given below and answer the questions that follow: **3**

Over a hundred countries of the world today claim and practice some kind of democratic politics: they have formal constitutions, they hold elections, they have parties and they guarantee rights of citizens. While these features are common to most of them, these democracies are very much different from each other in terms of their social situations, their economic achievements and their cultures. Clearly, what may be achieved or not achieved under each of these democracies will be very different.

(I) Explain the fascination for democracy amongst various countries.

(II) Explain democracy on the basis of expected and actual outcome.

**27.** Why is the tertiary sector becoming more important in India? Explain. **3**

**OR**

Why is organised sector preferred by the employees? Explain.

**28.** Describe the significance of the Reserve Bank of India. **3**

# SECTION - C

## (Long Answer Questions)

**29.** Read the sources given below and answer the questions that follows:

### Source-1: Religious Reform and Public Debates

There were intense controversies between social and religious reformers and the Hindu orthodoxy over matters like widow immolation, monotheism, Brahmanical priesthood, and idolatry. In Bengal, as the debate developed, tracts and newspapers proliferated, circulating a variety of argument.

### Source-2: New Forms of Publication

New literary forms also entered the world of reading lyrics, short stories, essays about social and political matters. In different ways, they reinforced the new emphasis on human lives and intimate feelings, about the political and social rules that shaped such things.

### Source-3: Women and Print

Since social reforms and novels had already created a great interest in women's lives and emotions, there was also an interest in what women would have to say about their own lives.

### Source-1: Religious Reform and Public Debates

(1) Evaluate how did the print shape the nature of the debate in the early nineteenth century in India. 1

### Source-2: New Forms of Publication

(2) To What extent do you agree that print opened up new worlds of experience and gave a vivid sense of diversity of human lives? **2**

### Source-3: Women and Print

(3) To what extent did the print culture reflect a great interest in women's lives and emotions? Explain. **2**

**30.** Explain the factors which are responsible for location of industries. **5**

**OR**

Explain the ways through which the industrial pollution of fresh water can be reduced.

**31.** 'Communalism can take various forms in politics.' Explain. **5**

**32.** Describe the necessity of political parties in democratic countries. **5**

**OR**

Describe the efforts to reform political parties in India.

**33.** "The impact of globalisation has not been uniform." Explain with examples. **5**

**34.** Why is sustainability important development? Explain. **5**

## SECTION - D

### (Map Based Question)

**35.** (a) Two places A and B are marked on the given political outline map of India. Identify them and write their correct names on the lines drawn near them.

**(1 × 2 = 2)**

(A) The place where Indian National Congress Session was held.

(B) The place where Indigo Planters organised Satyagraha.

(b) On the same outline Map of India, locate and label and label any four of the following with appropriate symbols: **(1 × 4 = 4)**

(i) Haldia - Major sea port

(ii) Mohali - Software technology park**

(iii) Vijayanagar - Iron and Steel Industrial Centre**

(iv) Naraura - Nuclear Power Plant

(v) Tehri - Dam

(vi) Thiruvananthapuram - International Airport**

---

---

**1.** The Napoleonic Code is also called the 'French Civil Code of 1804' defined the concept of equality before the law and also secured the right to property. This code was generated to simplify all the laws and systematized into a single document. This Code was spread to the regions under French control.

**2.** **(b)** Bankim Chandra Chattopadhayay was an Indian novelist, poet, Essayist and journalist. He was the author of the 1882 Bengali language novel Anandamath, which is one of the landmarks of modern Bengali and Indian literature. He was the composer of Vande Mataram, written in highly sanskritized Bengali, personifying Bengal as a mother goddess and inspiring activists during the Indian Independence Movement.

**3.** **(d)** The aristocracy is a social class that a particular society considers its highest order. Aristocracy was usually seen as rule by a privileged group. It was NOT the reason for the popularity of scientific ideas among the common people in eighteenth century Europe.

**4.** **Axis powers:** Germany, Italy and Japan.

**Allied powers:** France, Britain, USSR, USA, China.

### OR

In Bombay, Parsis like Dinshaw Petit and Jamsed jee Nusserwanjee Tata who built huge industrial empires in India, accumulated their initial wealth partly from exports to China, and partly from raw cotton shipments to England. Some industrialists in nineteenth-century Europe prefer hand labour over machines because: Machines were costly, ineffective, difficult to repair, and needed huge capital investments. Labour was available at low wages at that period of time. In seasonal industries only seasonal labour was required.

> **Note**
>
> *Jamsedji Nusserwanji Tata, regarded as the 'Father of Indian Industry', the founder of the Tata Group. He singlehandedly changed a nation's fortunes and steered it towards the path of industrialization.*

**5.** **(d)** Equality before the law, also known as equity before the law, freedom through the eyes of the law, moral equity, or moral egalitarianism, is the concept that of individual person must be viewed fairly by the law (concept of isonomy) and that both are entitled to the same principles of justice. Global populism was basically a 19th-century philosophy and party. The promotion of human and economic rights and of national supremacy was left-liberal priorities.

**6.** **(b)** Metternich is most well-known for his role in the Congress of Vienna in 1815, and resulting influence on subsequent European history. Metternich was appointed foreign minister in 1809 and, within a few years, he had pulled the Empire back from the brink of possible extinction.

7. **(d)** 4-3-1-2

   • Champaran Satygraha (1917)

   • Government of India act 1919 (1919)

   • Coming of Simon commission to India (1928)

   • Demand of Purna Swaraj in Lahore session of INC (1929)

8. A-pipeline, B-Overseas

   Pipeline transportation is a method of transportation which involves movement of solid, liquid or gaseous products over long distances through pipelines. This mode of transportation is mostly used for transport of crude and refined petroleum products such as oil and natural gas.

   Overseas shipping is the process of transporting goods between different countries, whether by sea, air, or road. When shipping overseas, freight forwarders must deal with the customs authorities to make sure the cargo can arrive safely at its destination.

9. Globalisation/International trade.

   • India is emerged as the software giant in the IT sector.

   • It can be enhanced in many ways to improve the export of information technology.

   • This platform can be promoted all over the world through planned and synchronized social media.

   • It can also be enhanced through digital media marketing techniques.

   • If this gets promoted with better and innovative ideas, countries all over the world would invest in our work and would also come forward to work with us.

10. Information Technology

*Business processes Outsourcing refers to when companies outsource business processes to a third-party (external) company. The primary goal is to cut costs, free up time, and focus on core aspects of the business.*

**OR**

   Cement

11. Laterite soil is commonly used as road pavement materials to provide a better sub base, gravel for roads and base materials. They are also good material for embankment construction. Laterite soils are good for tea, coffee and cashew cultivation. Laterite soils lack fertility due to intensive leaching. When manured and irrigated, some laterites are suitable for growing plantation crops like tea, coffee, rubber, cinchona, coconut, areca nut, etc.

12. Maize is grown in temperatures between 21°C and 27°C during the day and around 14°C during the night. But the most important factor is the 140 frost-free days. The crop is very susceptible to frost; therefore, its cultivation in temperate latitudes is limited.

**OR**

   Wheat requires rainfall of about 50 cm to 90 cm is most ideal. The optimum temperature range for ideal germination of wheat seed is 20-25° C though the seeds can germinate in the temperature range 3.5 to 35° C. Rains just after sowing hamper germination and encourage seedling blight. Areas with a warm and damp climate are not suited for wheat growing.

13. Secular/Secularism

*The Preamble has been amended only once so far, in 1976, by the 42nd Constitutional Amendment Act, 1976. The amendment added three new words: socialist, secular, and integrity.*

14. **(d)** As per Article 343(1) of the Constitution of India, Hindi in Devanagari script shall be the official language of the Union. There are 22 official languages in India and they are covered under the 8th schedule of the Indian Constitution. The languages are ---1) Assamese, (2) Bengali, (3) Gujarati, (4) Hindi, (5) Kannada, (6) Kashmiri, (7) Konkani, (8) Malayalam, (9) Manipuri, (10) Marathi, (11) Nepali, (12) Oriya, (13) Punjabi, (14) Sanskrit, (15) Sindhi, (16) Tamil, (17) Telugu, (18) Urdu (19) Bodo, (20) Santhali, (21) Maithili and (22) Dogri.

   There is no national language of India as per the constitution; Hindi and English both are considered the official language of India.

15. **(a)** Democracy is a form of government in which the nation's people rule the state directly by making legislation or indirectly through their elected representatives. In a democracy, the head of the state is an elected person who represents the government. So conduction of free, fair and regular elections, i.e., in a definite time interval, ensures the democracy of

the country. The fear of getting out of power in the next elections keeps them in check and motivates them to work for the country's welfare. The open debate, like the parliamentary discussion, helps the ordinary people understand the good and bad internal government proceedings and creates transparency between the government and the people. The second tool that ensures transparency is the Right to Information, which gives ordinary people the right to ask the government to explain its actions.

**16.** Peaceful demonstration or mass mobilisation.

**OR**

By reserving at least one third of the seats for women candidates. So that, women have their share in the party's decision making bodies so that steps can be taken for the betterment of women.

**17.** Removing barriers or restrictions by the government is known as Liberalisation.

**OR**

World Trade Organisation (WTO) is an organisation whose aim is to liberalise international trade.

The IMF aims to foster global monetary cooperation, secure financial stability, provide policy advice and financing for developing countries, promote exchange rate stability, and establish an international payment system, etc.

**18. (b)** RBI can issue any note of any denomination but NOT exceeding Rs. 10,000. The notes denomination is notified by Government and RBI acts accordingly. Under Section 22 of the Reserve Bank of India Act, RBI has sole right to issue currency notes of various denominations except one rupee notes. The Reserve Bank of India, chiefly known as RBI, is India's central bank and regulatory body responsible for regulation of the Indian banking system. It is under the ownership of Ministry of Finance, Government of India. It is responsible for the control, issue and maintaining supply of the Indian rupee. It also manages the country's main payment systems and works to promote its economic development. Bharatiya Reserve Bank Note Mudran (BRBNM) is a specialised division of RBI through which it prints and mints Indian currency notes in four of its currency printing presses located in Nashik (Maharashtra; Western India), Dewas (Madhya Pradesh; Central India), Mysore (Karnataka; Southern India) and Salboni (West Bengal; Eastern India).

**19. (c)** Potter, carpenter and factory workers are all workers in the secondary sector. The primary sector includes all those activities the end purpose of which consists in exploiting natural resources: agriculture, fishing, forestry, mining, deposits.

**20.** The per capita income is calculated by dividing the total income of the country by the population of the country. It represents the average income of an individual in a country.

**OR**

Literacy rate measures the proportion of literate population in the 7 and above age, who has the ability to read, write and understand.

**21.** The implications of First World War on the economic and political situation of India are discussed below:

**Economic**

(i) It led to a huge increase in defense expenditure which was financed by war loans.

(ii) Customs duties were raised and income tax introduced.

(iii) Villages were called upon to supply soldiers, and the forced recruitment in rural areas caused widespread anger.

(iv) The war created a demand for industrial goods like jute bags, cloth, rail, etc. and caused a decline in imports from other countries into India.

(v) Indian industries expanded during the war and earned fabulous profits.

(vi) Through the war years prices increased-doubled between 1913 and 1918-leading to extreme hardship for the common people.

**Political**

(i) In India, after the end of the war, the Punjabi soldiers returned, which aroused political activity against colonial rule in that province and became the spark for further, wider protests.

(ii) There was a surge of nationalism and the rise of mass civil disobedience when the Montagu-Chelmsford Reforms' failed to deliver on the expectation of home rule.

(iii) As the war dragged on, casualties mounted, forced recruitments occurred, and resentment grew to fuel nationalism.

**OR**

The roles of poor peasantry in the 'Civil Disobedience Movement' are discussed below:

(i) Areas like Rae Bareily, Agra, Lucknow, etc., and several other areas witnessed the participation of the peasantry in the Civil Disobedience Movement. Hence, this movement transformed into a mass movement.

(ii) As part of the Civil Disobedience Movement, the peasantry ceased paying taxes. They stopped paying taxes not only to the government but also to zamindars and landlords.

(iii) Peasant leaders like Rafi Ahmed Kidwai and Kalika Prasad took the leadership of the movement.

**22.** The Indian trades had been beneficial for the British during seventeenth century due to following reasons:

(i) Cotton, silk, indigo dye, saltpetre and tea were in demand in Britain and their availability from India enhanced the quality of life for the British.

(ii) Hand-made products came to symbolise refinement and class because they were better finished, individually produced and carefully designed.

(iii) Machine-made goods were for export to the colonies.

**OR**

The elite of British prefer hand made goods in the mid-nineteenth century because :

(i) Handmade products came to symbolise refinement and class.

(ii) Hand-made cloths were costlier and of better quality.

(iii) They were better finished, individually produced and carefully designed.

(iv) Machine-made goods were for masses, in the colonies not for classes.

**23.** Following are the steps to make use of minerals in a planned and sustainable manner:

(i) Reuse the waste to reduce the production cost.

(ii) Technologies need to be constantly evolved to allow the use of low grade ores at low cost.

(iii) Recycling of metals, using scrap metals and other substitutes.

**24.** The pace of change in the communication sector has been rapid in modern times because of following reasons:

(i) The Subscriber Trunk Dialing (STD) telephone facility strengthen telecom networks in India by integrating the development in space technology with communication technology.

(ii) Mass Communication served as means of entertainment as well as a medium of creating awareness through radio, television, newspapers, magazines, books, and films. Example: All India Radio (Akashvani), Doordarshan.

(iii) With the advent of mobile phones, long-distance communication became easier and the communication industry experienced growth.

(iv) The Indian postal network is one largest of its kind and handles letters, cards, envelopes, and periodicals like magazines, newspapers, and other media. All these are a part of personal communication.

**OR**

Roadways have an edge over Railways because of following reason:

(i) Road transport is easy to access in hilly areas whereas in rail transport it's difficult to reach such places.

(ii) Road transport operating cost is cheaper than rail transport.

(iii) Door to door transportation can only be provided by roadways.

(iv) Construction and maintenance cost is less in road transport.

(v) Road transport is also used as a feeder to other modes of transport, such as railway stations and air and sea ports.

(vi) Road transport is better to transport goods for short distance.

**25.** The rationales behind the implementation of decentralisation in India are:

(i) Since India is a vast country; central government is unable to hear the needs of people from different areas.

(ii) The local government can easily understand the needs and demands of their people.

(iii) To help women to participate in decision making process. 33% seats are reserved for women in local government.

(iv) To take off burden from central and state government.

(v) To strengthen democracy.

(vi) To make possible for the people to directly participate in decision making at local level.

(vii) Local government have better ideas on where to spend money and how to manage things more efficiently.

 **Note**

*Madhya Pradesh became the first state in the country to implement the 3-tier panchayati raj—gram panchayat (village-level council), janpad panchayat (block committee), and zilla panchayat (district council)—envisaged in the 73rd Constitution Amendment Act, 1992.*

**26. (I)**

(i) Democracy gives people freedom of life and freedom of speech.

(ii) A democratic country has a strong economic system and all the people get equal opportunities.

**(II) Expected Outcome:**

(i) Citizens right to information about the government and its functioning.

(ii) Regular, free and fair elections, open public debate on major policies and legislations.

**Actual outcome:**

(i) Every decision does not comes forward in a public debate.

(ii) Holding elections that offer a fair chance to everyone.

(iii) Sharing information with people rarely happens.

(iv) Democracies have never been free of corruption.

(v) Government has failed to pay attention to the needs and expectations of people.

**27.** The tertiary sector becoming more important in India because:

(i) The development of primary and secondary sectors increases the demand for services such as transport, trade, storage.

(ii) Demand for tourism, shopping, private schools, private hospitals, etc. increases with the increase in the level of income.

(iii) Liberalisation of financial sector provided an environment for faster growth of financial services.

(iv) Basic services like healthcare, education, banking, postal service, police stations and courts are required in a developing country like India, which are mostly taken care of by the government.

**OR**

The organised sector preferred by the employees because:

(i) It covers those enterprises or places of work where the terms of employment are regular.

(ii) It provides job security for all employees and a certain amount of money is kept apart from the salary every year to pay the lump-sum amount to the employees after retirement.

(iii) They follow its rules and regulations which are given in various laws such as the Factories Act, the Minimum Wages Act, the Payment of Gratuity Act, Shops Act, etc.

 **Note**

*The primary sector, which employs 60% of the population, contributes around 23% to the GDP; in contrast, the tertiary sector employs 24% of the workforce and contributes to 51% of the GDP.*

**28.** The significances of the Reserve Bank of India are discussed below:

(i) RBI acts as a banker to the government and is the custodian of the foreign exchange reserves of the economy.

(ii) It issues currency notes on behalf of the central government.

(iii) It supervises the functioning of formal source of loans.

(iv) RBI monitors the banks and make sure that they maintain minimum reserves as per the guidelines of Central Bank.

It sees that banks give loans not just to big traders but also to small borrowers, small cultivators etc.

Periodically banks have to submit information to RBI on how much they are lending, to whom, at what interest rate, etc.

(v) RBI ensure that the banking system of the country does not suffer from any setback and money market remains stable.

**29.** (1) Different religious groups confronted the changes happening within colonial society in different ways and offered a variety of new interpretations of the beliefs of different religions.

(2) The print opened up new worlds of experience and a vivid sense of diversity because of following reasons:

(i) Print created the possibility of wide circulation of ideas, and introduced a new world of debate and discussion.

(ii) Print created a new culture of reading because earlier there was a hearing public, now a reading public came into being.

Earlier, women had no means to share their lives and emotions. Print helped in developing many women authors. Even some male authors started to write about women's lives.

**30.** The factors which are responsible for location of industries are given below:

**(i) Closeness to the source of raw material:** Industries are located near the source of raw materials which saves the cost of transportation. Steel centres are developed where coal and iron are easily available.

**(ii) Power resources:** Coal, oil and water sources of power. Most of the industries are located near coal fields.

**(iii) Means of Transportation:** Industries need cheap, developed and quick means of transportation. Cheap means of transportation are required for the movement of workers, raw materials and machinery to the factories.

**(iv) Climate:** Stimulating climate increase the efficiency of the labourers. The cotton textile industry required humid climate. The aircraft industry needs clear weather.

**(v) Skilled Labour:** Cheap and skilled labour is essential for the location of industries.

**(vi) Market Availability:** Nearness to the market is important since finished goods should reach the market at the end of the manufacturing process

**(vii) Availability of Water:** Many industries are established near rivers, canals, and lakes. The iron and steel industry, textile industries, and chemical industries require large quantities of water for their proper functioning.

**OR**

The industrial pollution of fresh water can be reduced by following ways:

(i) Installation of water treatment plants at the industrial sites for recycling.

(ii) Treating hot water and effluents before releasing them in rivers and ponds.

(iii) Minimising the use of water for processing by reusing.

(iv) Regulation of use of ground water by industries.

(v) Harvesting of rain water to meet water requirement.

**31.** (i) In a democracy, communalism may take the form when the majoritarian community starts believing in the superiority of their religion and ignores the wishes of the minorities.

(ii) Communal violence is the worst form of communalism. It acquires the political form when it is sponsored by the state.

(iii) When religious beliefs of a person involve prejudices and stereotypes, claiming one religion's ideas to be superior to another.

(iv) Political mobilisation on religious lines involves the use of sacred symbols, religious leaders, emotional appeal and plain fear in order to bring the followers of one religion together in the political arena.

(v) When a majority community tries to establish its domination over the other communities with the help of the state. Minority communities under such circumstances, retaliates by demanding the formation of separate state for them.

**32.** The importance of a political party in democracy can be understood from the given points:

(i) Political party acts as a link between government and masses.

(ii) Political parties discuss the problems of the state, the working and failure of the government and give suggestion for the upliftment of masses.2

(iii) The rise of political parties is directly linked to the emergence of representative democracies. As society became larger and complicated, they also need some agency to gather different views on various issues and to present these to the government.

(iv) Political parties from and run governments. Various political leaders are assigned different ministries to carry out the task of governance.

(v) Elected representatives make promises regarding major policies for different sections of society, irrespective of sex, race, religion, etc.

**OR**

The following efforts have been made to reform political parties in India:

(i) Supreme Court made mandatory for every person contesting the election to give an affidavit regarding his wealth and criminal cases pending against him. With this people can acquire information about their leaders and this has also led to decline in criminalisation of politics.

(ii) Amendment was made in the constitution to prevent MPs and MLAs from changing parties. If anyone try to change his/her party, he/she lose his/her seat.

(iii) Election Commission has ordered all political parties to hold their organisational elections and file the income tax returns for the purpose of introducing internal democracy.

(iv) Regulating internal affairs in the party should be made compulsory. Registers of the existing members should be made. All parties should follow their constitution and regular elections should be held for the higher post of the party.

(v) Funds should provide for contesting elections. It can be either given in the form of cash or in the form of petrol, paper, telephone, etc. This may reduce the influence of money in the elections.

**33.** The impact of globalisation has not been uniform because:

(i) Small manufacturers and retailers have been hard hit due to globalisation.

(ii) Many illiterate and poor people lost their jobs due to closure of small units and change in technology.

(iii) The developed countries exploits resources from underdeveloped countries.

(iv) Competition from companies in developed countries also cripple industries of under developed and developing countries.

(v) Developed countries took resources from underdeveloped countries at cheap rate and exported costly finished products to underdeveloped countries.

(vi) Globalisation has been beneficial only for developed countries. And had a bad impact on the underdeveloped and developing countries.

**34.** The issue of sustainability is important for development because:

(i) With the passage of times the generation changes and with this change society wants more and more benefits from the resources. This increases Ecological footprint.

(ii) The increasing needs of people decaying things day by day and excessive use is making things worse. The available resources will be exhausted soon and our coming generation will stay deprived from all kind of needs if the speed of usage remain same.

(iii) The development should be done by keeping in mind the future usage.

(iv) If resources will not be sustained for future then our natural resources will be exhausted after some time and upcoming generations will not be able to take the advantage of these natural resources.

**35.  (a)**

**(b)**

(ii) Mohali
(v) Tehri Dam
(iv) Naraura
(i) Haldia
(iii) Vijayanagar
(iv) Thiruvananthapuram

# CBSE Board Solved Paper

## SECTION - A

**(Very Short Answer Questions)**

$(20 \times 1 = 20)$

1. Which of the following revolutions is called as the first expression of nationalism? **1**

   (a) French Revolution

   (b) Russian Revolution

   (c) Glorious Revolution

   (d) The Revolution of the liberals

2. Why was the Inland Emigration Act of 1859 troublesome for plantation workers? **1**

3. Why was the Vernacular Press Act passed in 1878? **1**

**OR**

Why was 'Gulamgiri' book written by Jyotiba Phule in 1871 ?

4. Define the term 'Veto.' **1**

**OR**

Define the term 'Carding.'

5. Fill in the blank. **1**

Buddhist missionaries from China introduced hand-printing technology into ______ around AD 768-770.

**OR**

By 1448, Gutenberg perfected the system of printing first book he printed was the ______.

6. Why was reading of manuscript not easy in India? Choose the appropriate reason from the following options: **1**

   (a) Manuscripts were highly cheap.

   (b) Manuscripts were widely spread out.

   (c) Manuscripts were written in English and Hindi.

   (d) Manuscripts were fragile.

7. Who were called 'Chapmen?' **1**

   (a) Book seller

   (b) Paper seller

   (c) Workers of printing press

   (d) Seller of 'penny chap books.'

8. Fill in the blanks. **1**

| Types of Resources | Examples |
|---|---|
| A? | Biotic and Abiotic |
| B? | Renewable and Non-renewable |

9. Which is the oldest artificial sea port of India? **1**

**OR**

Which is the deepest, landlocked and well protected sea port of India?

10. In which of the following States is Kalpakkam Nuclear Power Plant located? **1**

   (a) Gujarat      (b) Odisha

   (c) Kerala      (d) Tamil Nadu

11. Choose the correct option from columns A and B. **1**

| A | B |
|---|---|
| (a) Chandrapur Thermal power plant | (i) Odisha |
| (b) Mayurbhanj iron ore mines | (ii) Amarkantak |
| (c) Kalol oil fields | (iii) Gujarat |
| (d) Bauxite mines | (iv) Jharkhand |

12. Fill in the blank: **1**

______ industry is used for manufacturing aircraft, utensils and wires.

13. Which one of the following is a major caste group of Sri Lanka: **1**

   (a) Christian and Tamil

   (b) Buddhist and Hindu

   (c) Sinhali and Tamil

   (d) Sinhali and Christian

14. State any one step taken in Belgium to rule out the problem of regional differences and cultural diversities. **1**

15. Modern democracies maintain check and balance system. Identify the correct option based on the horizontal power sharing arrangement. **1**

(a) Central government, state government, local bodies.

(b) Legislature, executive, judiciary.

(c) Among different social groups.

(d) Among different pressure groups.

**16.** Suggest any one way to protect women from domestic oppression.                                                     1

**OR**

Suggest any one way to create communal harmony among various communities of India.

**17.** Choose the incorrect option from column A and column B.                                                            1

| Column A<br>(Category of Person) | Column B<br>(Developmental goals/Aspirations) |
|---|---|
| (a) Landless rural labourers | (i) More days of work and better wages |
| (b) Prosperous farmers from Punjab | (ii) Availability of other sources of irrigation |
| (c) Farmers who depend only on rain for growing crops | (iii) Assured a higher support prices for their crops |
| (d) A rural woman from a land owning family | (iv) Regular job and high wages to increase her income |

**18.** Study the table and answer the question given below:                                                              1

Some comparative data on Haryana, Kerala and Bihar

| State | Infant Mortality Rate per 1000 live births (2016) | Literacy Rate % 2011 | Net Attendance Ratio (per 100 persons) secondary stage (age 14 and 15 years 2013-14) |
|---|---|---|---|
| Haryana | 33 | 82 | 61 |
| Kerala | 10 | 94 | 83 |
| Bihar | 38 | 62 | 43 |

Source : Economic Survey, 2017-18 Vol. 2 Government of India: National Sample Survey Organisation (Report No. 575).

Question: In comparison to Kerala which state has the highest infant mortality rate.

**19.** Suggest any one way to create employment in semi-rural areas.                                                      1

**20.** How is GDP calculated?                                                                                            1

**OR**

How is Public sector different from Private sector?

GDP can be calculated by adding up all of the money spent by consumers, businesses, and the government in a given period.

## SECTION - B

### (Short Answer Questions)

**(8 × 3 = 24)**

**21.** Read the source given below and answer the question that follows.                                                 3

**Source: The Movement in the Towns**

The movement started with middle-class participation in the cities. Thousands of students left government-controlled schools and colleges, headmasters and teachers resigned and lawyers gave up their legal practices. The council elections were boycotted in most provinces except Madras, where the Justice Party, the party of the non-Brahmans, felt that entering the council was one way of gaining some power-something that usually only Brahmans had access to.

The effects of non-cooperation on the economic front were more dramatic. Foreign goods were boycotted. The import of foreign cloth halved between 1921 and 1922, its value dropping from 102 crore. In many places merchants and traders refused to trade in foreign goods or finance foreign trade. As the boycott movement spread, and people began discarding, imported clothes and wearing only Indian ones, production of Indian textile mills and handlooms went up.

1.   Explain the role of 'Justice Party in boycotting of Council elections'                                               1

2.   How was the effect of 'non-cooperation on the economic front dramatic'                                              1

3.   Explain the effect of 'Boycott movement on foreign textile trade'                                                    1

**22.** Explain any three effects of population growth in England in the eighteenth century.   **3**

**OR**

Why did the export of Indian textile decline at the beginning of the nineteenth century? Explain any three reasons.

**23.** Describe the importance of judicious use of resources. **3**

**OR**

Describe the different steps of 'resource planning.'

**24.** Efficient means of transport are pre-requisites for fast development of the country. Support the statement with examples.   **3**

**25.** Describe any three features of 'federal government'.

  **3**

**OR**

Describe any three features of 'unitary government'.

**26.** Mention any three features of 'secularism' described in the Indian Constitution.   **3**

**OR**

Mention the problem of 'Casteism' in Indian politics.

**27.** Suggest any three ways to maintain Body Mass Index (BMI).   **3**

**28.** "Tertiary sector activities help in the development of the primary and secondary sectors." Evaluate the statement.

  **3**

**OR**

"Primary sector was the most important sector of economic activity at initial stages of development." Evaluate the statement.

## SECTION - C

### (Long Answer  Questions)

(5 × 5 = 25)

**29.** How did ideas of national unity in early nineteenth century Europe allied to the ideology of liberalism? Explain.   **5**

**OR**

How did Greek war of independence mobilise nationalist feelings among the educated elite across Europe? Explain.

**30.** Why is agriculture called the backbone of Indian economy? Explain.   **5**

**31.** Describe any five functions of political party.   **5**

**32.** "Democratic system is better than any other form of government." Support the statement with examples.   **5**

**33.** "Bank plays an important role in the economic development of the country." Support the statement with examples.   **5**

**OR**

"Credit sometimes pushes the borrower into a situation from which recovery is very painful." Support the statement with examples.

## SECTION - D

### (Case Based Question)

(5 × 1 = 5)

**34.** Read the sources given below and answer the questions that follow:

**Source A: Production across countries**

Until the middle of the twentieth century, production was largely organised within countries. What crossed the boundaries of these countries were raw material, food stuff and finished products. Colonies such as India exported raw materials and food stuff and imported finished goods. Trade was the main channel connecting distant counties. This was before large companies called Multinational Corporations (MNCs) emerged on the scene.

**Source B: Foreign trade and integration of markets**

Foreign trade creates an opportunity for the producers to reach beyond the domestic markets, i.e., markets of their own countries, Producers can sell their produce not only in markets located within the country but can also compete in markets located in other countries of the world. Similarly, for the buyers, import of goods produced in another country is one way of expanding the choice of goods beyond what is domestically produced.

**Source C: Impact of globalisation in India**

Globalisation and greater competition among producers-both local and foreign producers-has been of advantage to consumers, particularly the well-off sections in the urban areas. There is greater choice before these consumers who now enjoy improved quality and lower prices for several products. As a result, these people today, enjoy much higher standards of living than was possible earlier.

**Source A: Production across countries**   **1**

**1.** How are MNCs a major force in connecting the countries of the world?

**Source B: Foreign trade and integration of markets2**

**2.** How does foreign trade become a main channel in connecting countries?

**Source C: Impact of globalisation in India.**   **2**

**3.** How is globalisation beneficial for consumers?

## SECTION - E
### (Map Based Question)

(2 + 4 = 6)

**35.** (a)  Two features 'A' and 'B' are marked on the given political outline map of India. Identify these features with the help of the following informations and write their correct names on the lines marked near them

(A) The place where the Indian National Congress Session was held.                                   1

(B) The place where the movement of Indigo planters was started.                                   1

(b)  Locate and label any four of the following with appropriate symbols on the same given political outline map of India.

4

| | | |
|---|---|---|
| (i) | Sardar Sarovar | Dam |
| (ii) | Bhilai | Iron and Steel Plant |
| (iii) | Pune | Software Technology Park |
| (iv) | Kochi | Major Sea Port |
| (v) | Indore | Cotton Textile Industry |
| (vi) | Naraura | Nuclear Power Plant |

## Solutions

1. **(a)** The French Revolution was a period of radical political and societal change in France that began with the Estates General of 1789 and ended with the formation of the French Consulate in November 1799. Many of its ideas are considered fundamental principles of liberal democracy, while the values and institutions it created remain central to French political discourse.

2. Under this act, the plantation workers were not permitted to leave the tea gardens without official permission. People were hardly got such permissions. They were not allowed to go to their homes.

3. The Vernacular Press Act was passed in 1878 to curtail the freedom of Indian press by restricting vernacular newspapers to publish any material that might excite feelings of dissatisfaction against the British government.

**OR**

Jyotiba Phule wrote book 'Gulamgiri' in 1871 to linked the conditions of the black slave in America with those of the lower castes people in India.

**Note**

*Jyotirao Phule was social reformer, activist, writer, and thinker. He is remembered for his socio-cultural reforms. He was the founder of Satyashodak Samaj in 1873. The primary emphasis of this Samaj was seeking truth and propagated caste equality.*

4. The term 'Veto' refers to a constitutional right to reject a decision or proposal made by a lawmaking body.

**OR**

Carding is a mechanical process that disentangles, cleans and intermixes fibers such as cotton or wool in order to produce a continuous web suitable for subsequent processing like spinning.

5. Japan

**OR**

Bible

6. **(d)** A manuscript is a handwritten composition on paper, bark, cloth, metal, palm leaf, or any other material. Some of the most common genres were Bibles, religious commentaries, philosophy, law, and government texts.

7. **(d)** Chapbooks were timeless books of jest and tales that often sprang out of folklore. Chapbooks were so called because they were sold by peddlers known as chapmen. Chap comes from the Old English for trade, so a Chapman was literally a. dealer who sold books.

8. **(a)** Biotic and abiotic factors are what make up ecosystems. Biotic factors are living things within an ecosystem; such as plants, animals, and bacteria, while abiotic are non-living components; such as water, soil and atmosphere. The way these components interact is critical in an ecosystem.

   Resources are characterized as renewable or nonrenewable; a renewable resource can replenish itself at the rate it is used, while a nonrenewable resource has a limited supply. Renewable resources include timber, wind, and solar while nonrenewable resources include coal and natural gas.

9. Chennai Port, formerly known as Madras Port, is the second largest container port of India, behind Mumbai's Nhava Sheva. The port is the largest one in the Bay of Bengal. It is the third-oldest port among the 13 major ports of India with official port operations beginning in 1881, although maritime trade started much earlier in 1639 on the undeveloped shore. It is an artificial and all-weather port with wet docks. Once a major travel port, it became a major container port in the post-Independence era.

**OR**

The port which is encircled by land from all sides with a water passage towards the sea or ocean is termed as a land-locked port. Vishakhapatnam is the deepest land locked and well protected port along the Eastern coast of India. It is the executive capital of the Indian state of Andhra Pradesh.

10. **(d)** Kalpakkam is located in Tamil Nadu. It is considered the house of India's modern and indigenous nuclear station – the Madras Nuclear Power Plant. This small town is famous for its facilities and industrial growth and has also become a popular tourist site due to its backwaters and flocks of migratory birds. The Kalpakkam Atomic Power Station is said to be the house of two nuclear reactors operating at 220 MW power along with a super-fast breeder reactor having a power generation capacity of 500 MWe. This is why this facility is said to be the first step the Indian government has taken toward a prospective nuclear future. its backwaters and flocks of migratory birds. The Kalpakkam Atomic Power Station is said to be the house of two nuclear reactors operating at 220 MW power along with a super-fast breeder reactor having a power generation capacity of 500 MWe. This is why this facility is said to be the first step the Indian government has taken toward a prospective nuclear future.

11.

| A | B |
|---|---|
| (a) Chandrapur Thermal power plant | (iv) Jharkhand |
| (b) Mayurbhanj iron ore mines | (ii) Odisha |
| (c) Kalol oil fields | (iii) Gujarat |
| (d) Bauxite mines | (iv) Amarkantak |

12.  Aluminum smelting

13.  **(c)** Sri Lanka has two major social groups, Sinhalese and Sri Lankan Tamils. People who speak Sinhala are known as the Sinhalese. People who speak Tamil are the Sri Lankan Tamils. The Sinhalese comprise 74 percent of the total population in Sri Lanka while Tamils make up for 18 percent of the total population in Sri Lanka.

14.  The constitution prescribes equal number of French and Dutch speaking people in central government so single community cannot make decisions. They gave equal representation to both communities in the Central Cabinet of Ministers.

15.  **(b)** The basic difference between legislature executive and judiciary is that the legislature is concerned with enacting laws and policies. The role of the executive body is the implementation of those laws and policies.The principal role of the judiciary is to protect rule of law and ensure supremacy of law. It safeguards rights of the individual, settles disputes in accordance with the law and ensures that democracy does not give way to individual or group dictatorship.The scope of executive power varies greatly depending on the political context in which it emerges, and it can change over time in a given country. In democratic countries, the executive often exercises broad influence over national politics, though limitations are often applied to the executive. The role of the legislature is to pass laws, which are then enforced by the executive, and interpreted by the judiciary. The executive can also be the source of certain types of law, such as a decree or executive order.

16.  The one way to protect women from domestic oppression is: Educating them about laws to protect them from, Domestic Violence and other types of exploitation. Also empowering them by providing education.

**OR**

The one way to create communal harmony among various communities of India are given below:

(i)  To show respect to the religion of others.

(ii)  To celebrate all religious functions together.

(iii) To make others aware about the religion and social practices of people belonging to different faiths.

*The Protection of Women from Domestic Violence Act, 2005, Mission Shakti, Sakhi One-Stop Centres, Stree Manoraksha, Beti Bachao Beti Padhao, Nirbhaya Fund, etc. are some initiatives by the Indian government.*

17.  **(d)** Developmental goal for the for a rural women from a land owing family is that- (i) the women want to grow crops in her land by keeping agriculture laborers with less wage, (ii) Women from a land owing family wants that her children would get proper education at low cost.

18.  According to given data-
Bihar (38/1000) has the highest rate of mortality. Kerala has a low Infant Mortality Rate because it has adequate provision of basic health and educational facilities. Bihar has the high infant mortality rate because Bihar has lack of health facilities and child rearing practices not every traditional practice is good.

19.  One important way to create employment in semi-rural areas is.
By starting cottage industries and small processing units. Also, give credit to those who start small businesses.

20.  GDP can be canculated by adding up all of the money spent by consumers, business and the government in a

**OR**

**Public Sector-**
Public sector organisations are owned, controlled and managed by the government or other state-run bodies.

**Private Sector-**
Private sector organisations are owned, controlled and managed by individuals, groups or business entities.

*Formula to calculate GDP:*
*GDP = C + I + G + (X - M), where, C: Total Consumption Expenditure; G: Total Government Expenditures; I: Total Investments; X: Exports; M: Imports.*

21.  1.  The Justice Party members were non-Brahmans and so far had not been able to win elections, as the Brahman candidates always won. They thought it was a golden opportunity for them to enter the councils. So, they decided not to boycott council elections.

2.  The movement was started with middle class participation in the cities. Thousands of students left government controlled schools and colleges, headmasters and teachers resigned and lawyers gave up their legal practices.

3.  The effects of 'Boycott Movement' on foreign textile trade was that the import of foreign cloth halved between 1921 and 1922, its value dropping from 102 crore.

22.  Europe's population doubled during the 18$^{th}$ century, from roughly 100 million to almost 200 million. The three effects of population growth in England in the eighteenth century are:

(i)  Increase in the demand for food grains in Britain.

(ii)  The expansion of urban centres and the growth of industries led to the increase in demand for agricultural products, which lead to the increase in food grain prices.

(iii) Due to the rapid population growth, cities and towns were overcrowded, which worsened living conditions. Many people lived in cramped, unhealthy conditions, which increased the spread of disease.

(iv) As raw cotton exports from India increased, the price of raw cotton shot up. Weavers in India were starved of supplies and forced to buy raw cotton at exorbitant prices.

**OR**

The export of Indian textile decline at the beginning of the nineteenth century because:

(i) Britain imposed import duties on cotton textiles, thus export market declined.

(ii) Exports of British goods to India increased.

(iii) Due to cheap machine made goods weavers could not compete with them.

*Curretly, the textile sector contributes 2.3% to Indian gross domestic product, 7% of industrial output, 12% of export earnings, and more than 21% of total employment. India is the 6th largest producer of technical textiles with a 6% global share and the largest producer of cotton and jute in the world.*

**23.** The importance of judicious use of resources are given below:

(i) The planning is an important step in country like India where resources are enormously diverse for judicious use of resources.

(ii) It provides economically viable and sustainable solution to the issues related to resources and serves efficiently and effectively.

(iii) The proper management is vital for the efficient and sustainable use of resources.

(iv) Irrational consumption and overutilization may lead to socioeconomic and environmental problems. Most of the non-renewable resources, if exhausted, may not be able to be recreated.

(v) Resources are available only in limited quantities.

(vi) The awareness plays an important role in planning, management and use of resources.

**OR**

Resource planning is consisting of complex processes which are given below:

(i) Developing a planning structure endowed with appropriate technology, skill and institutional set up for implementing resource development plans.

(ii) Identification and inventory of resources across the regions of the country which involves surveying mapping, qualitative and quantitative estimation and measurement of the resources.

(iii) Harmonizing the resource development plans with overall national development plans.

**24.** (i) Transportation help in the development of primary, secondary and tertiary sectors. Therefore, efficient means of transport and communication are necessity prerequisites for fast development.

(i) Transportation links areas of production with consumption, agriculture with industry, and villages with towns and cities.

(ii) The development of a country depends upon the production of goods and services as well as their movement over space.

*The second-largest road network in the world is found in India. The total road length is 6.4 million km, which includes both urban and rural roads as well as national and state highways. 64.5% of goods are transported by road, and 90% of passenger traffic is on roads.*

**25.** The features of 'federal government' are given below:

(i) There are two or more levels of government.

(ii) Each level of government has its own jurisdiction in matters of legislation, taxation and administration.

(iii) The Supreme Court has the power to settle disputes between federal governments.

(iv) Fundamental provisions of Constitution cannot be amended by any one level of government.

(v) The separation of powers are defined by the Constitution and the legislative power.  [Any Three]

**OR**

The three features of 'unitary government' prohibits are given below:

(i) All powers are centralised in the hands of the central government and the centre is the reservoir of all state powers. In this system, there are no provincial governments and the Constitution empowers the central government to legislate, execute and adjudicate with full autonomy.

(ii) In unitary government there are neither provincial assemblies and executives nor the upper chambers at the centre. There is a single central government at the centre. There is a unicameral legislature popularly elected. The central legislature is there to legislate, executive to execute and the judiciary to adjudicate without any share.

(iii) The laws of the unitary system, unlike in a federation, are uniform. Laws made by the centre are equally enforced in the rest of the state without any territorial distinction while in a federation; the nature of the law varies from province to province.

**26.** The three features of 'secularism' described in the Indian Constitution are as follows;

(i) The Constitution of India does not give special recognition to any one religion and there is no state religion in India.

(ii) All individuals and communities have been given freedom to practice, profess and propagate any religion.

(iii) The Constitution of India discrimination on grounds of religion.

**OR**

The problems of 'Casteism' in Indian politics are discussed below:

(i) During elections parties choose candidates keeping in mind the caste composition of the electorate and nominate candidates from different castes to get necessary support to win elections.

(ii) Universal adult franchise and the principle of one vote compelled political leaders to gear up to the task of mobilising and securing political support.

(iii) Political parties and candidates in elections make appeal to caste sentiment to muster support. Some political parties are known to favour some castes and are seen as their representatives.

**27.** Body Mass Index is a person's height in kilograms by the square of height in meters. It can be maintain be following ways.

(i) Through anaerobic activity.

(ii) Through aerobic exercise.

(iii) Through and individual sports and team games.

**28.** "Tertiary sector activities help in the development of the primary and secondary sectors" because of following reasons:

(i) Tertiary sector activities, do not produce any good but they are an aid or support for the primary and secondary sectors production process.

(ii) Tertiary sector comprises of services such as hospitals, educational institutions, post and telegraph services, police stations, courts, defence, transports, banks, etc. All these are required as a basic service that helps the primary and secondary sectors.

(iii) Sometimes, it becomes necessary to store goods in godowns, communicate, and borrow money from banks. Hence, tertiary activities like storage, communication, and banking facilities help in these processes.

(iv) New services such as those based on information and communication technology have become important and essential.

**OR**

"Primary sector was the most important sector of economic activity at initial stages of development" because of:

(i) The primary sector was the most important sector as the methods of farming changed and agriculture sector began to prosper, it started producing much more food than before and most people were also employed in this sector.

(ii) This sector is still the largest economic sector and plays a significant role in the overall socio-economic development of the country.

(iii) The well being of the secondary sector depend on the on the primary sector. This sector generally takes the output of primary sector as raw material to manufacture finished goods.

(iv) Flourishing primary sector help in the development of strong secondary and tertiary sectors.

**29.** The ideas of national unity in early nineteenth Europe allied to the ideology of liberalism because of following reasons:

(i) It stood for the end of autocracy and clerical privileges.

(ii) It stood for freedom for the individual and equality of all before law.

(iii) It believed in a constitution and representative government through Parliament.

(iv) It emphasised on the concept of government by consent.

(v) It emphasised the inviolability of private property.

**OR**

The Greek war of independence mobilise nationalist feelings among the educated elite across Europe are discussed below:

(i) Greek nationalists received support from other Greeks living in exile.

(ii) estern Europeans had sympathy due to the ancient Greek culture.

(iii) Greece was viewed as a part of Europe that had been annexed by Ottomans and now needed to be liberated.

(iv) Greece perceived as the foundation and cradle of civilisation in Europe by poets and artists and this led to a rise in nationalist consciousness.

(v) The Treaty of Constantinople of 1832 recognised Greece as an independent nation.

*In 1821, the Greeks began their struggle for independence. The Treaty of Constantinople was signed in 1832, recognising Greece as an independent nation.*

**30.** (i) Agriculture is called the backbone of Indian economy because 70% of Indian population are engaged in agriculture.

(ii) The raw material for the Industrial sectors like food processing company, textile industry comes from the agricultural sector.

(iii) Agriculture sectors serves as the source of raw material for non-agricultural sectors.

(iv) Agricultural and industrial sectors always go hand in hand not as alternatives.

(v) India earns foreign exchange by exporting agricultural products. It contributes around 29% of GDP.

*Agriculture is an important sector of the Indian economy, as it contributes about 17% to the total GDP and provides employment to around 58% of the population. Over 70 percent of rural households depend on agriculture.*

**31.** The five functions of political party are given below:

(i) The running political party, plays an important role in making the laws of the country.

(ii) Parties campaign for themselves during the election process.

(iii) Parties contest election through their candidates and these candidates are chosen by the top leaders or by the members of the party.

(iv) A political party is a link between the government and the people.

(v) The people can easily approach the local leader than the government official.

**32.** Democratic system is better than any other form of government because:

(i) It provides a method to resolve conflicts.

(ii) It enhances the dignity of the individual.

(iii) It improves the quality of decision making.

(iv) It promotes equality among citizens.

(v) If allows room to correct mistakes.

**33.** Bank plays an important role in the economic development of the country in many ways:

(i) Provides loan in rural area for crop production and small businesses ultimately resulting in the development of many places.

(ii) Provides loan to create fixed assets that will create employment opportunities.

(iii) Acts as a link between savers and investors.

(iv) The Bank accepts the deposit and pay an amount as interest on the deposit which encourage savings.

(v) Deposits are used to extend loan for various profitable events.

**OR**

Bank is a formal source of credit and in some situations the borrower would not able to repay loan. This pushes them in the situation of debt trap.

**Example:**

(i) In case of rural areas, if crop fails due to natural factors it will be difficult for the farmers to pay loan.

(ii) In case of failure of a business, it will be difficult for the businessman to repay the credit.

(iii) In case of high risk business, failure without some support can push borrower in painful situation.

(iv) In many cases, people has to sell their land and fixed assets to repay loan.

**34.** 1. MNCs play an important role in the process of globalisation. They bring their products, new business policies and cultures to a country. They also help in increasing competitiveness among the Indian companies. At present, most of us are able to use the latest models of cars and this could be possible because of globalisation. Because of hordes of MNCs in our country, most of the urban Indians have become broad-minded in their outlook.

2. The foreign trade becomes a main channel in connecting countries because trade in the past was restricted to finished goods being produced in one market, and sold being produced in one market, and sold in other markets. In today's time, besides trade; capital, technology, people, and service flow is also taking place all over the world. Today, the world is connected in a way that even production takes place across different countries.

3. (i) It enhances choices to the consumers and increased movement of goods, people, and ideas.

(ii) It has led to the establishment of many foreign brands in the country.

(iii) It created opportunities in terms of investment, employment for many developing and underdeveloped countries.

(iv) It has expanded the scope of the market.

**[Any two]**

SOCIAL SCIENCE-10

**35.  (b)**

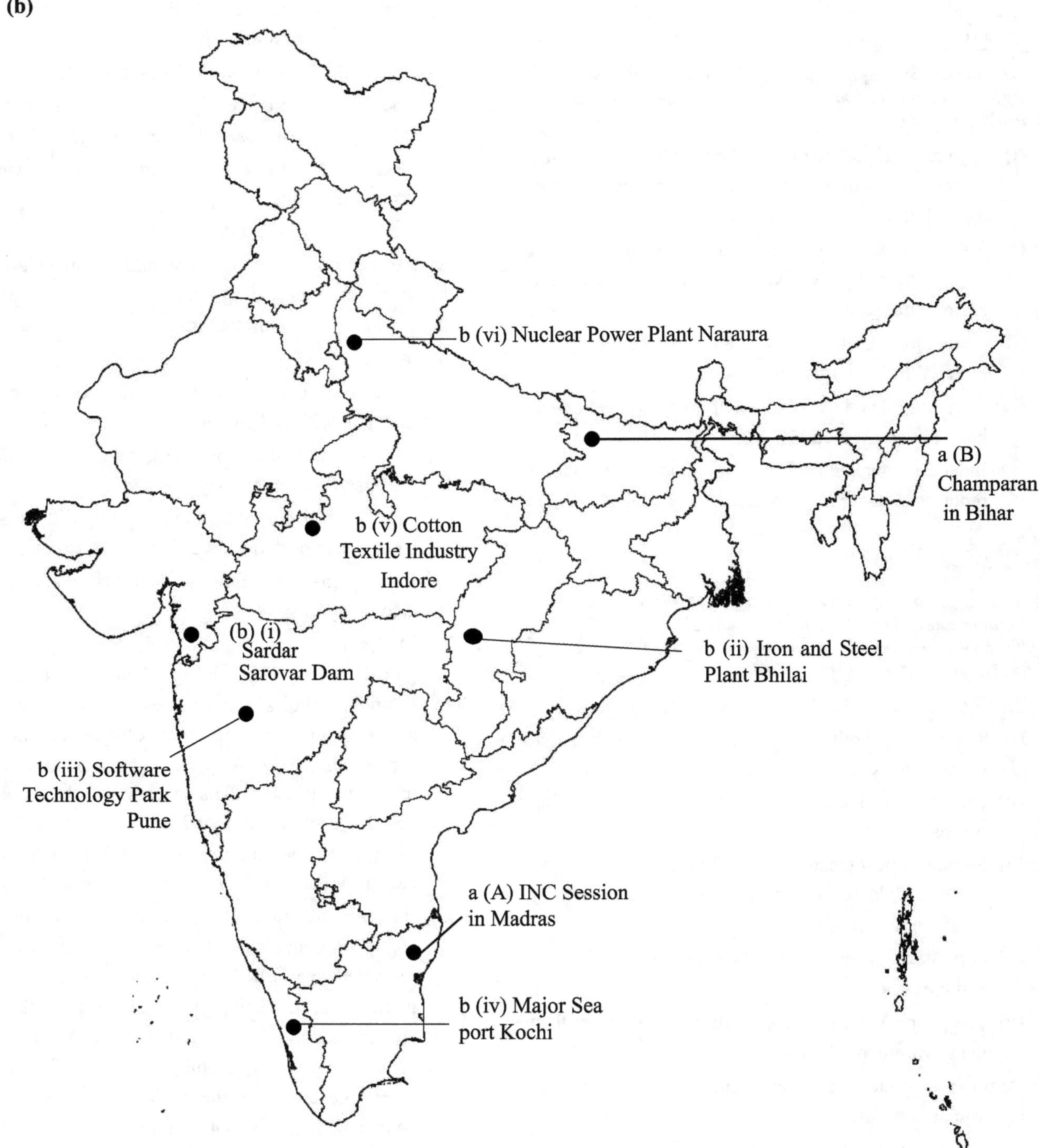

## SECTION - A
**(Very Short Answer Questions)**

$(7 \times 1 = 7)$

1. Explain the aim to form 'Zollverein', a Customs Union, in 1834 in Germany. **1**

**OR**

Explain the main reason responsible for the eruption of a major protest in Saigon Native Girls School in Vietnam in 1926.**

2. Why was printing of textbooks sponsored by the Imperial State in China? **1**

**OR**

Why did Chandu Menon give up the idea of translation of 'English Novels' in Malayalam?**

3. How has Shillong solved the problem of acute shortage of water? **1**

**OR**

How has Tamil Nadu solved the problem of acute shortage of water?

4. How did the feeling of alienation developed among the Sri Lankan Tamils? **1**

5. What may be a developmental goal of farmers who depend only on rain for growing crops? **1**

**OR**

What may be a developmental goal of urban unemployed youth?

6. Give one example each of modern currency and older currency. **1**

7. If you want to purchase an electrical valuable good, what logo would you like to see to confirm its quality?** **1**

## SECTION - B
**(Short Answer Questions)**

$(11 \times 3 = 33)$

8. Describe the great economic hardships that prevailed in Europe during the 1930s. **3**

**OR**

Describe the serious problem faced by the modern part of Hanoi in 1903.**

9. How had the printing press created a new culture of reading in Europe? Explain with examples. **3**

**OR**

How had Charles Dickens depicted the terrible effects of industrialisation on peoples lives and characters? Explain with examples.**

10. Describe any three main features of 'Alluvial soil' found in India. **3**

**OR**

Describe any three main features of 'Block soil' found in India.

11. "The dams that were constructed to control floods have triggered floods." Analyse the statement. **3**

12. Name any two subjects that are included in Concurrent List. How are laws made on these subjects? Explain. **3**

**OR**

How is sharing of power between the Union and the State Governments basic to the structure of the Constitution of India? Explain.

13. "Every social difference does not lead to social division." Justify the statement.** **3**

14. How can caste take several forms in polities? Explain with examples. **3**

---

*Note: (**) Marked questions are out of syllabus so these are not explained or answered.*

**15.** "Crude oil reserves are limited all over the world. If people continue to extract it at the present rate, the reserves would last only 35-40 years more" Explain any three ways to solve this problem.     **3**

**16.** Why is it necessary to increase a large number of banks mainly in rural areas? Explain.     **3**

**OR**

Why are service conditions of formal sector loans better than informal sector? Explain.

**17.** "How can the Government of India play a major role to make globalization more fir? Explain with examples.   **3**

**OR**

How has globalization affected the life of Indians? Explain with examples.

**18.** How are consumers enjoying the 'right to be informed' in their daily life? Explain with examples.**     **3**

## SECTION - C
### (Long Answer Questions)

**(7 × 5 = 35)**

**19.** How had the 'First World War' created economic problems in India? Explain with examples.     **5**

**OR**

How had a variety of cultural processes developed a sense of collective belongingness in India during the 19$^{th}$ century? Explain with examples.

**20.** Describe the role of 'technology' in transformation of the world in the nineteenth century.     **5**

**OR**

Describe the life of workers during the nineteenth century in England.

**OR**

Describe various steps taken to clean up London in the nineteenth century.**

**21** Name the two major beverage crops grown in India. Describe their growing areas.     **5**

**22.** How can the industrial pollution of fresh water be reduced? Explain various ways.     **5**

**23.** "Democracies do not appear to be very successful in reducing economic inequalities." Justify the statement. **5**

**OR**

"Democracy is a better form of government than any other form of government." Justify the statement.

**24.** What is a political party? Explain any four characteristics of a political party.     **5**

**25.** Compare the economic activities of the private sector with that of the public sectors.     **5**

## SECTION - D
### (Map Based Question)

**(3 + 5 = 8)**

**26.** (A) Two features 'a' and 'b' are marked on the given political outline map of India. Identify these features with the help of the following information and write their correct names on the lines marked near them:

(a) The place where the Indian National Congress Session was held.

(b) The place where Gandhiji violated the salt law.

**[1×2=3]**

(B) Locate and label any three of the following with appropriate symbols on the same given outline political map of India:     **[1×3=5]**

(i)   Bokaro**          –   Iron and Steel Plant

(ii)  Gandhinagar      –   Software Technology Park

(iii) Tarapur          –   Nuclear Power Plant

(iv)  Salal            –   Dam

(v)   Tuticorin        –   Seaport

## Solutions

1. In 1834, Zollverein, a customs union formed at the initiative of Prussia. The union abolished tariff barriers and internal custom dues and was willing to establish free trade with neighbouring states it reduced the number of currencies from thirty to two. It was joined by most of the German states.

**OR**

(**)

2. The printing of textbooks were sponsored by the Imperial State in China because China possessed a large bureaucratic system, which recruited their personnel through Civil service examinations. That is why, textbooks were printed in large numbers to provide them with study material.

3. Shillong set up Bamboo drip irrigation systems and Roof top rainwater harvesting. This helped Shillong meet its total requirement of each household.

**OR**

Tamil Nadu adopted rooftop water harvesting techniques. This practice was made mandatory under the law for all houses across the state.

Bamboo Drip Irrigation System is a 200-year-old technology for draining stream and spring water using bamboo pipes. It is commonly used in Meghalaya. The procedure delivers 20–80 drops per minute at the plant site.

4. The measures of the act of 1956 introduced by Sinhalese Government made the Sri Lankan Tamils feel alienated. They felt that none of the major political parties led by the Buddhist Sinhalese were sensitive towards their language and culture. They also felt that the constitution and policies of the government denied them equal political rights, discriminated against them in terms of jobs and other opportunities by ignoring their interests.

5. To have access to better water harvesting and irrigation techniques or be compensated in the absence of rain.

**OR**

To get a decent job suitable to his/her qualifications and skills or get proper career counselling.

The southwest monsoon plays a crucial role in India's agriculture and affects the livelihood of a fifth of the world's population. Around 55% of India's arable land is dependent on rain.

6. Modern currency: The plastic money that we use in the form of debit and credit cards.

Older currency: The bronze coins that were used in earlier times.

7. (**)

8. Great economic hardships were faced by the people of Europe in 1930s. Some of the difficulties that they faced were:

(i) Small producers in towns were often overthrown by the cheap machines.

(ii) Rise of food prices and unemployment led to widespread pauperism in the country.

(iii) Peasants suffered the burden of feudal dues and obligations in some regions of Europe.

(iv) The rise of population was larger than that of employment generation. People were migrating from rural areas to cities in search of employment, which was not easily available because of overcrowding.

9. The introduction of the printing press created a new wave of print culture in Europe:

(i) Mass production of books lead to decrease in the prices of the books and their circulation increased.

(ii) The reading culture was not restricted only to the elites but, even the common people had access to these books.

(iii) Printers also focused on publishing folk tales and ballads, well-illustrated with pictures so that the books could be enjoyed even by a less educated audience from the villages.

(iv) Through these books more and more people to come in contact with the ideas of philosophers and leading thinkers of the time.

**OR**

(**)

**10.** Major characteristics of Alluvial Soil are:

(i) It is one of the most fertile soils amongst all soil types.

(ii) Alluvial soil covers the entire northern plains in India.

(iii) Alluvial soil contains sand, silt and clay mainly due to silt deposited by the Indo-Gangetic-Brahmaputra rivers.

(iv) It is classified into Bhangar (old alluvial) and Khadar (new alluvial) according age.

(v) If contains good amount of potash, phosphoric acid and lime. And, this soil is ideal for the growth of crops like sugarcane, wheat and rice etc.

**OR**

Major characteristics of Black soil are:

(i) It is fine textured and clayey in nature and suitable for growing cotton.

(ii) It has high amount of lime, iron, magnesium and generally low quantities of Phosphorus, Nitrogen and organic matter.

(iii) It has a high clay content and therefore is highly retentive of water. It is extremely fertile in most of the places where it is found.

(iv) It is formed from weathered lava rocks, thus is black in colour.

*Note*

*About 40% of the country's total land area is covered by alluvial soil. It stretched across the coastal regions of northern Gujarat, the Narmada and Tapi basins, as well as from Punjab in the west to West Bengal and Assam in the east.*

**11.** Dams have been constructed to support the economic development of the country but they can be destructive at times due to the following reasons:

(i) Sometimes, they are constructed without proper planning and sometimes low standard construction material is used which cause floods.

(ii) Inferior quality of construction material increases the chances of floods.

(iii) Construction of these dams can make the area, in which they are constructed, 'earthquake prone', which may lead to landslides and the water to flow out of dams.

*Note*

*The Tehri Dam is located in the state of Uttarakhand. It is the highest Dam in India with a height of 260.5 metres.*

**12.** The Concurrent List is a list of 52 items given in the Seventh Schedule to the Constitution of India. It includes subjects of common interest to both the Union and State government. These subjects are education, forest, trade unions, marriage, adoption, and succession etc.

Both the Union and the State governments can make laws on these subjects. But if the laws made by both the government contradict each other, or a dead lock is created, then the law made by the Union government will prevail.

**OR**

Distribution of power is well embedded in the provisions of the constitution and is thus is its basic structure due to following reasons.

(i) The Constitution has distributed the legislative powers between the state government and Union government by dividing the subjects in Union list and State list.

(ii) There is a Concurrent list which, both the governments can make laws. Also, State governments enjoy their own power in states like Jammu and Kashmir.

(iii) Many provisions of the Indian Constitution are not applicable in the states without the approval of the state government.

(iv) The Union government enjoys its own hold over some of the union territories.

**13.** (**)

**14.** A caste is a fixed social group into which an individual is born within a particular system of social stratification. It is considered to be the sole basis of social community. People belonging to the same caste have the same interests which they share amongst themselves and no one else. Caste can take various forms in politiCs in following ways:

(i) One's caste can control access to political power, land, and police or judicial assistance. Castes also tend to influence local politics by being local to certain areas.

(ii) Political parties often favour some castes and are even recognized as representatives of these castes. This brings prejudice and biasness in terms of decisions, ideologies and other such important matters.

(iii) Principle of one person one vote or Universal Adult franchise has helped in compelling the political parties to mobilize and have an inclusive approach towards the castes that were earlier ignored by them.

(iv) Parties favour certain caste and secure vote bank. Parties also incite people on the pretext of casteism, thus create political disasters.

(v) Caste composition of an electorate is always kept in mind when the nominations are decided by the party during elections. Parties tend to nominate candidates of different castes so as to muster necessary support to win elections. When governments are formed, the parties make sure that these candidates of different castes find a place in the set up.

**15.** Crude oil is a type of fossil fuel which occurs naturally. It is an unrefined petroleum product composed of hydrocarbon deposits and other organic materials. It is a non-renewable resource of energy. It takes millions of years for the formation of this fuel. It is used to propel vehicles, to heat buildings, and to produce electricity. This type of fuel is being used at a faster rate than they are being produced. This causes depletion and scarcity of crude oil.

Following step which can be under taken to conserve this non-renewable source of energy:

(i) Instead of petroleum based commercial wax bees was to wax can also be beneficial floor.

(ii) Use of cycles wherever possible instead of using motorbikes or cars.

(iii) Use of public transport like buses and trains instead of self-owned vehicles.

Saudi Arabia is the world's largest oil producer. The country produces 13.24% of the oil consumed in the entire world daily. Saudi Arabia has the second-largest reserves of naturally occurring oil in the world after Venezuela.

**16.** Increased the number of banks needed in rural areas due to the following reasons:

(i) To develop the habit of saving among the villagers and to give loans to the farmers for boosting production

(ii) The informal sector charges a higher rate of interest which make loans very expensive. Also, there are no external organizations controlling the credit activities of lenders. This purural poor into debt trap.

(iii) Informal sector involves high degree of risk as there are no proper set of rules for repayment and there is a lot of exploitation of poor farmers.

(iv) Informal sector lenders may exploit the borrowers, they may engage in threats and intimidation to ensure repayment of loans. There is no written agreement between the lender and the borrower.

**OR**

**Formal sector:**

(i) It consists of banks and cooperatives, thus every clause is in writing and clear to comprehend.

(ii) It is supervised by the RBI.

(iii) Collateral is required but this sector is less risky.

(iv) It provides loans comparatively at lower rates.

**Informal sector:**

(i) The lenders are mainly money lenders, friends, relatives, traders and landowners etc.

(ii) No external organisation supervises this sector.

(iii) Collateral is not required, thus it involves high risk.

(iv) This sector charges higher interest rates. which could lead to a debt trap.

**17.** Fair globalization would create equal opportunities for all and would ensure that the benefits of globalization are shared better. The government can play a major role in making this possible through the following ways:

(i) The policies of the government must protect the interests of all the people of the country, not only of the rich and powerful.

(ii) The government must ensure that the labour laws are properly implemented and the workers get their rights.

(iii) The government must support the domestic and smaller producers by making them strong enough to enter the competitive global market.

(iv) The government should negotiate at the WTO for fairer rules and regulations.

**OR**

Globalization has affected the life of Indians in following ways:

(i) MNCs have increased their investments in India, this has helped in the inflow of capital and employment generation.

Globalisation is the word used to describe the growing interdependence of the world's economies, cultures, and populations, brought about by cross-border trade in goods and services, technology, and flows of investment, people, and information.

(ii) Consumers get a wide variety of choices in goods and services due to greater competition among producers due to globalisation.

(iii) The local companies supplying raw materials to industries that have been set as a result of the globalization, have prospered leaps and bounds.

(iv) Emergency of large Indian companies as multinational companies. This helped India to increase its contacts around the world.

(v) Globalisation had helped increase our GDP and per capita income, thus making the living standards better across the globe.

*Note*

*The World Trade Organisation (WTO) is the only international organisation dealing with global trade rules. Its main function is to ensure that trade flows as smoothly, predictably, and freely as possible.*

**18.** (**)

**19.** The economic effects due to the First World War were:

(i) Villages were supplying soldiers for the war forcefully. It caused widespread resentment and anger amongst the people.

(ii) It led to huge expenditures in defence. These expenditures were to be financed by increasing the taxes and by raising custom duties.

(iii) The food prices mere doubled between 1913 and 1918. This increased the hardships of the poor people of India.

(iv) The crop failure resulted in acute shortage of food.

(v) There was spread of influenza epidemic which contributed to the hardships of the people.

(vi) The drain on the Indian economy in the form of cash, kind and loans to the British government came to about 367 million pounds.

**OR**

(i) Nationalism is the feeling when people of a country develop a sense of common belonging and are united in a common thread. Their struggles unite them, and they tend to form a common identity.

(ii) This sense of collective belonging unites people of different communities, regions or languages by experience of many united struggles.

(iii) and fiction, folklore, and songs, popular poems and symbols, all played a vital role in the awakening of the spirit of nationalism. The identify of a nation is often symbolised by a figure or image.

(iv) In the early 19th century, with the growth of nationalism that the identity of India came to be visually associated with the image of Bharat Mata

(v) The image was first created by Bankim Chandra Chattopadhyay and in the 1870s he wrote 'Vande Mataram a hymn to the motherland.

(vi) Abanindranath Tagore painted his famous image of Bharat Mata which portrayed as an ascetic figure, she is calm, composed, divine and spiritual.

(vii) In the late 19th century India, nationalists began recording folk tales sung by bards and they toured villages to gather folk songs and legends.

(viii) When people would hear these songs, they would be filled with a spirit of belongingness to the country.

*Note*

*World War I (WW I), also known as the Great War, lasted from July 28, 1914, to November 11, 1918. WWI was fought between the Allied Powers (France, Russia, Britain, and the US) and the Central Powers (Germany, Austria-Hungary, the Ottoman Empire, and Bulgaria).*

**20.** The technological inventions helped the world develop in these ways:

(i) Development of the printing press that lead to the print revolution.

(ii) Railways, steamships, telegraphs led to easy transportation of goods and raw materials

(iii) Technological advancements stimulated the process of industrialization, which expanded production of goods and trade.

(iv) Refrigerated ships made transportation of perishable products, like meat, over long distances easy.

(v) With the invention of telephones, computers and other things like cables, network towers etc communication was made easy.

**OR**

The life of the workers in the 19th century was miserable.

(i) Workers were given lower wages and were made to work for longer hours.

(ii) Poverty was more prominent in cities as compared to villages.

(iii) They work on machines without proper training and education, which was dangerous.

(iv) The living conditions were very poor, it was expected of such people to die in a workhouse, hospital or lunatic asylum rather than in some decent working areas.

(v) The over-congestion was leading to epidemic diseases in the whole city.

(vi) There was no proper drinking water available.

(vii) Life expectancy of these poor people was nearly 29 years of age while it was near about 55 years of age for the middle and upper class people.

(viii) The real value of their earnings fell significantly due to a sharp increase in prices. The income of workers was also impacted by the period of employment which was highly inconsistent. In the 1830s, the percentage of unemployed people was anywhere between 35–75%.

**OR**

(**)

**21.** The two most important beverage crops of India are tea and coffee Tea:

Assam is a major tea producing state in India along with West Bengal Kerala and Tamil Nadu. The cropping season begins as early as March and extends almost to mid-December.

(i) The tea plant grows in tropical and sub-tropical climates.

(ii) Tea bushes require moist, frost-free and warm climate all through the year.

(iii) It requires deep and fertile well-drained soil, rich in humus and organic matter.

(iv) Conditions required for tea cultivation:

- Temperature-10-30 degrees Celsius.

- Rainfall- average yearly rainfall of 200 cm.

- Altitude-ground level of between 600-2000 m above sea level.

**Coffee:**

It is a tropical plant grown in semi-tropical climate. Coffee tree requires heat, humidity and abundant rainfall.

In India, coffee is traditionally grown in the Western Ghats spread over Karnataka, Kerala and Tamil Nadu. Karnataka is the largest producer accounting for about 70% of the total coffee production.

(i) The temperature of the place is 23°C to 28°C.

(ii) Bright sunshine and warm weather are necessary for the harvesting.

(iii) Requires rainfall between 60-85 inches but water stagnation is very harmful for coffee plants.

Soil requires presence of humus and other nitrogenous matter.

*Brazil is the largest coffee producer in the world. The climate is perfect for growing Arabica and Robusta beans. In 2021, Brazil exported nearly six billion U.S. dollars' worth of coffee to other countries, making it the world's leading coffee exporter by far.*

**22.** The wastes discharged from factories, refineries into water bodies causes water pollution. These wastes contains harmful chemicals and toxic metals like mercury, lead, arsenic etc. Which kill aquatic life.

The following steps can be taken to reduce the industrial pollution:

(i) Restructuring the manufacturing processes to reduce or eliminate pollutants and installing chimneys for treating of gaseous waste.

(ii) Create man-made cooling ponds to cool the heated waters of industries by evaporation, condensation and radiation.

(iii) Encourage industries to promote 'green' methods of product production including environment-friendly operating processes.

(iv) Recycling as much polluted water in industries as possible through increased recycling efforts will reduce industrial pollution in freshwater.

(v) Attach water treatment plant in industries for filtration of sewage before it enters the water bodies.

**Note**

*0.5% of the earth's water is available as fresh water. Over 68 percent of the fresh water on Earth is found in ice caps and glaciers, and just over 30 percent is found in groundwater. Only about 0.3 percent of our fresh water is found in the surface water of lakes, rivers, and swamps.*

**23.** According to a report, in India, more than 40% of the wealth created in the country from 2012 to 2021 had gone to just 1% of the population. The share of the rich class is increasing, whereas those who are at the bottom of the society, have very little to depend upon.

The poor constitute a large proportion of the voters. Yet, democratically elected government do not appear to be keen on addressing the question of poverty as is expected of them. People in several poor countries are now dependent on the rich countries even for basic food supplies.

Democracies are based on political equality. All citizens have equal right in electing representatives, but this is not so in the economic field. Economic equality comes by the equitable distribution of wealth. The poor sometimes find it difficult to even meet the basic needs of life like food, shelter, health and education.

Many factors can contribute to unequal wealth distribution:

(i) **Unemployment:** Because of population explosion, the number of job opportunities are very less compared to the people. A large number of educated people are still without jobs.

(ii) **Low literacy rate:** According to National Statistical Office (NSO) data, as of the year 2021, India's average literacy rate was 77.70%. Education is still considered to be a dream for many.

(iii) **Cycle of poverty:** Poor people still have to be depend on money lenders to borrow money at higher interest rates, which falls them into a vicious debt trap..

**OR**

Abraham Lincoln has said, "Democracy is the government of the people, by the people and for the people". Democracy is better than other forms of government because:

(i) No particular religion, region, race or language is given special preference. Everybody has equal rights and freedom, and there is no discrimination.

(ii) Every individual has a right to vote and choose his representatives in the government. Thus, it is more representative and popular.

(iii) The government is of the people and by the people. Laws are made to protect the liberty and freedom of the people.

(iv) In the opposition parties are allowed to criticise the government. Democracy, they creates a system of checks and balance.

(v) Every individual is given equal rights, there is less danger of conflict based on caste, religion or region and less social tensions in society. Equal distribution of opportunities is encouraged.

(vi) It is an accountable form of government and improves the quality of decision-making.

**24.** Political party is an organised groups of people having common ideology and its aim is to contest elections and come to power.

(i) It gain control over the government through the process of election.

(ii) They ensure that a country is governed as per set ideologies and run the government.

(iii) They frame their own policies in the form of manifestos which includes their vision on the basis of which they would establish governance in the country.

(iv) Political parties make laws and policies for the country and gives representation to diverse interest in society and give recognition to minorities.

(v) A political party has a leader, active members and followers who support the party.

**25.**

| S. No. | Private Sector | Public Sector |
|--------|----------------|---------------|
| 1. | Ther main motive is to earn profit. | The main motive is public welfare. |
| 2. | The ownership of assets and delivery of services is in the hands of the private individual. | The government owns most of the assets and provides all services. |
| 3. | The motive is to earn profit due to which it does not invest funds to construct infrastructures for public utility/facility. | Due to motives of public welfare, it invests funds to construct infrastructures for public utility/facility, like construction of roads, bridges, etc. |
| 4. | It collects money for the services they provide. | It raises money for various activities through taxes. |
| 5. | Here, the capital comes from the profits of business operations. | Here, the capital comes from the collection of tax, excise, and other duties, bonds, treasury bills, etc. |
| 6. | Examples: Tata Iron and Steel Company Ltd. (TISCO). | Examples: Railways, post office, etc. |

**26.**

Salal
(26 (B) (iv))
Gandhinagar
(26 (B) (ii))
Dandi (26 A(b)
Tarapur
(26 (B) (iii))
Bokaro
(26 (B) (i))
(a) (A) Chennai
(Madaras)
(B) Tuticorin
(26 (B) (v))

# Delhi 2019

# CBSE Board Solved Paper Term-II

## SECTION - A

### (Very Short Answer Questions)

$(7 \times 1 = 7)$

1. Interpret the concept of liberalisation in the field of economic sphere during the nineteenth century in Europe. **1**

**OR**

Interpret the contribution of French in the economic development of Mekong delta region.**

2. How had hand printing technology introduced in Japan? **1**

**OR**

How had translation process of novels into regional languages helped to spreed their popularity?**

3. How is over irrigation responsible for land degradation in Punjab? **1**

**OR**

How is cement industry responsible for land degradation?

4. How can democratic reforms be carried out by political conscious citizens? **1**

5. What may be a goal of landless rural labourers regarding their income **1**

**OR**

What may be a goal of prosperous farmer of Punjab?

6. Distinguish between 'Primary' and 'Secondary' Sector. **1**

7. Why do banks or lenders demand collateral against loans? **1**

## SECTION - B

### (Short Answer Questions)

$(11 \times 3 = 33)$

8. How had Napoleonic code exported to the regions under French control? Explain with examples. **3**

**OR**

Explain with examples the three barriers that are responsible to economic growth in Vietnam.**

9. How had the Imperial State in China been the major producer of printed material for a long time? Explain with examples. **3**

**OR**

How had novels been easily available to the masses in Europe during nineteenth century? Explain with examples.**

10. Describe any three main features of 'Rabi crop season.' **3**

**OR**

Describe any three main features of 'Kharif crop season.'

11. "Water scarcity may be an outcome of large and growing population in India." Analyse the statement. **3**

12. "The assertion of social diversities in a democratic country is very normal and can be healthy." Justify the statement with arguments.** **3**

**OR**

"Social divisions affect politics." Examine the statement.**

13. "Women still lag much behind men in India despite some improvements, since independence." Analyse the statement. **3**

14. How are political parties recognized as regional and national parties in India? Explain with examples. **3**

15. "Consequences of environmental degradation do not respect national or state boundaries." Justify the statement. **3**

16. Why is the 'tertiary sector, becoming important in India? Explain any three reasons. **3**

*Note: (**) Marked questions are out of syllabus so these are not explained or answered.*

**OR**

How do we count various goods and services for calculating Gross Domestic Product (G.D.P.) of country? Explain with example.

17. Describe the importance of formal sources of credit in the economic development. **3**

**OR**

Describe the bad effects of informal sources of credit on borrowers.

18. How can consumers use their 'Right to Seek Redressal'? Explain with example.** **3**

## SECTION - C

### (Long Answer Questions)

**(7 × 5 = 35)**

19. Who had organized the dalits into the 'Depressed Classes Association' in 1930? Describe his achievements. **5**

**OR**

Define the term 'Civil Disobedience Movement.' Describe the participation of rich and poor peasant communities in the 'Civil Disobedience Movement.'

20. "Indian trade had played a crucial role in the late nineteenth century world economy." Analyze the statement. **5**

**OR**

"Series of changes affected the pattern of industrialization in India by the early twentieth century." Analyze the statement.

**OR**

"Industrialization had changed the form of urbanization in the modern period." Analyze the statement with special reference of London.**

21. How are industries responsible for environmental degradation in India? Explain with examples. **5**

22. "Roadways still have an edge over railways in India." Support the statement with examples. **5**

23. Compare the situation of Belgium and Sri Lanka considering their location, size and cultural aspects.

**5**

**OR**

How is the idea of power sharing emerged? Explain different forms that have common arrangements of power sharing.

24. Describe the importance of democratic government as an accountable and legitimate government. **5**

25. Why do multinational corporations (MNCs) set up their offices and factories in certain areas only? Explain any five reasons. **5**

## SECTION - D

### (Map Based Questions)

**(2 + 3 = 5)**

26. (A) Two features a and b are marked on the given political outline map of India. Identify these features with the help of the following information and write their correct names on the lines marked near them. **2**

(a) The place where the Indian National Congress Session was held.

(b) The city where Jallianwala Bagh incident took place.

(B) Locate and label any three of the following with appropriate symbols on the same given outline political map of India. **3**

(i) Kalpakkam - Nuclear Power Plant

(ii) Vijayanagar - Iron and Steel Plant**

(iii) Noida - Software Technology Park

(iv) Paradeep - Sea Port

(v) Sardar Sarovar - Dam

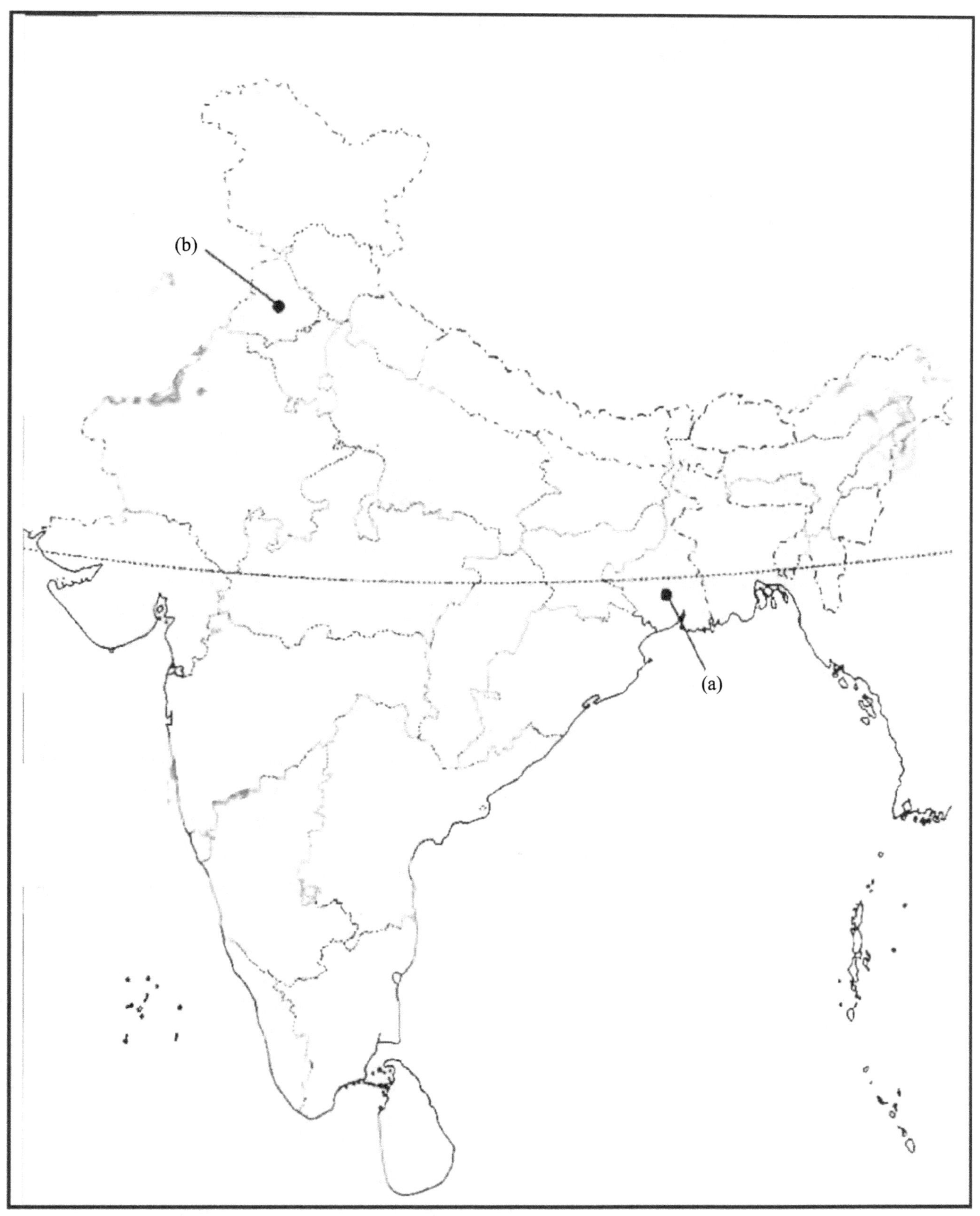
(b)
(a)

## Solutions

1. 'Liberalism' refers stood for the freedom of market and the abolition of state-imposed restrictions on the movement of goods and capital.

   (i) Duties were levied according to the weight or measurement of the goods which were different for different states.

   (ii) Liberalisation meant reduction of custom duties and removal of these quotas.

   (iii) A unified economic system allowing the unhindered movement of goods, people and capital was the need of the hour.

   (iv) In 1834, Zollverein, a customs union abolished tariff barriers and reduced number of currencies from over thirty to two.

2. Buddhist missionaries from China introduced hand printing technology in Japan around 768-770 AD.

**Note**

*The Buddhist Diamond Sutra which was printed in 868 AD was the oldest Japanese book.*

3. Over irrigation results into is responsible for land degradation due to water logging which leads to increase in salinity and alkalinity in the soil. Over irrigation and continuous use of Pesticides over land over a long period of times without taking appropriate measures to conserve and manage land has resulted in land degradation in Punjab.

   **OR**

   It generates heavy amount of dust which is released in the atmosphere. Later, it settles down in the surrounding areas which slows the process of infiltration of water into the soil.

4. The most important goal is to increase and improve the quality of political participation by ordinary citizens. The politically conscious citizens are aware of their duties and rights as entitled by the constitution, it gives them an upper hand. They are also able to spread this awareness around by holding discussion or generally through word of mouth and help in formation of Public opinion. Politically aware citizens have better knowledge of diplomacy and world around them.

5. Goals of a landless rural labourer are:

   (i) Better wages.

   (ii) More days of work

   (iii) Quality education from their children.

   **OR**

   Goals of a prosperous farmer of Punjab are:

   (i) High family income.

   (ii) Availability of cheap labourers.

6. **Primary Sector:**

   It covers those activities that involve production of goods directly using natural resources. E.g. Agriculture, fishing etc.

   **Secondary Sector:**

   It covers those activities in which natural products are changed into other forms. through manufacturing. This is the next step after primary activity. E.g. Textile, Automobile etc. Industries.

**Note**

*India is the world's second-largest fish producer, with exports worth more than Rs 47,000 crore. Fisheries are the country's single-largest agriculture export, with a growth rate of 6 to 10 percent in the past five years.*

7. Collateral is an asset or property that the borrower pledges when getting a loan, such as land, building, vehicle etc. This is used as a guarantee by the lender until the loan is repaid. If the borrower fails to repay the loan, the lender is free to sell the collateral and reimburse his amount. Thus, collateral acts like a guarantee against loan.

8. Napoleonic code exported to the regions under the French control:

   (i) It secured the right to property.

   (ii) It abolished feudal dues.

   (iii) It established equality before the law.

   (iv) It did away with all privileges based on birth.

   Napoleon had incorporated revolutionary principles in order to make the whole system more rational and efficient.

1. In Dutch Republic, Switzerland, Italy and Germany, Napoleon simplified administrative divisions, abolished the feudal system and freed peasants from serfdom and manorial dues.

2. In the towns too, guild restrictions were removed.

3. Transport and communication systems were improved.

4. Peasants, artisans, workers and new businessmen enjoyed a new-found freedom.

5. Businessmen and small-scale producers of goods, in particular, began to realise that uniform laws, standardised weights and measures, and a common national currency would facilitate the movement and exchange of goods and capital from one region to another.

9. (i) Books in China were printed by rubbing paper against the inked surface of woodblocks from AD 594 The imperial state in China was, for a very long time, the major producer of printed material.

   (ii) China possessed a huge bureaucratic system which recruited its personnel through civil service examinations. Textbooks for this examination were printed in vast numbers under the sponsorship of the imperial state.

   (iii) From the sixteenth century, the number of examination candidates went up and that increased the volume of print.

   (iv) By the seventeenth century, as urban culture bloomed in China, the uses of print diversified. Reading increasingly became a leisure activity.

   (v) Women, revolutionaries, poets and even merchants used print in everyday life.

10. Features of Rabi crop season :

   (i) Rabi crops are sown in the minter months of October through December.

   (ii) At the time of harvesting, it requires bright sunshine and is harvested is Summer from April to June.

   (iii) Crops depend on sub-soil moisture.

   (iv) Requires less rainfall between 50-75 cm. Availability of precipitation during winter months due to western temperate cyclones help in success of these crops.

   (v) Major Rabi crops are wheat, gram, peas, barley etc.

**OR**

Features of Kharif crop season:

(i) It was sown with the onset of the monsoon in May.

(ii) Crops are harvested in September - October.

(iii) Requires more rainfall between 100-110 cm and requires a lot of water and hot weather to grow.

(iv) It requires loamy or alluvial soil.

(v) Rice, maize, pulses such as urad, moong dal and millets are among the key kharif crops.

 *Note*

*India is the world's largest producer of milk, pulses and jute, and ranks as the second largest producer of rice, wheat, sugarcane, groundnut, vegetables, fruit and cotton.*

11. A large population requires more water not only for domestic use but also to produce more food. Hence, to facilitate higher food grain production, water resources are being over exploited to expand irrigated areas for dry season agriculture. Irrigated agriculture is the largest consumer of water. Post independent India witnessed intensive industrialization and urbanization, creating vast opportunities for us. Today, large industrial houses are as common place as the industrial units of many MNCs. The ever-increasing number of industries have made matters worse by exerting pressure on existing freshwater resources. Industries, apart from being heavy users of water, also require power to run them. Much of this energy comes from hydroelectric power. Most of these have their own groundwater pumping devices to meet their water needs, which results in fragile water resources being over exploited. This has caused falling ground-water levels in several of these cities.

 *Note*

*India extracts the most groundwater in the world, more than the 2nd and 3rd largest extractors (China and the United States) together. According to the Composite Water Management Index, NITI Aayog estimates that more than 600 million people are facing acute water shortages. It is also projected that the country's water demand will be twice the available supply by 2030.*

12. (**)

**OR**

(**)

**13.** Women still lag much behind men in the following ways:

(i) Political participation of women in India is very less when compared to other countries. Less than 15% the total members in the Lok Sabha are women. The situation is worse in State Assemblies where less than 10% of the total members are women.

(ii) The Women reservation bill to encourage the participation of women is still pending since the past decade.

(iii) Women are paid less than their male counter parts. Proportion of women in highly paid jobs is still less and studies have shown that on an average they work more than men and yet are paid less. Although the Equal Remuneration Act provides provision for equal wages to be paid for equal work.

(iv) The literacy rate amongst women is also low when compared to men. Literacy rate is only 77% as compared to 84.7% among men. This shows the discrimination women have to face.

(v) Men are still considered to be the head of the family. A lot of dowry issues still emerge everywhere. Men are known to dominate women in every field using strength as a factor. Women are made to stay quiet even in cases of rapes, betrayal etc.

> **Note**
>
> *Around 52–75% of Indian women engaged in agriculture are illiterate. There is an average gender wage disparity, with women earning only 70 percent of men's wages, according to a report on agricultural statistics released by the Minister of Agriculture and Farmers' Welfare.*

**14.** Every party in the country has to register with the Election Commission. Parties that get a unique symbol and some other special facilities are 'recognized' by the Election Commission for this purpose. That is why these parties are called, 'recognized political parties'.

A party that secures at least six percent of the total votes in an election to the Legislative Assembly of a State and wins at least two seats is recognized as a 'State Party.' For example - Trinamool Congress, Shiv Sena, DMK etc.

A party that secures at least six percent of the total votes in Lok Sabha elections or Assembly elections in four states and wins at least four seats in the Lok Sabha is recognized as a 'National party.' For example - BJP, Indian National Congress.

> **Note**
>
> *India has eight recognised national parties: the All India Trinamool Congress (AITC), Bahujan Samaj Party (BSP), Bharatiya Janta Party (BJP), Indian National Congress (INC), Communist Party of India (CPI), Communist Party of India, National People's Party (NPP), and the National Congress Party (NCP).*

**15.** Environment is degraded through the depletion of resources like air, water and soil. It leads to destruction of ecosystem and extinction of wildlife.

(i) Deforestation in some countries may disturb the rainfall pattern in the surrounding countries.

(ii) Land degradation and dam burst can bring massive siltation and flood like situation.

(iii) Pollution in one country may effect the other in form of acid rain, climate change etc.

This shows that environmental degradation does not respect land boundaries.

**16.** (i) As income rises, certain sections of people start demanding more services like tourism, shopping, hospitals, schools etc. This helps in increasing the GDP of the country.

(ii) Certain new services such as Information and communication technology have become essential in India.

(iii) This sector offers employment for poor and unskilled workers.

(iv) It determines the national income and per capita income.

(v) It helps in the development of agriculture and other industries such as transport, storage, and trade.

(vi) It flourishes in tourism, retail, schools, and private hospitals.

**OR**

Gross Domestic Product (GDP) is the market value of the final goods and services produced during a year within the domestic territory of a country.

For eg, a farmer sold wheat to a flour mill for ₹8 per kg. The mill grinds the wheat at and sells the flour to a biscuit company for ₹10 per kg. The biscuit company uses the flour, sugar and butter to make 5 biscuit packets. It sells the biscuit to the consumer at ₹20 per biscuit packet. Here biscuits are the final goods that are purchased by the consumer. Wheat and wheat flour are the intermediate goods used in the production of final good. The value of ₹20 already includes the value of flour ₹10. Hence, only the value of final goods and services are included in GDP.

17. Importance of formal sources of credit in economic development are as follows:

(i)  It provides fixed interest rate to all sections of society.

(ii) It limits the scope of using unfair means to repay the payment.

(iii) The formal credit charge less interest rate and accessible to all, rich or poor.

(iv) Monitored by the Reserve Bank of India or regulated by the Government of India and thus helps in bringing order to the system of lending and borrowing in the country.

**OR**

The bad effects of informal sources of credit are:

(i)  They are not subordinate to any government organisation like RBI, thus there is no official backing or monitoring agency.

(ii) There is absence of a fixed interest rate which increases the scope of exploitation.

(iii) Higher interest rates, with no official records, often lead to debt traps.

(iv) It increases the probability of scope of using unfair means to get back their payment.

18. (**)

19. Dr. B.R. Ambedkar had organised the dalits into the Depressed Classes Association in 1930.

His achievments are as follows :

(i)  The 'Depressed Classes Association' was in favour of separate electorate for dalits.

(ii) It enhanced the dignity of marginalised section of society such as SC, ST, OBC.

(iii) He uplifted the dalits against the dominance of upper caste Hindus.

(iv) It gave the depressed classes, reserved seats in Provincial and Central Legislative Councils in proportion to their population.

(v)  In the field of social reform, he published five weekly papers, Mook Nayak, Bahishkrit Bharat, Bahishkrit Bharat, and Samta Janata, to fight untouchability.

(vi) In 1924, he founded the Bahishkrit Hitkarini Sabha to fight the evils of untouchability. The Sabha started a free school for the young and the old and ran reading rooms and libraries.

*Note*

*Dr. Bhimrao Ambedkar is known as the father of the Indian constitution. He was the first law minister of an independent India and the first Indian to pursue an economics doctorate degree abroad.*

**OR**

'Civil Disobedience' means "Refusal by people to obey particular laws or pay taxes, usually as a form of peaceful political protest".

In the countryside,

(1) Rich peasant communities like the Patidars of Gujarat and the Jats of Uttar Pradesh were active in the movement.

(2) They are the producers of commercial crops, they were hit hard by the trade depression and falling prices.

(3) The rich peasants organise their communities, and at times forcing reluctant members, to participate in the boycott programmes.

(4) For the rich peasants, the fight for Swaraj was a struggle against high revenues.

(5) Poor peasants wanted the unpaid rent to the landlord remitted. They joined a variety of radical movements, often led by socialists and communists.

20. Indian trade has played a crucial role in the late nineteenth century world economy by the following ways :

(i)  India provided raw materials to the developing industries of the world.

(ii) India became a major market for the final goods especially for cotton textile industry of Britain.

(iii) In the 19th century, India was a major exporter of raw materials to Britain.

(iv) Indian markets were flooded with British-manufactured goods. There was a trade surplus for Britain while trading with India.

(v) Britain's trade surplus in India also helped to pay the so called 'home charges' that included private remittances by British officials and traders, interest payments on India's external debts and pensions of the British officials in India.

(vi) Thousands of Indian and Chinese labourers went to work on plantation, in mines, and for roads and railways construction projects around the world.

**Note**

*The US emerges as India's biggest trading partner in FY23 at $128.55 billion, with China in second place. Major export items from India to the U.S. include petroleum, polished diamonds, pharmaceutical products, jewellery, light oils and petroleum, frozen shrimp, make-up, etc.*

**OR**

As the Swadeshi movement gathered momentum, nationalists mobilised people to boycott foreign cloth. Industrial groups organised themselves to protect their collective interests, pressurising the government to increase tariff protection and grant other concessions. From 1906, the export of Indian yarn to China declined since produce from Chinese and Japanese mills flooded the Chinese market. So industrialists in India began shifting from yarn to cloth production. Cotton piece goods production in India doubled between 1900 and 1912. Yet, till the First World War, industrial growth was slow. The British mills busy with war production to meet the needs of the army, Manchester imports into India declined. Suddenly, Indian mills had a vast home market to supply. As the war prolonged, Indian factories were called upon to supply war needs: jute bags, cloth for army uniforms, tents and leather boots, horse and mule saddles and a host of other items. New factories were set up and old ones ran multiple shifts. Many new workers were employed and made to work longer hours. Over the war years, industrial production increased.

21. Industries are responsible for environmental degradation in India in following ways :

(i) The construction activities, machinery and factory equipment, generators, saws and pneumatic and electric drills make a lot of noise in environment.

(ii) The release of high proportion of undesirable gases such as sulphur dioxide, and carbon monoxide are a product of these industries.

(iii) Air-borne waste particle contains both solid and liquid particles like dust, sprays, mist and smoke which pollutes the environment.

(iv) The paper, pulp, chemical and textile industries that let out dyes, detergents, acids, salts and heavy metals etc., with carbon, plastic and rubber into the water bodies.

(v) The solid industrial waste is dumped into isolated pockets of land. This leads to land and soil pollution in adjoining areas.

22. Roadways have more importance than Railways due to the following reasons :

(i) it provides door to door service.

(ii) it can traverse comparatively more dissected areas and undulating topography.

(iii) it goes to higher gradients of slopes and can traverse mountains such as Himalayas.

(iv) construction cost of roads is much less than that of railways lines.

(v) it is also used as feeder to other modes of transport such as they provide link between railway stations, air and sea ports.

| **Belgium** | **Sri Lanka** |
|---|---|
| 1. It is a European country which shares its boundaries with Netherlands, Luxembourg and ermany. | 1. It is an island nation, a South Asian country, situated south to India. |
| 2. It is a very small country in Europe. | 2. As compared to Belgium, it is much bigger in area. |
| 3. The ethnic composition is very complex. 59% are living in Flemish region and speak Dutch language. Another 40% people live in the Wallonia region and speak French and the remaining one percent of the Belgians speak German. | 3. It has a diverse population. Social composition of population of Sri Lanka is as follows:<br>• Sinhalese speaking - 74%<br>• Tamil speaking - 18%<br>• Christians - 7% |

**OR**

Power sharing has emerged as a strong substitute to the idea of undivided political power, which believed in giving power to one person or a group of people located in one place. The core principle of power sharing is that people are the source of all political powers/Common forms of power sharing are:

(i) Power is shared among different social groups such as religious and linguistic groups, e.g. community government.

(ii) Power sharing arrangement can also be seen in the way political parties, pressure groups and movements control or influence those in power.

(iii) Horizontal division of power: the power is divided among different organs of the government, such as legislature, the executive and the judiciary. It places different organs of the government at the same level.

(iv) Vertical division of power: Here the sharing of power can be done at different levels of the government - a central government for the entire country and governments at provincial or regional level, usually called federal government.

**24.** (i) It give its citizens the right to information about the government and its functioning.

(ii) Democracy provides a responsive government as it is formed by elected representatives of the people.

(iii) The representatives also ensure that the programmes for the welfare of the different groups are implemented.

(iv) Democracy facilitates periodic, free and fair elections regularly.

(v) Open discussions are held on all major issues and legislations and decisions are taken on the basis of popular public opinion.

(vi) Democracy follows the rules given in the constitution which generates trust among citizens.

**25.** MNCs set up their production units in a particular areas due to the following reasons :

(i) Where skilled and unskilled labour is available at low costs.

(ii) Where markets are near.

(iii) Where the favourable government policies which look after their interests.

(iv) Where the other factors of production such as raw materials, water, electricity and transport are available and assured.

(v) Where there are standard safety measures for assured production.

26.

26(A) (b)
Amritsar
26 (B) (iii)
Noida Software
Technology
Park
26 (A) (a)
Culcutta
26 (B) (iv)
Paradeep
Sea Port
26 (B) (v)
Sardar
Sarovar
Dam
26 (B) (ii)
Vijayanagar
26 (B) (i)
Kalpakkam

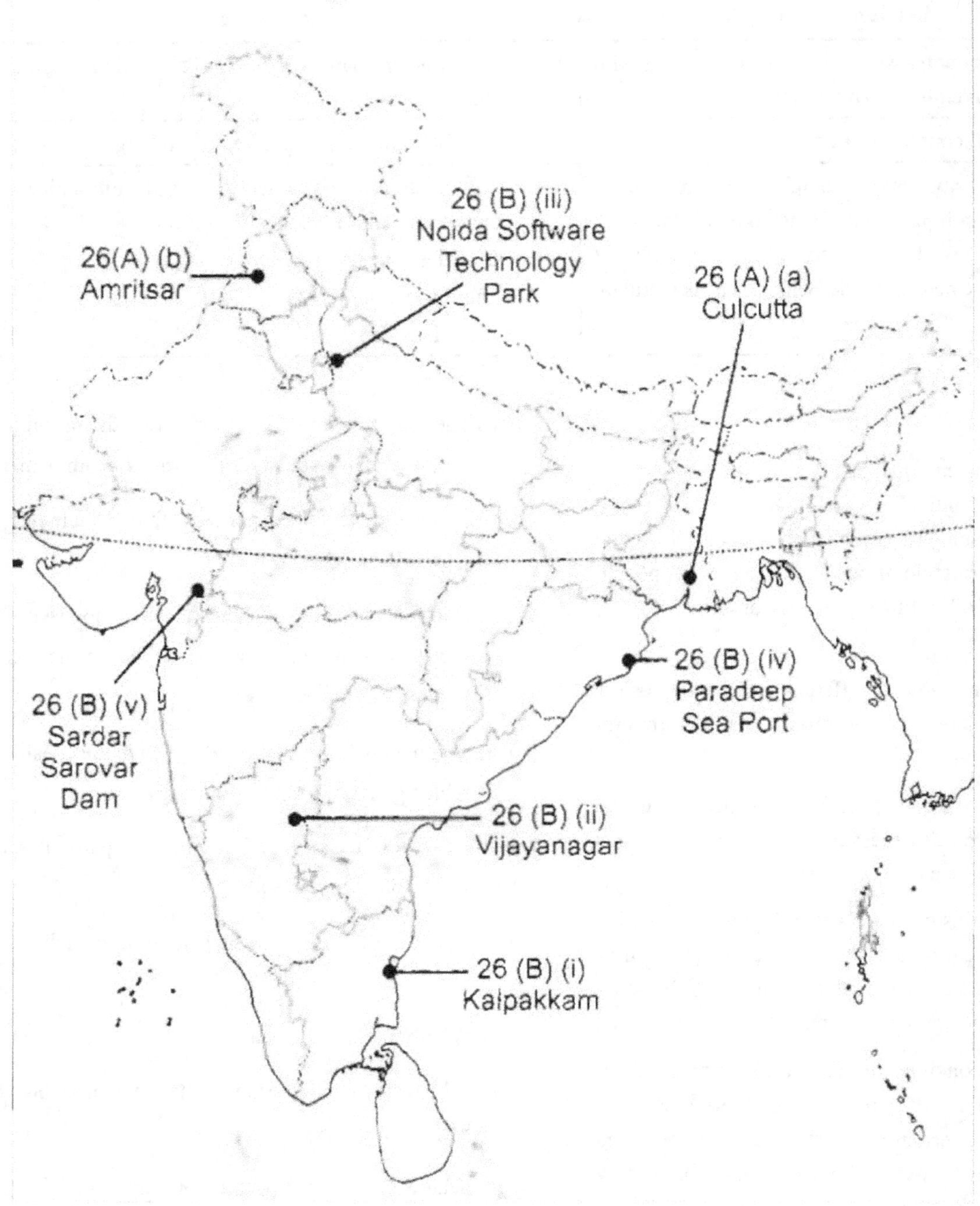

# 2018
# CBSE Board Solved Paper

## SECTION - A

### (Very Short Answer Questions)

**(20 × 1 = 20)**

1. Why were big European powers met in Berlin in 1885?

    1

    **OR**

    Why were merchants from towns in Europe began to move countryside in seventeenth and eighteenth centuries?

    **OR**

    Why did Charles Booth, a Liverpool ship owner conduct the first social survey of low skilled workers in the East End of London in 1887?**

2. Why did the Roman Catholic Church impose control over publishers and booksellers?

    1

    **OR**

    Why do novels use vernaculars?**

3. Classify resources on the basis of origin.

    1

4. 'A challenge is not just any problem but an opportunity for progress.' Analyse the statement.**

    1

5. State any two goals of development other than income.

    1

6. When we produce goods by exploiting natural resources, in which category of economic sector such activities come?

    1

7. Give any two examples of informal sector of credit.

    1

## SECTION - B

### (Short Answer Questions)

**(11 × 3 = 33)**

8. Describe the impact of 'Rinderpest' on people's livelihoods and local economy in Africa in the 1890s.

    3

    **OR**

    Describe any three major problems faced by Indian cotton weavers in nineteenth century.

**OR**

Describe any three steps taken to clean up London during nineteenth century.**

9. "The 'Print Revolution' had transformed the lives of people changing their relationship to information and knowledge." Analyse the statement.

    **[3 × 1 = 3]**

    **OR**

    Distinguish between the themes of 'Pride and Prejudice' and 'Jane Eyre' novels written by Jane Austen and Charlotte Bronte respectively.**

10. How has the ever increasing number of industries in India made worse position by exerting pressure on existing fresh water resources? Explain.

    3

11. "Dense and efficient network of transport is a prerequisite for local and national development." Analyse the statement.

    3

12. Describe any three provisions of amendment made in 'Indian Constitution' in 1992 for making 'Three-Tier' government more effective and powerful.

    3

13. Explain the three factors that are crucial in deciding the outcome of politics of social divisions.**

    3

14. "Secularism is not an ideology of some political parties or persons, but it is one of the foundations of our country." Examine the statement.

    3

15. How is the issue of sustainability important for development? Explain with examples.

    3

16. Distinguish the service conditions of organized sector with that of unorganized sector.

    3

17. Why is cheap and affordable credit important for the country's development? Explain any three reasons.

    3

18. How can consumer awareness be spread among consumers to avoid exploitation in the market place? Explain any three ways.**

    3

*Note: (**) Marked questions are out of syllabus so these are not explained or answered.*

## SECTION - C

### (Long Answer Questions)

(7 × 5 = 35)

19. Describe the explosive conditions prevailed in Balkans after 1871 in Europe. **5**

**OR**

Describe the role of different religious groups in the development of anti-colonial feelings in Vietnam.**

20. How did Non-Cooperation Movement start with participation of middle class people in the cities? Explain its impact on the economic front. **5**

**OR**

Why was Congress reluctant to allow women to hold any position of authority within the organisation? How did women participate in Civil Disobedience Movement? Explain.

21. "The Government of India has introduced various institutional and technological reforms to improve agriculture in the 1980s and 1990s." Support this statement with examples. **5**

**OR**

Compare 'intensive subsistence farming' with that of 'commercial farming' practiced in India.

22. Why is the economic strength of a country measured by the development of manufacturing industries? Explain with examples. **5**

23. Describe any five major functions of political parties performed in a democracy. **5**

24. "Democracy stands much superior to any other form of government in promoting dignity and freedom of the individual." Justify this statement. **5**

**OR**

"Democracies lead to peaceful and harmonious life among citizens." Justify this statement.

25. How has foreign trade been integrating markets of different countries? Explain with examples. **5**

**OR**

How do we feel the impact of globalisation on our daily life? Explain with examples.

## SECTION - D

### (Map Based Questions)

(1 × 2 = 2)

26. (A) Two features a and b are marked on the given political outline map of India. Identify these features with the help of the following information and write their correct names. on the lines marked near them:

(a) The place where the Indian National Congress Session was held. **1**

(b) The place where Gandhiji organized 'Satyagraha' in favour of cotton mill workers. **1**

(B) Locate and label the following with appropriate symbols on the same given outline political map of India. **(1 × 3 = 3)**

(i) Raja Sansi-International Airport **1**

(ii) Bhadravati-Iron and Steel Plants** **1**

(iii) Software Technology Park of West Bengal** **1**

**Solutions**

**1.** The conference was organised by Otto Von Bismarck, first Chancellor of Germany. The European powers met to decide the carving up of Africa among them. The states were Germany, Spain, Netherlands, Belgium, Portugal, France and Great Britain. No African was invited to this conference.

**OR**

To supply money to peasants and artisans persuading them to produce for an international market.

**OR**

(**)

**2.** The Roman Catholic Church imposed control over publishers and booksellers because printed religious literature started writing about God and his creation in different ways. They were afraid of the impacts of books on people's mind.

**OR**

(**)

**3.** Resources classification on the basis of origin:

**(i) Biotic resources :** All living organisms in our environment are known as biotic resources. Example: Tree, animal, insects etc.

**(ii) Abiotic resources:** All non-living things present in our environment are known as abiotic resources. Example: earth, air, water, metals, rocks etc.

**4.** (**)

**5.** Important goals of development other than income, such as:

(i) Safe and secured environment for women.

(ii) Equal treatment, security and dignity for all citizens.

**6.** When we produce goods by exploiting natural resources, it comes under the category of 'Primary sector'.

**7.** The two informal sectors of credit are:

(i) Moneylenders

(ii) Traders

**8.** The impact of 'Rinderpest' on people's livelihoods and local economy in Africa were:

(i) Rinderpest killed 90% of cattle in Africa.

(ii) The loss of cattle destroyed Africa livelihood and forced Africans into labour market.

(iii) Planters, mine owners, and the colonial government successfully monopolised what scarce cattle resources remained.

(iv) Control over the cattle resources enabled European colonisers to conquer and subdue Africa.

*Note*

*Rinderpest was introduced into sub-Saharan Africa in 1887 when infected cattle from India were imported into Ethiopia to feed Italian soldiers. The disease infected local cattle with 90% mortality, and over the next decade spread across the continent.*

**9.** 'Print Revolution' influenced popular perception and opened up new ways of looking at things in following ways:

(i) Before print revolution, books were not only expensive but they could not be produced in sufficient numbers. Now books can reach out to wider sections of people.

(ii) Printing reduced the cost of books. The time and labour to produce each book came down and multiple copies were being produced with ease.

(iii) Due to easy access to books, illiterate persons could listen to the sacred texts of religious books, folk tales and ballads being recited.

*Note*

*In Germany, around 1440, goldsmith Johannes Gutenberg invented the movable-type printing press, which started the printing revolution. Four years later, he would print what became known as the Gutenberg Bible, which is really what kicked off the age of print.*

**10.** (i) The increasing number of industries has made matter worse by exerting pressure on existing fresh water resources. Fresh water is required in thermal energy plants and steel industries on a large scale.

(ii) Industries dump the chemical waste in the river, lake, etc. which then consequently pollute the water dangerously for human survival.

(iii) Industries, apart from being heavy users of water also require power to run it which in turn needs additional water.

(iv) Industries also contaminate the groundwater through seepage of industrial wastes. So, the increasing number of industries exerts pressure on existing fresh water resources.

**11.** (i) Good transportation facilities in rural areas enhance the quality of life of people, as they can easily access health and medical facilities.

(ii) Transportation ensures the extension of trade and networks.

(iii) The improvements and reforms in the transport sector enhance the dynamicity of freight and passengers in a region.

(iv) With efficient roads and means of transport in place, industries and markets also develop, giving the economy a boost.

(v) It increases job opportunities and decreases regional imbalances.

(vi) Transportation offers a lot of tourism and business opportunities for the government.

**12.** The constitution was amended to make the third tier of democracy more powerful and effective as follows :

(i) The 73rd amendment of 1992 make it mandatory to hold regular elections for local government bodies.

(ii) Seats are reserved in the elected bodies and the executive heads of these institutions for SC/ST/ Backward classes.

(iii) At least one third of all positions are reserved for women.

(iv) An independent institution called the State Election Commission, has been created in each state to conduct Panchayat and Municipal elections.

(v) The State Governments are required to share some powers and revenue with local government bodies.

### Note

*Balwant Rai Mehta is known as the father of panchayati raj institutions. Balwant Rai Mehta Committee (1957): Constituted to look into the workings of the community development program.*

**13.** (**)

**14.** (i) The Indian constitution provides all individuals and communities freedom to profess, practice and propagate any religion, or not to follow any.

(ii) The constitution prohibits discrimination on grounds of religion.

(iii) At the same time, the constitution allows the state to intervene in the matters of religion in order to ensure equality within religious communities. For example, Article 17 which bans untouchability.

### Note

*The terms "socialist,", "secular,", and "integrity" were added to the Preamble of the Indian Constitution in 1976 through the 42nd Constitutional Amendment.*

**15.** (i) Sustainability focuses on environmental protection and check environmental degradation, moreover, to stop over exploitation and over use of resources.

(ii) Instead of using coal, oil and natural gas to provide electricity and to power vehicles. We should take advantage of the abundance of solar, wind, wave, tidal and thermal energy that is free, renewable and sustainable. These resources will provide more than enough green electricity which can then power all the industries, homes and transport that we need.

(iii) Sustainable use of natural resources is the process by which economic, industrial and social needs are met but the resources are to be managed and exploited in such a way that the biodiversity, and the biological cycle like carbon, nitrogen and water cycle are not destroyed.

**16.** Major differences between both such units are as follows:

| Units of organised sector | | Units of unorganised sector | |
|---|---|---|---|
| (1) | These sectors are registered by the government and have to follow its rules and regulations. | (1) | These sectors cover small and scattered units which are out of government's control. |
| (2) | Workers are covered by security of employment. | (2) | Low paid jobs and often not regular. Employment is not secured. |
| (3) | Workers are expected to work only for a fixed numbers of hours, if they work more, then they get overtime payment. | (3) | There are no provisions of overtime, paid leave, holidays, leave due to sickness, etc. |
| (4) | The factories follow government rules such as Factories Act, Minimum Wages Act, Payment of Gratuity Act etc. | (4) | They do not follow government rules. When there is less work, due to season or other reasons some people may be asked to leave without salary or payment. |

*In India, there are 93% of unorganised labour. Only 7% of employees in India have access to jobs in the organised sector.*

17. Cheap and affordable credit plays a crucial role for the country's developmeny due to the following reasons :

   (i) To meet the on going expenses of production and thereby develop their business in agricultural and industrial areas.

   (ii) It raises the standard of living and social status of the common man.

   (iii) For middle class people, loans help a lot in constructing their houses and to get rid of monthly rents.

*According to the World Bank's Global Financial Inclusion Database, or Global Findex report (2017), 80% of Indian adults have a bank account, compared to 53% estimated in 2014. 85% of loans taken by poor households in urban areas are from informal sources like relatives, money lenders, etc.*

18. (**)

19. The Balkans was a region of geographical and ethnic variation comprising modern day Romania, Bulgaria, Albania, Greece, Macedonia, Croatia, Bosnia-Herzegovina, Slovenia, Serbia and Montenegro whose inhabitants were broadly known as the Slavs. In 19th century, the Ottoman Empire had sought to strengthen itself through modernisation and internal reforms but with very little success. One by one, its European subject nationalities broke away from its control and declared their own independence. The Balkan peoples based their claims for independence or political rights on nationality and used history to prove that they had once been independent but had subsequently been subjugated by foreign powers. Hence, the rebellious nationalities in the Balkans thought of their struggle as their attempts to win back their long lost independence which converted the region into a battle ground.

**OR**

(**)

20. Non-Cooperation Movement started with middle class participation in the cities:

   (i) Teachers, Headmasters resigned and lawyers gave up their legal practices.

(ii) The council elections were boycotted in most provinces except made as where the justice party, the party of non-Brahmans felt that entering power the council was one way of gaining.

(iii) Its aims were to show resentment to actions considered oppressive like Jallianwala Bagh and Rowlatt Act. Thousands of students left government controlled school and colleges.

Impact on Economic Front-

(i) Traders and merchants refused to trade in foreign goods and sometimes they even refused to finance foreign trade. The import of foreign trade halved between 1921 and 1922.

(ii) People started wearing only Indian clothes and began to discard foreign clothes. As a result, production of Indian textile mills and handloom went up largely.

(iii) Foreign goods were boycotted, liquor shops picketed, and foreign clothes were burnt hugely.

**OR**

Gandhiji was convinced that it was duty of a woman to look after her family and home, they should be good mothers and good wives. And for a long time the Congress was reluctant to allow women to hold any position of authority within the organisation.

Women' participation took its way in the following ways:

(i) During Gandhiji's Salt March thousands of women came out of their houses to listen to him.

(ii) Women participated in protest marches, manufactured salt and picketed foreign cloth and liquor shops.

(iii) Women broke doors of shops, came on the roads and helped the movement leaders.

(iv) Many women were arrested and were sent to jail. In urban areas these women were from high caste families. E.g., Sarojini Naidu, Satyavati Devi, Kamla Nehru etc. In rural areas they came from rich peasant household.

(v) A large section of women of Gujarati community was influenced by Gandhiji's idealism and participated in National Movement in Bombay. Bengal being the nerve centre of female education in India, increased the women's participation in nationalism. In 1930, women rallied before Bethune College, Calcutta in support of Gandhiji's Civil Disobedience Movement.

**21.** The Government of India has introduced various institutional and technological reforms under comprehensive Land Development Programme to improve agriculture in the 1980s and 1990s.

**About Land Development Programme:**

(i) Provision for crop insurance against drought, flood, cyclone, fire and disease.

(ii) Establishment of Grameen banks, cooperative societies and banks for providing loan facilities to the farmers at lower rates of interest.

**Other Reforms:**

Government has initiated many other benefit schemes for the farmers. These are as follows :

(i) Government also announced Minimum Support Price (MSP) for various agricultural products like cereals, pulses etc.

(ii) Weather bulletins and agricultural programmes for farmers were introduced through radio and television channels.

(iii) Kisan Credit Card (KCC): Scheme for giving easy and cheap loans to small farmers. Personal Accident Insurance Scheme (PAIS) for Kisan Credit Card (KCC) holders.

**OR**

| Intensive Subsistence Farming | | Commercial Farming | |
|---|---|---|---|
| (i) | Here, crops produced by the farmers are mainly consumed by their families. Surplus production is sold in the nearby local markets. | (i) | Here, the farmers grow crops for the purpose of trade, it is called commercial farming. |
| (ii) | More than one crop is cultivated in the agricultural field. | (ii) | One crop is cultivated in the field. |
| (iii) | It is labour intensive farming. | (iii) | Farming is mechanised. and is prevalent in areas where farms are large and market economy is well developed. |
| (iv) | It depends on monsoon. | (iv) | It uses modern irrigation methods. |
| (v) | It is practiced in small area. | (v) | It is practiced in large area. |

| (vi) | Major crops are: Food grains, fruits and vegetables. | (vi) | Major crops are: cash crops and cereals. |
|---|---|---|---|

**22.** Economic strength of a country, is measured by manufacturing industries because :

(i) Industrial development is a precondition for eradication of unemployment and poverty from a country.

(ii) Manufacturing industries help in modernising agriculture which forms the backbone of the economy, they also reduce the dependency of people on agriculture.

(iii) Manufacturing Industries transform their raw materials into a wide variety of furnished goods of higher value are prosperous and developed.

(iv) Export of manufactured goods expands trade and brings much needed foreign exchange on international level.

(v) Manufacturing industries help reduce regional inequities by building industries in tribal and underdeveloped areas.

**23.** The fire functions of Political Parties:

(i) Political parties put forward candidates to contest elections. These candidates may be chosen by the top leaders or by members of the party.

(ii) Political parties play a major role in making laws for the country. No law can become a bill unless majority parties support it.

(iii) Parties put forward their policies and programmes for voters to choose from them. A government is expected to base its policies on the line taken by the ruling party.

(iv) Parties shape public opinion. They raise and highlight issues. Parties also launch movements for the resolution of the problem faced by the people.

(v) Political parties provide people access to government machinery and welfare schemes. It is easy for the public to approach their local party leader than a government officer.

**24.** Democracy stands much superior to any other form of government in promoting dignity and freedom of individual.

Following points can support this statement:

(i) It promotes equality among citizens.

(ii) It improves the quality of decision making opposition parties play important role.

(iii) Since, it provides methods to resolve conflicts since every citizen has the right to go in courts.

(iv) It allows room to correct mistakes and is an accountable, responsive and legitimate government.

(v) It reduces poverty. Every citizen has right to work. It also accommodates social diversity.

(vi) India is a secular state. All religions are equal here.

(vii) The passion for dignity and freedom are the basis of democracy. Equal treatment to women are necessary ingredients of democratic society.

**OR**

Democracy leads to peaceful and harmonious life among citizens in following ways :

(i) Democracy has had greater success in setting up regular, free and fair elections.

(ii) Every citizen has equal right to vote, to profess his/ her religion and to get education.

(iii) Every citizen can take part in any debate.

(iv) It ensures that the rights of its people are protected by the state and the government functions according to the laws.

(v) In democracy, there is no distinction between people based on race, religion, caste, colour or birth.

(vi) Equal opportunities are provided to all to be educated to grow as good citizens and to earn their living.

**25.** (i) The foreign trade provides an opportunity for both producers and buyers to reach beyond the markets of their own country.

(ii) There is a huge competition among producers of one country and producers of other country. Since goods transported from one country to another.

(iii) Now there is competition among buyers they have more choice of goods, over domestically produced goods.

(iv) With the opening of trade, goods travel from one market to another and varieties of goods on the markets rises. Price of similar goods in two markets tend to become stabilise.

For e.g., During Diwali season, buyers in India have the option of choosing between Indian and Chinese lights and bulbs, Chinese lights manufacturers gets an opportunity to expand their business as these lights are cheap and available in larger quantities.

**OR**

Impact of Globalization in our daily life are :

(i) Employment have been created in industries where MNCs have invested.

(ii) Transportation technology has made much faster delivery of goods across long distances possible at lower cost.

(iii) Prices of products have come down due to competition among the producers and manufacturers.

(iv) The invention of computers, internet, mobile phones and fax has made contacting each other around the world quite easy.

(v) Some Indian companies have become multinational themselves due to globalisation which increases jobs.

**26.**

(26. B.i)
Raja Sansi-International Airport Amritsar
b
Ahmedabad (1918)
(26. B.iii)**
West Bengal software and technology park, Kolkata
(26. B.ii)**
Bhadravati Iron and Steel Plant
a
Madras (Chennai) (1927)

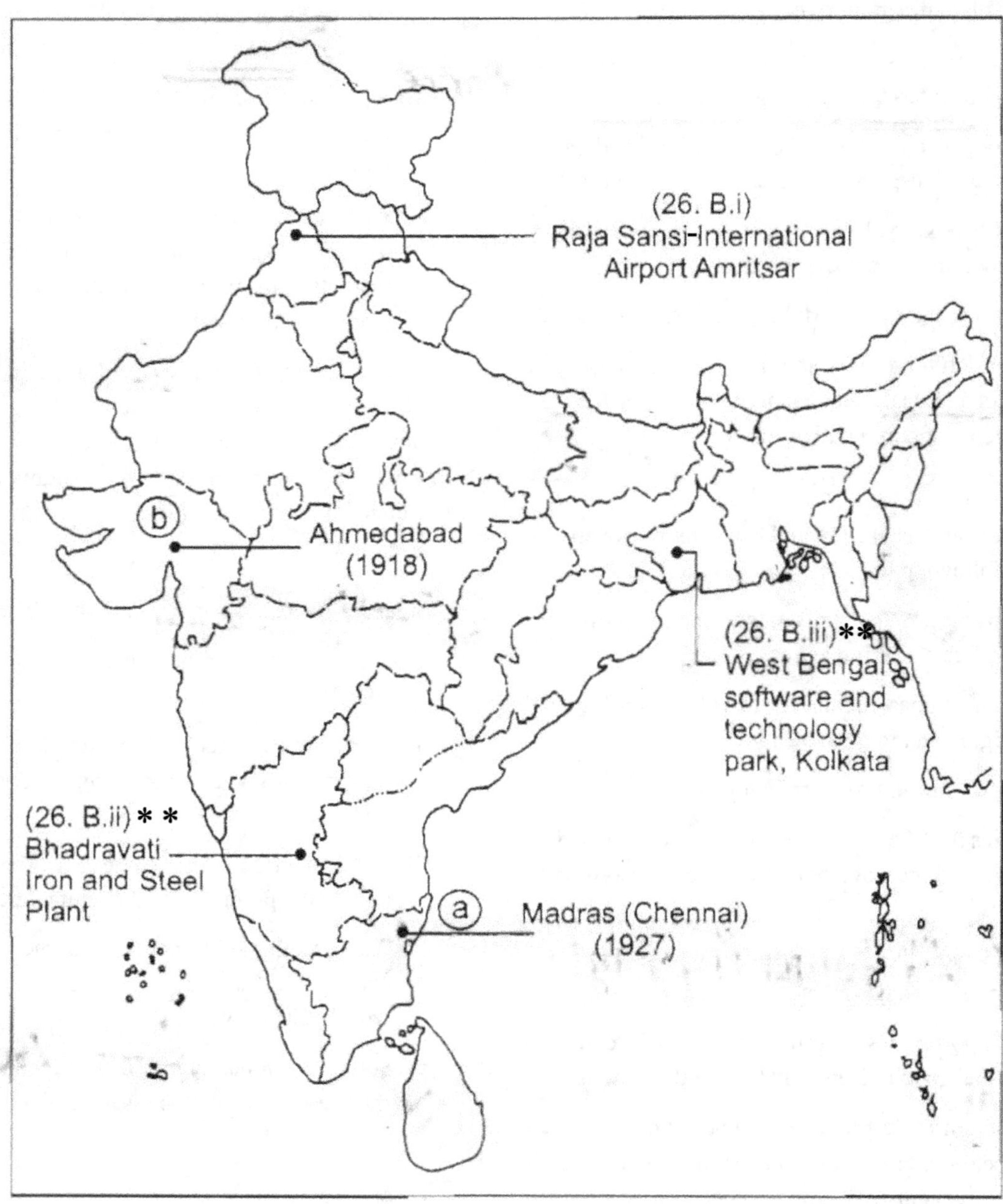

# CBSE Board Solved Paper Term-II

## SECTION - A

**(Very Short Answer Questions)**

**(8 × 1 = 8)**

1. Name the writer of the book '*Hind Swaraj*'. 1

2. Name the river related to National Waterways No. 2. 1

3. Explain any one difference between a pressure group and a political party**. 1

4. Explain the meaning of democracy. 1

5. Name any one political party of India which grew out of a movement.** 1

6. How does the use of money make it easier to exchange things? Give an example. 1

7. Given an example of violation of consumer's right to choose.** 1

8. How is the maximum retail price printed on packets beneficial for you?** 1

## SECTION - B

**(Short Answer Questions)**

**(12 × 3 = 36)**

9. Describe any three economic hardships faced by Europe in the 1830s. 3

**OR**

Describe any three problems faced by the French in the sphere of education in Vietnam.** 

10. Why did Gandhiji decide to withdraw the 'Non-Cooperation Movement' in February, 1922? Explain any three reasons. 3

11. Evaluate the role of business classes in the 'Civil Disobedience Movement'. 3

12. Describe any three characteristics of Durg-Bastar-Chandrapur Iron-ore belt in India. 3

13. Analyse the role of the manufacturing sector in the economic development of India. 3

14. Examine with example the role of means of transport and communication in making our life prosperous and comfortable. 3

15. Analyse the role of popular struggles in the development of democracy.** 3

16. How do pressure groups and movements strengthen democracy?** 3

17. On the basis of which values will it be a fair a expectation that democracy should produce harmonious social life? Explain. 3

18. Explain any three loan activities of banks in India. 3

19. How do Multi-National Corporations (MNCs) interlink production across countries? Explain with examples. 3

20. Analyse the importance of the tree-tier judicial machinery under Consumer Protection Act (COPRA), 1986 for redressal of consumer disputes.** 3

## SECTION - C

**(Long Answer Questions)**

**(8 × 5 = 40)**

21. "The first clear expression of nationalism came with the 'French Revolution' in 1789." Examine the statement. 5

**OR**

Examine the reasons that forced America to withdraw from the Vietnam war.** 

22. How did the Colonial Government repress the 'Civil Disobedience Movement' Explain. 5

23. Why is it necessary to conserve mineral resources? Explain any four ways to conserve mineral resources. 5

24. Analyse the role of chemical industries in the Indian economy. 5

25. Describe any five characteristics of democracy. 5

26. "It is very difficult to reform politics through legal ways." Evaluate the statement.** 5

27. Analyse any five positive effects of globalisation on the Indian economy. 5

28. What is liberalisation? Describe any four effects of liberalisation on the Indian economy. 5

## SECTION - D

### (Map Based Questions)

(3 + 3= 6)

29. Three features A, B and C are marked on the given political outline map of India. Identify these features with the help of the following information and write their correct names ons the lines marked on the map:                    **3 × 1= 3**

A.  The city associated with the Jallianwala Bagh incident.

B.  The place where the Indian National Congress session (1927) was held.

C.  The place where Gandhiji violated the salt Law.

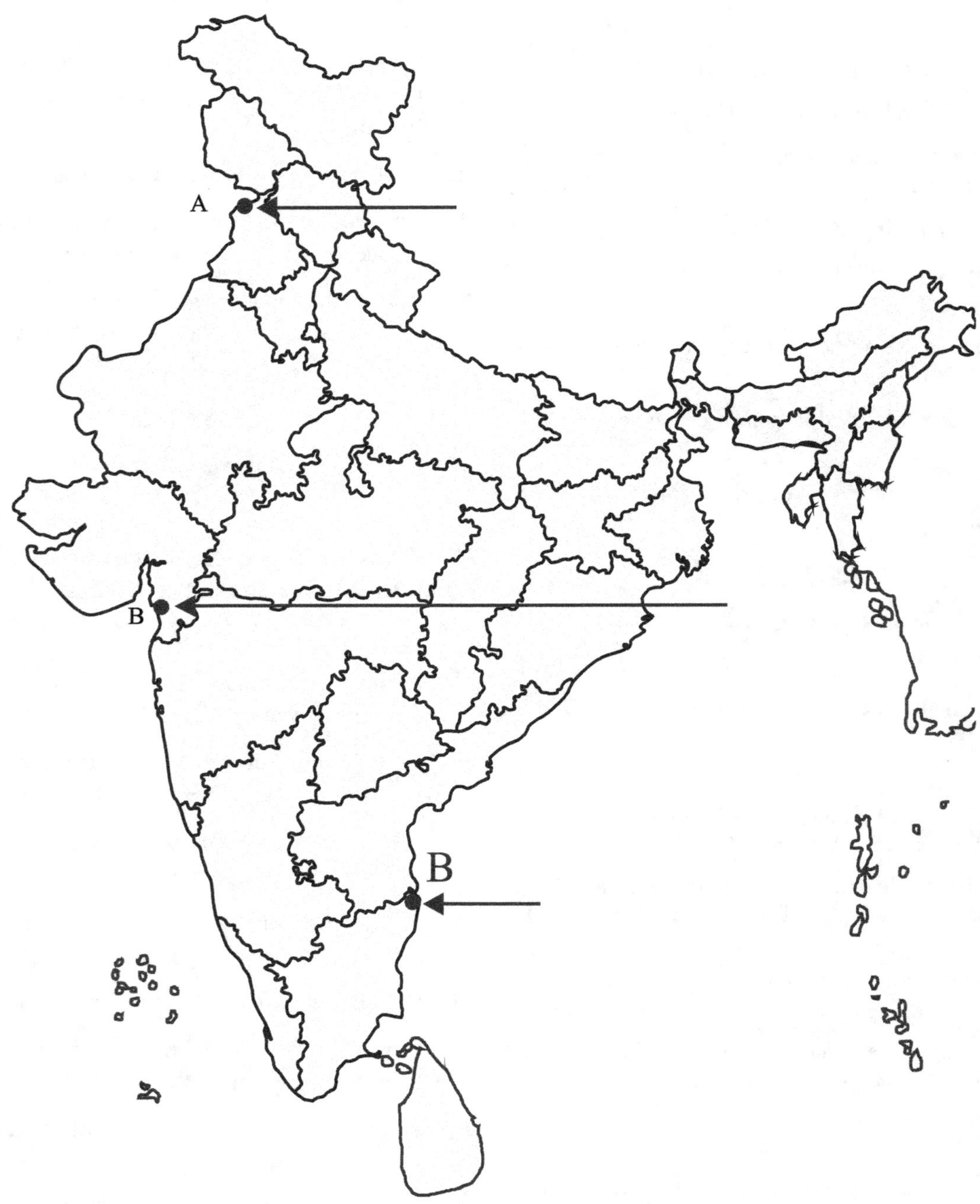

**30.** On the given political outline map of India locate and label the following features with appropriate symbols:     **(3 × 1= 3)**

   A.   Narora – Nuclear Power Plant.

   B.   Tuticorin – Major Sea Port.

   C.   Bhilai – Iron and Steen Plant.**

## Solutions

1. The book '*Hind Swaraj*' was written by Mahatma Gandhi.

2. National Waterways No. 2 is related with the river '*Brahmaputra*'.

3. (**)

4. Democracy is a from of government in which the supreme power is vested in the people and the representative of the people are elected by the voters on the basis of universal franchise.

5. (**)

6. Money makes exchanging things easier as:

   (i) Money has general acceptability.

   (ii) Its price remains constant compared to other commodities.

   (iii) It can be stored easily and doesn't need much space.*

   (iv) It is in the form of authorised paper currency which gives the gaurantee of the mentioned price to the owner.

   A shoe manufacturer wishes to sell his shoes and buy potatoes. He would sell his shoes in the market for money and then use the money to buy potatoes.

*Note*

*The Reserve Bank of India (RBI) prints and manages currency in India, whereas the Indian government regulates what denominations to circulate. The RBI prints all currency notes except the one rupee denomination notes and its subsidiary coins. The designing and minting of coins is the responsibility of the Government of India.*

7. (**)

8. (**)

9. Economic hardships faced by Europe in 1830s were:

   (i) Unemployment, migration and price rise.

   (ii) Increase in population.

   (iii) Rising competition in the market.

   (iv) Poor condition of peasants.

10. Causes of withdrawal of Non-Cooperation Movement are as follows:

    (i) Some of the activists set a police station on fire at Chauri-Chaura (Gorakhpur), Uttar Pradesh in which 21 policeman were burnt alive.

    (ii) Many members of the India National Congress felt that the Non-Cooperation Movement was tiresome and unnecessary, since they wanted to contest the election.

    (iii) Gandhiji felt that people of India were not ready for a nation-wide movement of mass struggle.

11. The role of business classes in the Civil Disobedience Movement is as follows:

    (i) The business classes supported Civil Disobedience Movement and Protested against colonial policies that restricted business activities.

    (ii) They wanted protection against import of foreign goods and a rupee sterling foreign exchange ratio that would discourage imports. Business classes formed the Indian Industrial and Commercial congress in 1920 and the Federation of the Indian Chamber of Commerce and Industries (FICCI) in 1927.

    (iii) The business community interpreted Swaraj in their own way. They came to see Swaraj at the time when colonial restriction on business would no longer exist and the trade industry would flourish without constraint.

12. The characteristics of Durg-Bastar-Chandrapur Iron-ore belt in India are as follows:

    (i) Durg-Bastar-Chandrapur belt of high grade haematite iron-ore. It is suitable for steel-making.

    (ii) The steel made from this ore is used to produce automobiles, railway equipment and in defence sector.

    (iii) 50% of the iron ore is exported to Japan and South Korea from the Vishakhapatnam port as building new steel plant is a very costly affair.

*Note*

*Odisha- Jharkhand belt, Durg-Bastar-Chandrapur belt, Ballari-Chitradurga-Chikkamagaluru-Tumakuru belt, Maharashtra-Goa belt are the major iron ore belts in India.*

13. The contribution of Manufacturing sector to national economy:

    (i) The industrial labourers and other employees get higher wages and enjoy higher standard of living compared to landless agricultural labourers.

    (ii) Manufacturing reduces dependence on agriculture by providing alternative employment opportunities in factory.

(iii) Increase in use of fertilizers, pesticides, plastics, electricity and diesel in agriculture has been possible due to the growth and competitiveness of the manufacturing industries.

**14.** Transportation and communication have made our life prosperous and comfortable in the following ways:

(i) Through transportation raw materials reach the factory and finished products reach to consumers. The pace of development of a country depends upon the production of goods and services as well as their movement over time.

(ii) The ease and mode of communications, like mobiles, internet, and Wi-Fi makes seamless flow of information possible.

(iii) Railways, airways, waterways, newspaper, radio, television, cinema and internet have been contributing to its socio-economic progress in many ways. The trade from local to international level has added to the vitality of its economy.

(iv) Transportation helps in generating employment for labourers as well as supplying labour in agriculture and the industrial sector. Communication has also helped in the transfer of information, which has led to technology transfer.

**15.** (**)

**16.** (**)

**17.** Democracy is a from of government in which the supreme power is vested in the people and the representatives of the people are elected by the voters on the basis of adult franchise. It promotes equality among citizens. It looks after the interest of the people. It allows accommodation of social diversity.

The basic values of democracy which provides fair expectation that democracy will produce harmonious social life are : (a) Social Equality, (b) Freedom, (c) Justice, (d) Economic justification, (e) Political freedom, civil and fundamental rights.

**18.** Activities of banks in India who are involved in providing loan:

(i) Bank intermediate between the depositors and borrowers.

(ii) Banks offer less interest on deposits than what they demand on loans.

(iii) Banks provide loans for various economic activities.

(iv) Reserve some cash deposits.

*The "Bank of Hindustan", established in 1770, was the first bank in India. It is located in the then-Indian capital, Calcutta.*

**19.** Multinational Corporations (MNCs) interlink their production across countries in following ways:

(i) MNCs set up offices and factories for production in regions of other country where they can easily get cheap labour and other resources. This minimise the cost of production end to maximise the profit.

(ii) The production process is divided into small parts and spread out across the globe.

(iii) The MNCs not only sell its finished products globally, but more importantly, the goods and services are produced globally.

(iv) Also, MNCs control production by placing orders around the world with a large number of small producers of items, like garments, footwear, sports items, etc. Then MNC sells these products under its brand name.

(v) The common route for MNC investments is to buy local companies and then to expand production. For example: Cargill Foods an American MNC had bought over an Indian company Parakh Foods which had their large marketing network in various parts of India and also has a good reputation. With this advantage, Cargill is now the largest producer of edible oil in India.

**20.** (**)

**21.** "The first clear expression of nationalism came with the 'French revolution' in 1789 in the following ways:

(i) France was a full-fledged territorial state under the rule of absolute monarch till 1789. The political and constitutional changes led to the transfer of sovereignty from monarchy to the body of French citizen.

(ii) The revolution proclaimed that it was the people who would hence forth constitute the nation and shape its destiny. The French revolutionaries introduced various measures and practices that could create a sense of collective identity, and a feeling of nationalism among the French people.

(iii) Regional dialects were discouraged and French, as it was spoken and written in Paris, became the common language of the nation.

(iv) A new French flag, the tri-colour, was chosen to replace the former royal standard.

(v) The Estates General was deleted by the body of active citizens and renamed as National Assembly. New hymns were composed, oaths were taken and martyrs were commemorated, all in the name of nation.

(vi) The revolutionaries further declared that they would help other people of Europe to become free nations. The students and other members of educated middle classes began setting up Jacobin Clubs. Their activities and campaigns prepared the way for the French armies which moved into Holland, Belgium, Switzerland and much of Italy in 1709s.

### Note

*Formed in 1789 as the Society of the Friends of the Constitution, it was known as the Jacobin Club because it met in a former convent of the Dominicans (known in Paris as Jacobins). It was originally formed by deputies of the National Assembly to protect the revolution's gains against a possible aristocratic reaction.*

22. The 'Civil Disobedience Movement' boycotted foreign cloth and picketed liquor shops. Peasants refused to pay revenue and taxes, village officials resigned. The Colonial Government repressed the members participating in movement in the following ways:

(i) Abdul Ghaffar Khan, a devout disciple was arrested in April 1930. Many people were killed who protested it.

(ii) Mahatma Gandhi was arrested by Colonial government due to which the industrial workers of Sholapur attacked police posts, municipal buildings, law courts and railway stations.

(iii) Peaceful Satyagrahis were attacked, women and children were beaten and about one lac people were arrested.

(iv) British government was worried and frightened by these development of movement and it followed a policy of brutal repression included lathi charge.

(v) In many places, forest people violated forest laws by going into reserved forests to collect wood and graze cattle. Worried by the developments, the colonial government began arresting the peoples and Congress leader one by one.

23. Minerals require millions of year to form. These are non-renewable resource and their stock is limited. Continuous extraction of minerals raises the cost of extraction as they have to be dug from greater depths.

A concerned effort has to be made in order to use our mineral resources in a planned and sustainable manner.

These are :

(i) Encouraging the use of substitutes in order to save minerals.

(ii) Improved technologies need to be constantly evolved to allow the use of low grade ores at low costs.

(iii) Recycling of minerals using scraps metals and other substitutes.

(iv) Reducing wastage in the process of mining.

24. The chemical industry contributes approximately percent 7% of GDP in India. It is the third largest in Asia and occupies sixth in the world. It comprises both large and small scale manufacturing units. Rapid growth has been recorded in both inorganic and organic sectors. Inorganic chemicals include sulphuric acid, nitric acid, alkalies, soda ash and caustic soda. These industries are widely spread over the country.

Organic chemicals includes petrochemicals, which are used for manufacturing of synthetic fibres, plastics, dye-stuffs, drugs and pharmaceuticals. Organic chemical plants are located near oil refineries and petrochemical plants.

The chemical industry has its own largest consumers. Basic chemicals undergo processing for the further production of other chemical that are used for industrial application, agriculture or directly for consumer markets.

25. The main characteristics of democracy are:

(i) In democracy, the rulers are elected by the people.

(ii) In a democracy, the final decision of making power must rest with elected representatives.

(iii) In a democracy, each adult citizen have one vote and each vote have one value.

(iv) A democracy is based on a tree and fair election, where those who are currently in power have a fair chance of losing.

(v) A democratic government rules within limits set by constitution.

26. (**)

27. The positive impacts of globalisation on Indian economy are:

(i) The improvements in the transportation technology has made much faster delivery of goods across long distances possible lower rates.

(ii) New jobs have been created in industries where MNCs have invested such as electronics, cell phones etc.

(iii) The invention and use of computer, internet, mobile phone, fax, etc., has made contact with each other around the world quite easy.

(iv) Now these exists a wide choice of goods and services in the market. The latest models of digital cameras, mobile phones and television made by the leading manufactures of the world are available in the markets. These products are affordable as well as within reach of the people.

(v) Some Indian companies have become multinational by due to globalisation, such as Tata Motors, Ranbaxy, Infosys etc.

**28.** Liberalisation of the economy means minimising the controls imposed by the government in return for higher involvement of privates organisations. The four effects of liberalisation on the Indian economy are:

(i) Since, barriers on foreign trade and foreign, investment were removed to a large extent. Now, goods could be imported and exported easily.

(ii) Competition would improve the performance of producers within the country.

(iii) Liberalisation allows to make decisions freely.

(iv) Foreign companies could set up factories and offices to boost up production.

(v) Competition improve the performance of producers within the country since they have to improve their quality of the product.

### Note

*Economic liberalization in India was initiated in 1991 by Prime Minister P. V. Narasimha Rao and his then-Finance Minister Dr. Manmohan Singh. The objectives are industrialization, expansion in the role of private and foreign investment, and introducing a free market system.*

**29.**

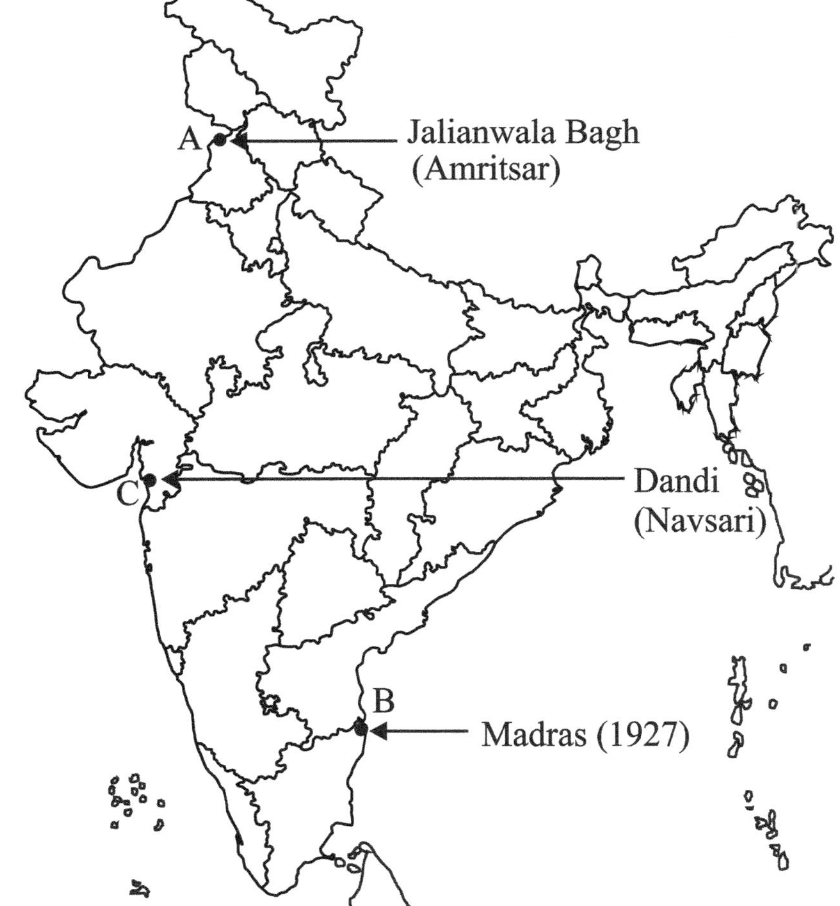

30.

Narora (Nuclear Power Plant,
Bulandshahar, U.P.)
A
C
Bhilai (Iron
and Steel Plant)
Tuticorin (Major Sea Port)
B

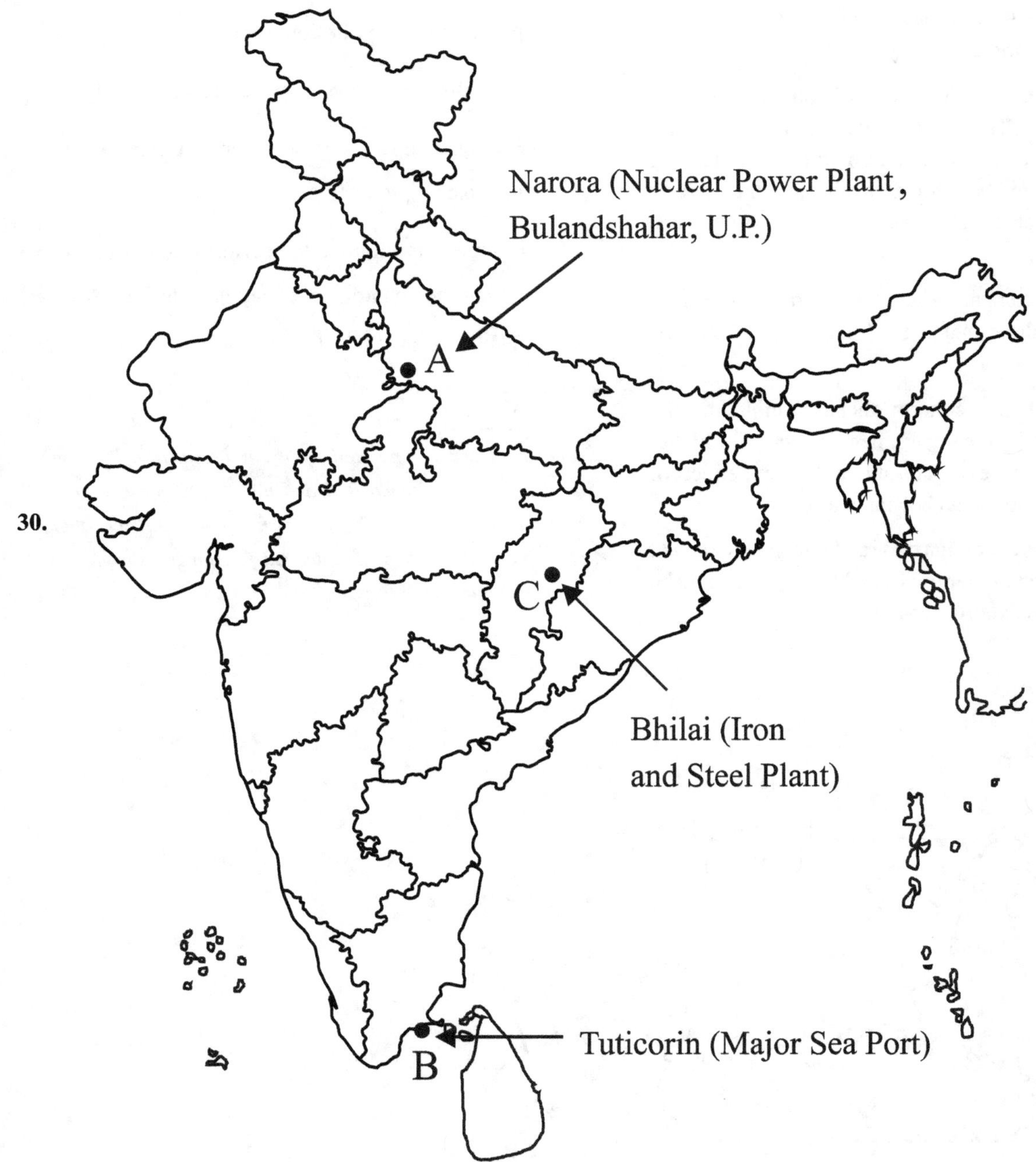

# CBSE Board Solved Paper Term-II

## SECTION - A
### (Very Short Answer Questions)

(8 × 1 = 8)

1. Name the writer of the novel 'Anandmath'. **1**

2. Name the river which is related to 'National Waterways' No. 1. **1**

3. How 'pressure groups' are formed?** **1**

4. Explain the meaning of 'challenge'.** **1**

5. Given an example of any 'pressure group' of India which functions as a branch of 'political party'.** **1**

6. Highlight the inherent problem in double coincidence of wants. **1**

7. Give any one example of consumer's 'right to choose'.** **1**

8. If you want to extract information about the functions of any government department, which right would you exercise?** **1**

## SECTION - B

### (Short Answer Questions)

(12 × 3 = 36)

9. Describe any three steps taken by the French revolutionaries to create a sense of collective identity amongst the French people. **3**

**OR**

Describe any three changes that came in the life of Vietnamese after the colonisation of Vietnam by the French.**

10. Why did Gandhiji decide to launch a nationwide Satyagraha against the proposed Rowlatt Act 1919? Explain any three reasons: **3**

11. Evaluate the contribution of folklore, songs, popular prints etc., in shaping the nationalism during freedom struggle. **3**

12. Describe any three characteristics of 'Odisha-Jharkhand belt' of iron ore in India. **3**

13. Explain with examples the interdependence of agriculture and industries. **3**

14. Why do the movement of goods and services from one place to another require fast and efficient means of transport? Explain with examples. **3**

15. Differentiate between Nepal's movement and Bolivia's popular struggle.** **3**

16. How do the pressure groups and movements influence politics. Explain with examples.** **3**

17. Analyse any three values that make democracy better. **3**

18. "Banks are efficient medium of exchange." Support the statement with arguments. **3**

19. Examine any three conditions which should be taken care of multinational companies to set up their production units. **3**

20. Analyse any three reasons for the beginning of the consumer movement in India.** **3**

## SECTION - C
### (Long Answer Questions)

(8 × 5 = 40)

21. Who hosted 'Vienna Congress' in 1815? Analyse the main changes brought by the 'Vienna Treaty'. **5**

**OR**

Analyse the role of 'Hoa-Hao' movement to arouse anti-imperialist sentiments in Vietnam.**

22. "Plantation workers had their own understanding of Mahatma Gandhi's ideas and the notion of "Swaraj". Support the statement. **5**

*Note: (**) Marked questions are out of syllabus so these are not explained or answered.*

**23.** 'Energy saved is energy produced'. Assess the statement. **5**

**24.** Explain any two main challenges faced by the jute industry in India. Explain any three objectives of National Jute Policy. **5**

**25.** "Democracy is very important for promoting dignity and freedom of citizens." Support the statement with arguments. **5**

**26.** Describe any five efforts made to reform political parties in India. **5**

**27.** "Self Help Groups" help borrowers to overcome the problems of lack of collateral" Examine the statement. **5**

**28.** Describe the contribution of technology in promoting the process of globalisation. **5**

## SECTION - D

### (Map Based Question)

**(3 × 2 = 6)**

**29.** Three features A, B and C are marked on the given political outline map of India. Identify these features with the help of the following information and write their correct names on the lines marked on the map: **3 × 1 = 3**

A. The place, related to the calling off the 'Non-Cooperation Movement'.

B. The place where the 'Peasants Satyagraha' was started.

C. Name the place where 'Indian National Congress' session (September 1920) wss held.

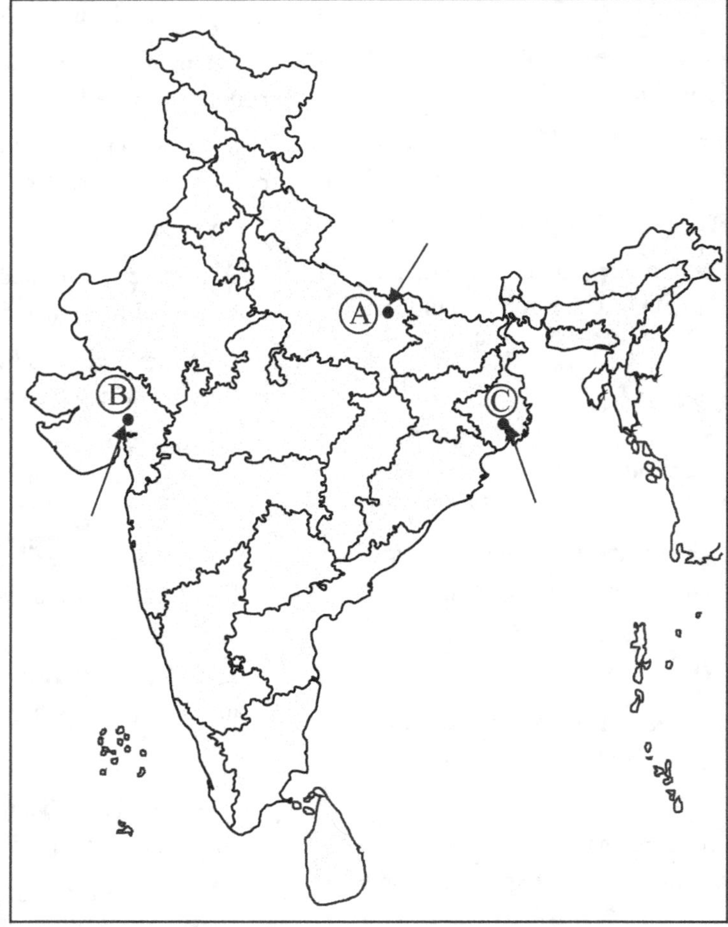


**30.** On the given political outline map of India locate and label the following with appropriate symbols. **3 × 1 = 3**

A. Salem-Iron and Steel Centre.**

B. Kandla-Major Sea Port.

C. Hyderabad-Sofware Technology Park.

## Solutions

1. The writer of the novel 'Anandmath' is Bankim Chandra Chattopadhyay.

> **Note**
>
> *Anandamath is a Bengali novel written by Bankim Chandra Chattopadhyay and published in 1882. It is inspired by and set in the background of the Sannyasi Rebellion in the late 18th century.*

2. The river related with 'National Waterways' No. 1 is Ganga. Ganga-Bhagirathi-Hooghly river system from Allahabad to Haldia was declared as 'National waterways No. 1'.

3. (**)

4. (**)

5. (**)

6. The inherent problem in double coincidence of wants is that both the sides must agree to sell and buy each other's commodities at the same time. For examples:

   For example, one person has tomatoes but is in need of mangoes, and another has mangoes but is in need of tomatoes. Then they will exchange their goods.

7. (**)

8. (**)

9. Steps taken by the French revolutionaries to create a sense of collective identity among the French people were:

   (i) A new French flag, the tricolor, was adopted to replace the former Royal standard.

   (ii) Internal custom duties and dues were abolished.

   (iii) Uniform system of weights and measures was adopted.

   (iv) The ideas of Le Partie (the father land) and Le Citoyen, Patne the Citizen emphasized the notion of a united community enjoying equal rights under the constitution.

   (v) A centralised administrative structure was established, and it produced uniform laws for all of the country's residents.

10. Gandhiji decided to launch a nationwide Satyagraha against the proposed 'Rowlatt Act' in 1919 due to the following reasons:

    (i) It also provided for preventive indefinite detention and arrest without a warrant. Other provisions included juryless trials for forbidden political acts.

    (ii) Convicted people were to deposit securities upon their release, and they were also to refrain from taking part in any political, religious, or educational activities.

    (iii) This act severely curbed the freedom of the press.

11. History and fiction, folklore and songs, popular prints and symbols, played a vital role in shaping the nationalism during freedom struggle. It can be described in the following points:

    (i) Khadi and charkha used by Mahatma Gandhi became symbol of agitation and resistance.

    (ii) The identity of India came to be visually associated with the image of Bharat Mata created by Bankim Chandra Chattopadhyay. He also wrote '*Vande Matram*' as a hymn to the motherland.

    (iii) Nationalists began recording folk tales sung by bards and they toured villages to gather folk songs and legends.

12. The Odisha-Jharkhand belt produced best quality of iron-ore. Its main characteristics are:

    (i) High grade haematite ore is found in Odisha.

    (ii) It is found in Badampahar mines in Mayurbhanj and Kendujhar districts.

    (iii) In the adjoining Singbhum district of Jharkhand, haematite iron-ore is mined in Gua and Noamundi.

> **Note**
>
> *Kudermukh deposits are known to be one of the largest deposits of iron ore in the world and are situated in Bellary-Chikmaglur-Chitradurga Belt.*

13. Agriculture and industries are interdependent on each other in the following ways:

    (i) Industries obtain raw material such as jute sugar etc., from agriculture and produce finished products.

    (ii) Manufacturing industries, which are involved in the production of tools and equipments, have helped in modernizing agriculture.

(iii) Developments and competitiveness of the manufacturing industries have assisted agriculturists in increasing their productions and made the production processes very efficient.

**14.** Fast and efficient means of transport plays a vital role in the development of a country because:

(i) We use different materials and services in our daily life. Some of these are easily available in our immediate surroundings, while other requirements are met by bringing things from other places.

Goods and services do not move from supply location to demand location on their own. The movement of these goods and services needs transportation.

(ii) The products come to the consumers by transportation.

(iii) The development of a country depends upon the production of goods and services as well as their movement over space.

(iv) It is necessary to carry raw materials from production centres and from manufacturing hubs to markets in as little time as possible to achieve efficiency, particularly for perishable goods.

**15.** (**)

**16.** (**)

**17.** Values that makes democracy better are:

(i) It provides equality among citizens all individuals.

(ii) Citizens of state country have equal rights in electing their representatives.

(iii) Enhances the respect, dignity and freedom of an individual.

(iv) It improves the quality of decision making

(v) It allows for negotiations and room to correct mistakes.

(vi) Every citizen has the right and means to examine the process of decision making.

(vii) It produces a government that is accountable to the citizens and responsive to the needs and expectations of citizens.

**18.** "Banks are efficient medium of exchange " because:

(i) Banks accept the deposits and also pay an amount as interest on the deposits.

(ii) The facility of cheque against demand deposit makes it possible to directly settle payments without the use of cash.

(iii) Demand deposits are accepted widely as a medium of payment.

 *Note*

*The State Bank of India (SBI) is the largest bank in India and also one of the biggest corporations in the world. At present, SBI has 159 computerised banks and 11,274 listed branches.*

**19.** An MNC is a company which owns and controls productions or provides consultancy in more than one nation. Following are the conditions before setting up their production units that are:

(i) MNCs require good quality raw materials for their factories.

(ii) MNCs set up offices and factories for production in region where the can get cheap labour.

(iii) MNCs look for good transport mode to take their product to consumers or to other countries.

(iv) MNCs set up production where it is close to the markets.

(v) MNCs might look for government policies that protect their interests.

**20.** (**)

**21.** In 1815, representative of the European Powers-Britain, Russia, Prussia and Austria, who had collectively defeated Napolean, met at Vienna congress. The congress was hosted by the Austrian Chancellor Duke Metternich.

The main changes brought by the treaty are as follows:

(i) France lost the territories, it had annexed under Napolean.

(ii) The Bourbon dynasty, was restored to power.

(iii) A series of states were set up on the boundaries of France to prevent French extension in future.

(iv) Prussia was given important new territories on its western frontiers while Austria was given control of Northern Italy.

(v) The Kingdom of Netherlands, including Belgium was set up.

(vi) In the east, Russia was given a part of Poland while Prussia was given a portion of Saxony

(vii) The intention was to restore the monarchies that have been overthrown by Napolean, and to create a new conservative order in Europe.

**22.** Plantation workers had their own understanding of Mahatma Gandhi ji's ideas and the notion of "Swaraj" as follows:

(i) Freedom means retaining a link with the village from which they had come.

(ii) For plantation workers, freedom meant the right to move freely in and out of the confined space in which they were enclosed.

(iii) Plantation workers were not permitted to leave the tea gardens without permission so when they heard of the Non-Cooperation Movement, thousands of workers defied the authorities, left the plantations and headed home.

(iv) Plantation workers believed that Gandhi Raj was coming and every one would be given land in their own villages.

*Note*

*Swaraj is an ancient word of Sanskrit where 'swa' means self, or one's own, and 'raj', means rule. Mahatma Gandhi pioneered the ideology of 'Swaraj' during the British rule. His concept of 'Swaraj' was to empower masses and give them the real sense of self-rule.*

**23.** India is one of the least energy efficient country in the world. We have to following are the cautious approach for judicious use of our limited energy resources:

(i) Switching off the electrical appliances when not in use. This will reduce the electricity bill and save energy.

(ii) Use power saving deices, meaning in place of ordinary bulbs, and tubelight, we can use LED bulbs, similarly AC and other units which consume less power, should be used.

(iii) Use public transport systems such as buses, metro etc., instead of individual vehicles, so that petrol, diesel and CNG can be saved.

(iv) Use non-conventional source of energy i.e., as far as possible water heating and cooking can be done through solar energy.

(v) Use a slow cooker, toaster oven, or microwave oven over a conventional oven. Also, use utensils made of ceramic and glass.

*Note*

*India is the world's third largest producer of renewable energy, with 40% of its installed electricity capacity coming from non-fossil fuel sources.*

**24.** (**)

**25.** According to Abraham Lincoln, democracy is a government of the people, by the people, and for the people. It is very important for promoting dignity and freedom of the citizens.

We support the statement through the following argument:

(i) Democracy is based on equality, whether rich or poor, or belongs to any religion and caste to be treated equally.

(ii) The respect and freedom are the basis of democracy.

(iii) Respect and equal treatment of women are important ingredients of a democratic society.

(iv) Democracy works on legal basis which works on the principles of individual freedom and dignity.

(v) Democracy has strengthened the disadvantaged and discriminated castes for equal status and equal opportunity.

**26.** Efforts have been made and further efforts should be made for the reforms of political parties in India. These are as follows:

(i) The constitution was amended to prevent MLAs and MPs from changing parties to stop defection. This law known as anti-defection law.

(ii) The supreme court passed an order to reduce the influence of money and criminals for active participation in fighting MLA/MP elections.

(iii) It become mandatory for every candidate who contests elections to file an affidavit giving details of his property and criminal cases pending against him.

(iv) The election commissioner makes it necessary for political parties to hold their organizational elections and file their income tax returns.

(v) The cash donations to political parties have been reduced to ₹ 2000. All cheque payments/transfer of money have tobe  shown in every party's balance sheets.

(vi) The new system has made parties a amountable to the public regarding elections.

**Note**

*The Tenth Schedule, popularly known as the Anti-Defection Act, was included in the Constitution via the 52nd Amendment Act, 1985. Its purpose was to bring stability to governments by discouraging legislators from changing parties. It punishes individual Members of Parliament (MPs) and MLAs for leaving one party for another.*

27. "Self Help Groups" help borrowers to overcome the problems of lack of collateral in the following ways:

   (i) In a "Self Help Group" most of the important decisions regarding savings and loan activities are taken by the group members.

   (ii) The group responsible for the repayment of the loan.

   (iii) In case of non-repayment of loan by any member is followed up seriously by other members in the group.

   (iv) Because of this banks are willing to lend to the poor woman. When organised in SHGS, even though they have no substantial collateral.

28. The technology has contributed immensely in promotion the process of globalisation in the following ways:

   (i) Faster made delivery of goods faster across long distances possible at cheaper costs.

   (ii) The technology in the areas of telecommunication, computers, internet, mobiles has changed rapidly. It technology has facilitated the satellite communication devices.

   (iii) Telecommunication facilities are used to make contact with one another around the world at any time.

   (iv) The facility of video conferencing or one to one video calling has become common in present days.

   (v) It also allows us to send instant electronic mail (e-mail), and voice mail across the world at negligible costs.

29.

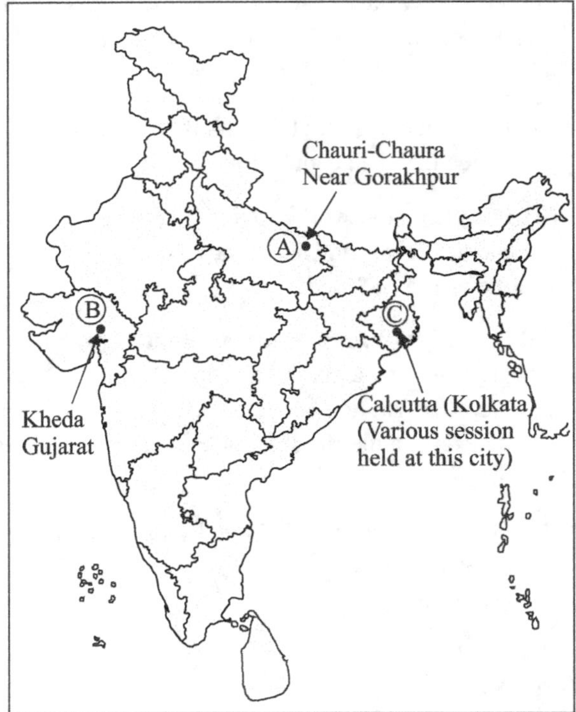



30.

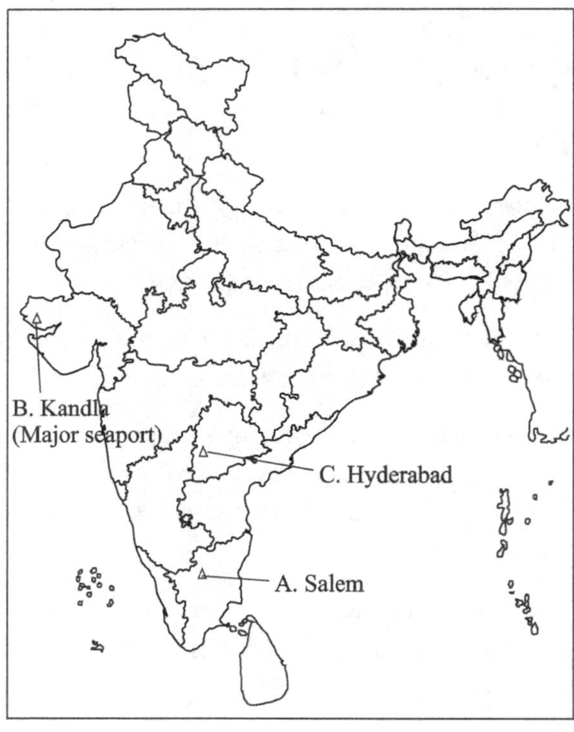

# CBSE Board Solved Paper Term-II

## SECTION - A

**(Very Short Answer Questions)**

**(8 × 1 = 8)**

1. Who remarked "when France sneezes the rest of Europe catches cold." **1**

**OR**

Who were called colons in Vietnam?**

2. Why should the use of cattle cake as fuel be discouraged? **1**

3. Distinguish between Pressure Groups and Political Parties by stating any one point of distinction.** **1**

4. Why did India adopt multi-party system? **1**

5. Name any two sectional interest groups.** **1**

6. Why do MNCs set up their offices and factories in those regions where they get cheap labour and other resources? **1**

7. If any damage is done to a consumer by a trader, under which consumer right can one move to consumer court to get compensation.** **1**

8. Why is the supervision of the functioning of formal sources of loans necessary? **1**

## SECTION - B

**(Short Answer Questions)**

**(12 × 3 = 36)**

9. "The decade of 1830 had brought great economic hardship in Europe", Support the statement with arguments.

**3**

**OR**

"The Ho Chi Minh Trail became advantageous to Vietnamese in the war against U.S." Support the statement with arguments.**

10. What type of flag was designed during the 'Swadeshi Movement' in Bengal? Explain its main features. **3**

11. "The plantation workers in Assam had their own understanding of Mahatma Gandhi and the notion of Swaraj". Support the statement with arguments. **3**

12. Classify industries on the basis of source of raw material. How are they different from each other? **3**

13. 'Consumption of energy in all forms has been rising all over the country. There is an urgent need to develop a sustainable path of energy development and energy saving'. Suggest and explain any three measures to solve this burning problem. **3**

14. Suggest any three steps to minimise the environmental degradation caused by the industrial development in India. **3**

15. What is meant by regional political party? State the conditions required to be recognised as a 'regional political party'. **3**

16. What are public interest pressure groups? Describe their functioning.** **3**

17. Which three challenges do you feel are being faced by political parties in India? Give your opinion. **3**

18. "Deposits with the banks are beneficial to the depositers as well as to the nation." Examine the statement. **3**

19. Why had the Indian government put barriers to foreign trade and foreign investments after independence? Analyse the reasons. **3**

20. "Rules and regulations are required for the protection of the consumers in the market place." Justify the statement with arguments.** **3**

## SECTION - C

**(Long Answer Type Questions)**

**(8 × 5 = 40)**

21 "Napoleon had destroyed democracy in France but in the administrative field he had incorporated revolutionary principles in order to make the whole system more rational and efficient." Analyse the statement with arguments. **5**

**OR**

"The peace negotiations in Geneva followed the division of Vietnam that set in motion a series of events that turned Vietnam into a battle field." Analyse the statement with arguments.**

---

*Note: (**) Marked questions are out of syllabus so these are not explained or answered.*

**22.** Why did Mahatma Gandhi decide to call off the Civil Disobedience Movement? Explain. **5**

**23.** Explain the importance of conservation of minerals. Highlight any three measures to conserve them. **5**

**24.** "Roadways still have an edge over railways in India." Support the statement with arguments. **5**

**25.** Describe the popular struggle of Bolivia.** **5**

**26.** "Political parties are a necessary condition for a democracy". Analyse the statement with examples. **5**

**27.** How can the formal sector loans be made beneficial for poor farmers and workers? Suggest any five measures. **5**

**28.** Describe the impact of Globalization on Indian economy with examples. **5**

## SECTION - D
### (Map Based Questions)

**(1 + 2 = 3)**

**29.** Three features A, B and C are marked on the given political outline map of India. Identify these features with the help of the following information and write their correct names on the lines marked in the map: **3**

A. The place where cotton mill workers organised Satyagraha.

B. The place related to the calling off the Non-Cooperative Movement.

C. The place where the Indian National Congress Session was held in September 1920.

**30.** On the given political outline map of India locate and label the following with appropriate symbols: **(3 × 1 = 3)**

A. Oil Field - Digboi

B. Iron and Steel Plant - Bhilai**

C. Major Sea Port - Kochi

## Solutions

1. Metternich said, "When France sneezes, the rest of Europe catches a cold."

*Duke Metternich was a well-known politician and diplomat who served as the Foreign Minister of the Austrian Empire from 1809 until 1848. He was born in Koblenz, Germany, in 1773 and belonged to a noble family.*

2. The use of cattle cake as fuel is undesirable because, it releases harmful gases like carbon monoxide which is toxic in nature.

3. (**)

4. Due to its huge socio-cultural diversity, varying geography and due to its huge population with different religions, India adopted multi-party system. It is not possible to accommodate such variations in one single party. So, there are multiple parties present in India.

5. (**)

6. MNCs set up their offices and factories in those regions where they get cheap labour and other resources to minimise the cost of production and maximise profit earning.

7. (**)

8. Supervision of the functioning of formal sources of loans is necessary because banks have to submit information to the RBI on how much they are lending, to whom they are lending and at what interest rate.

9. The decade of 1830 had brought great economic hardship or crisis in Europe due to the following reasons:

   (i) Due to enormous increase in population all over Europe, unemployment became a common feature in most of the countries.

   (ii) Migration of rural people to the cities further made the situation worse.

   (iii) Due to increased population, the demand of food increased. It led to the rise of food prices. This increased price along with a year of bond harvests led to widespread poverty in town and country.

   (iv) Small scale producers in towns sometimes faced stiff competition from rural areas where production was carried out mainly in homes or small workshops. These products imported from rural areas were obviously cheaper than the town-made products.

**OR**

(**)

10. During the Swadeshi movement in Bengal, a tricolour flag with red, green and yellow colours was designed. It had 8 lotuses which represented 8 provinces and a crescent moon representing Hindus and Muslims.

*The flag was designed by Pingali Venkayya during the Swadeshi movement in Bengal. It was the first Indian flag that was designed.*

11. The plantation workers too had their own understanding of Gandhiji's notion of Swaraj:

    (i) Under the Inland Emigration Act of 1859, plantation workers were not permitted to leave the tea gardens without permission, and they were rarely given such permission.

    (ii) When they heard of the Non-Cooperation movement thousands of workers defied the authorities, left the plantations, and headed home.

    (iii) For plantation workers in Assam, freedom meant the right to move freely in and out of the confined space in which they were enclosed and it mean retaining a link with the village from which they had come.

    (iv) They interpreted the term Swaraj in their own ways, imagining it to be a time when all sufferings and troubles would be over.

12. On the basis of source of raw materials, industries are classified into four categories. They are:

    (i) **Agro-based Industries**: The industries which use agriculture products as their raw material are called agro-based industries.

    For example: vegetable oil, cotton textile, dairy products, leather, juice, pickle and spices etc.

    (ii) **Forest-based industries:** The industries use forests as their raw material and are called forest-based industries. Paper, rayon, bamboo, resin, honey, furniture, are some examples of forest based industries.

(iii) **Mineral-based Industries:** These industries are those industries, which get raw material from minerals like-Iron and steel and cement industries.

Iron made from iron ore is the product of mineral based industry. This is used as raw material for the manufacturing of a number of other products, such as heavy machinery, building materials and railway coaches.

(iv) **Pastoral-based industries:** These industries depend upon animals for their raw materials. Hides, skins, shoes, dairy product, etc. are some of the examples.

13. Consumption of energy in all forms has been rising. To take care of this concern various measures that need to be adopted are as follows:

(i) Increase in the use of renewable energy resources like-solar, wind, biogas, tidal and geothermal energies. This will decrease the dependence on non-renewable sources.

(ii) Judicious use of limited energy resources.

(iii) Use of public transport system in place of individual vehicle.

(iv) Energy conservation, through switching off electrical devices when not in use, using power saving devices etc.

*The Sihwa Lake Tidal Power Station in South Korea has the largest electricity generation capacity at 254 megawatts (MW).*

14. Three steps that can be taken to minimise environmental degradation by the industries:

(i) Fitting smoke stacks in factories with electrostatic precipitators.

(ii) Reduce smoke by using oil or gas instead of coal in factories.

(iii) Treating waste matter and effluents before releasing them in rivers and ponds.

15. Regional Political Party exists, operates and functions at the regional level. It gives prominence to regional issues, specific problems of the region and it has influence on the people of that region. It lays more stress on regional culture identify, which it wants to preserve and promote.

Conditions required to be recognised as a regional political party are:

(i) Party should have polled at least 6% valid votes in an election to the Legislative Assembly.

(ii) Party has reached in at least three states in last general election.

(iii) Party had won at least two seats in Legislative Assembly elections.

*According to the Election Commission of India, in 2021, the total number of parties registered was 2858, including 6 national parties, 56 state parties, and 2796 unrecognised parties.*

16. (**)

17. Political parties face the following challenges:

(i) Lack of internal democracy: Parties do not conduct internal regular elections, organisational meetings are not conducted, and they do not maintain a register of the membership.

(ii) Money and muscle power: Candidates who can raise money are nominated, such powers are visible during the time of elections.

(iii) Dynastic succession: Leaders on top have the unfair chance of favouring their families and friends, thus the top positions end up being controlled by families.

18. Deposits with banks are beneficial to the depositors as well as to the nation because:

Benefit to the depositor.

(i) People's money is safe with the bank.

(ii) People can withdraw the money as and when they require.

(iii) Bank accepts the deposits and pays interest to the depositor.

Benefits to the nation

(i) Banks mediate between those who have surplus funds and those are in need of these funds.

(ii) Huge demand for loans for various economic activities.

(iii) Banks use the major proportion of the deposit to extend loans.

19. The Indian government put up barriers to foreign trade and foreign investments because:

(i) To protect the producers within the country from foreign competition.

(ii) In the 1950s and 1960s, industries were coming up in India and external competition due to imports at that stage would not have been conducive for development of domestic industries in India.

(iii) Indian government permitted imports of only essential items such as-machinery, fertilisers, petroleum, etc.

**20.** (**)

**21.** (i) Due to Napoleon's uniform laws, transport and communications network improved and peasants, artisans, workers and businessmen enjoyed freedom.

(ii) Also in the towns, guild restrictions were removed.

(iii) Napoleon simplified administrative divisions thereby abolishing feudal system. He freed the peasants and other sections of society from serfdom and manorial dues.

(iv) The Napoleonic code did away with privileges based on birth, established equality before the law and secured the right to property.

(v) The Civil code of 1804 also known as Napoleonic code spread to all countries including Switzerland, Italy and Germany.

 *Note*

*Napoleon Bonaparte (1769–1821), also known as Napoleon I, was a French military leader and emperor who conquered much of Europe in the early 19th century.*

**OR**

(**)

**22.** Mahatma Gandhi decided to call off the Civil Disobedience Movement because:

(i) Worried by the development of Civil Disobedience Movement the colonial government began arresting the Congress leaders one by one.

(ii) This led to violent clashes in many places.

(iii) Abdul Ghaffar Khan, a devout disciple of Mahatma Gandhi was arrested in April 1930, angry crowd demonstrated in the streets of Peshawar, facing armoured cars and police firing in ?. Which many people were killed.

(iv) When Mahatma Gandhi was arrested, industrial workers attacked police force, municipal building, law courts, railway stations and all other structures that symbolized British rule.

(v) The peaceful Satyagrahis were beaten and about 1 lakh people were arrested.

Due to the violence at large scale Mahatma Gandhi called off the Civil Disobe-Dience Movement.

 *Note*

*Civil disobedience can be defined as refusing to obey a law, a regulation, or a power judged unjust in a peaceful manner. Civil disobedience is, therefore, a form of resistance without violence.*

**23.** Importance of Conservation:

(i) Mineral are being rapidly consumed which takes millions of years to be created.

(ii) They are finite and non-renewable.

(iii) Continued extraction of mineral ores leads to increasing costs as mineral extraction comes from greater depths along with deceasing quality.

Three measures to conserve them are:

(i) Recycling of metals.

(ii) Finding substitutes.

(iii) It should be used in a planned and sustainable manner.

(iv) Improved technology needs to be constantly evolved to allow use of low grade ores at low costs.

(v) Using scrap metals.

(vi) Any other relevant point.

**24.** As of 2022, the total length of National Highways in the country was 144634 km. The growing importance of road transport vis-a-vis rail transport is rooted in the following reasons:

(i) Construction cost of roads is much lower than that of railway lines.

(ii) It is economical in transportation of few persons and relatively smaller amount of goods over short distances.

(iii) Roads provide door-to-door service, thus the cost of loading and unloading is much lower.

(iv) Roads can traverse comparatively more dissected and undulating topography.

(v) Roads can negotiate higher gradients of slopes and as

such can traverse mountains such as the Himalayas.

(vi) Road transport is also used as a feeder to other modes of transport. They provide a link between railway stations, air and sea ports.

**25.** (**)

**26.** Political parties are necessary for democracy due to the following reasons:

(i) Political Parties provide voters with alternative ways of governance and economic management.

(ii) They provide candidates in elections who, go to the legislature to make laws after running elections.

(iii) They provide the leaders who form the government.

(iv) They also form the opposition party in the legislature to act as a check on the ruling government.

(v) These parties provide a means for the general people to make their voices heard in the legislature and government.

(vi) They represent the people in the legislature and ensure that laws are passed to reflect the will of the general people.

**27.** The various sources of loans are:

(i) Formal sector loan.

(ii) Informal sector loan

Formal sector loan: They are given by banks and cooperatives. The informal lenders include money lenders, traders, employers, relatives, friends etc.

Informal Sector loans: Poor people and workers get much of their loans from the informal sectors, which are exploitative and charges very high interest rate.

The measures to make formal sector loan beneficial for poor farmers and workers are as follows:

(i) The formal sector should ensure that every needy receivers loans.

(ii) The formal sector like, banks and cooperatives should lend more to poor people and workers, particularly in rural areas.

(iii) Providing Self Help Group (SHG) bank linkage.

(iv) The formal sector should provide cheap and affordable credit.

(v) Increase the number of cooperatives and banks in rural areas.

**28.** The globalisation has impacted Indian economy in the following ways:

(i) Over the past twenty years, the foreign investment has increased.

(ii) Globalisation has created new opportunities for Indian companies, particularly providing services like it.

(iii) It has created new jobs and has helped in reducing the unemployment rate to an extent.

(iv) Services such as data entry, accounting, engineering are now being done cheaply in India.

(v) Indian companies like- Tata Motors, Infosys have been able to get benefits from the increased competition created as a result of Globalization.

**29.**

 **Note**

*The first session of the Indian National Congress was held in Bombay in 1885. Its first president was W.C. Bannerjee.*

30.

Digboi
A
B
Bhilai
C
A. Oil Field : Digboi
B. Iron & Steel Plants : Bhilal
C. Major Sea Port : Kochi

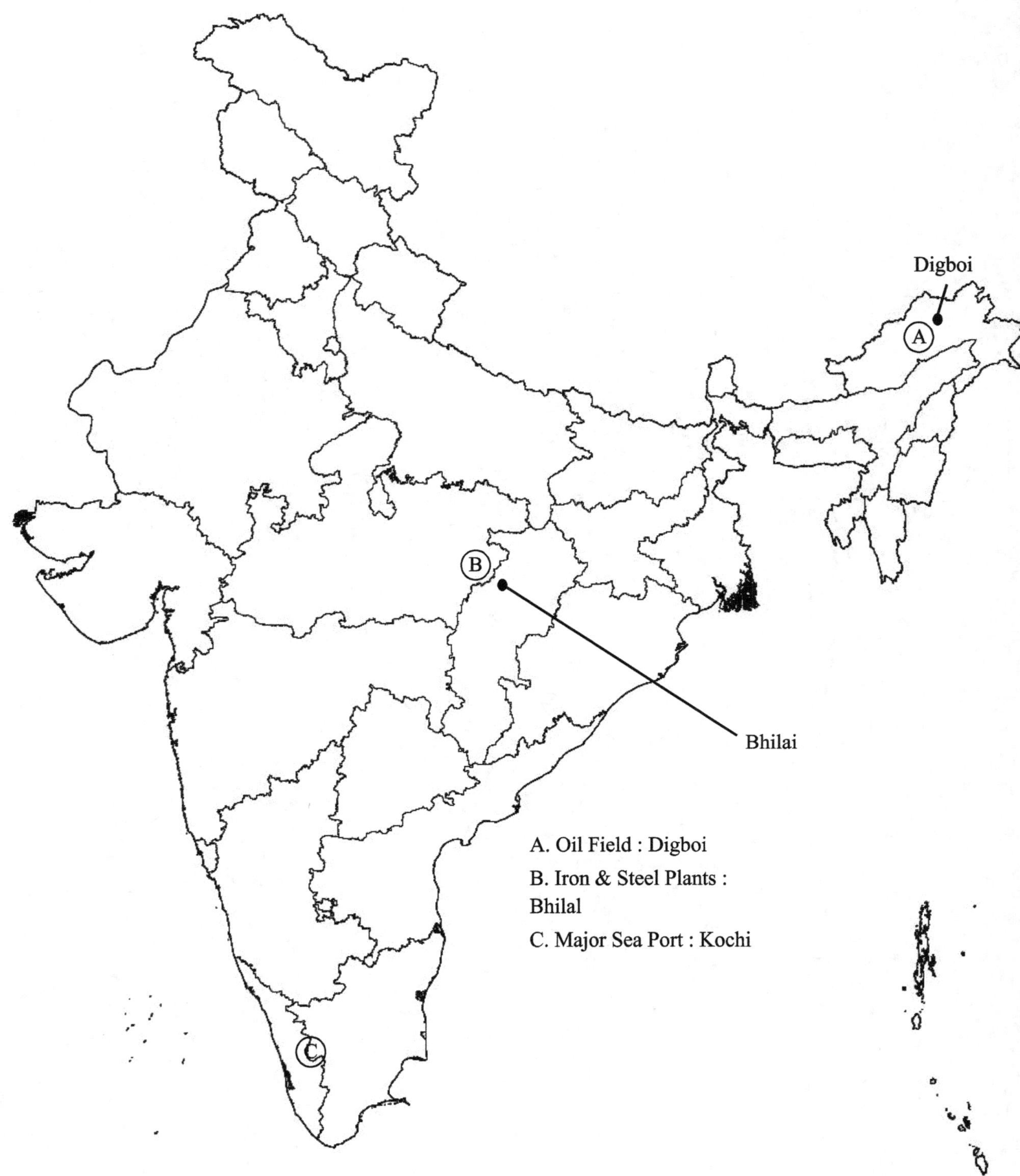

# 2016

# CBSE Board Solved Paper Term-I

## SECTION - A

### (Very Short Answer Questions)

(8 × 1 = 8)

1. (a) Who invented printing press and when? 1

   **OR**

   (b) What is referred to as "Kissa-goi"?**

2. What is the position of India, in the world, in terms of sugarcane production? 1

3. Give one point to differentiate between Civil Rights Movement and Black Power Movement.** 1

4. What is another popular name of Rural local government in India? 1

5. What is meant by Majoritarianism? 1

6. If there are four members in a family and their total income is ₹20,000/- what would be the average income of each person? 1

7. Which sector helps in the development of the primary and secondary sectors? 1

8. Define secondary sectors. 1

## SECTION - B

### (Short Answer Questions)

(13 × 3 = 39)

9. (a) "The multinational companies (MNCs) choose China as an alternative location for investment?" Explain the statement. 3

   **OR**

   (b) Highlight any three benefits of industrialization on the society.

   **OR**

   (c) What led to the expansion of population in Bombay in the mid 19th century? Give any three reasons.**

10. (a) The silk routes are a good example of trade and cultural link between distant parts of the world. Explain with examples. 3

    **OR**

    (b) Why were there clashes between the weavers and the Gomasthas? Explain.

**OR**

(c) Why did people of London call underground railway 'the iron monster'. Give any three reasons.**

11. (a) Give any three reasons for the enhancement of literacy in the 17th and 18th centuries in most parts of Europe. 3

    **OR**

    (b) "Premchand's novels are filled with powerful characters from all levels of society." Justify the statement.**

12. (a) Why did British government curb the freedom of the Indian press after the revolt of 1857? 3

    **OR**

    (b) How were the concerns of Oriyan Society depicted in the Oriyan novels of 19th century? Explain.**

13. Why has the land under forests not increased much from 1960-61? 3

14. Describe the Project Tiger launched by the Indian government.** 3

15. Why is the rooftop rainwater harvesting the most common practice in Shillong inspite of the fact that Cherrapunjee and Mawsynram receiving highest rainfall in the world are situated only at a distance of 55 kms from there? Explain. 3

16. Which features of Panchayati Raj do you like the most and why? Explain. 3

17. Why do social differences emerge in a society? Does every social difference lead to social division? Explain your answer with the help of an example. 3

18. Explain any three forms of power sharing among different organs of government in India. 3

19. Explain common, different and conflicting goals by giving suitable examples. 3

20. Explain the problem of underemployment in the service sector in urban areas with examples. 3

21 What is the basis for determining for developmental goals of different people? Give one example to prove that development for some may cause harm to others. 3

---

*Note: (**) Marked questions are out of syllabus so these are not explained or answered.*

## SECTION - C
### (Long Answer Questions)

$(8 \times 5 = 40)$

22. (a) Describe the factors that led to the Great Depression of 1929.  **5**

**OR**

(b) How did cotton factories become an intimate part of the English landscape in the early 19<sup>th</sup> century? Explain.

**OR**

(c) Explain the changes in the work available to women in London during 19<sup>th</sup> and 20<sup>th</sup> century.**

**OR**

23. (a) Why did the Roman Catholic Church being keeping an Index of Prohibited Books from the mid 16<sup>th</sup> century/ Explain by giving five reasons.  **5**

**OR**

(b) Assess the involvement of women in the growth of novels in 18<sup>th</sup> century and give two examples of it.**

24. "The declining share of agriculture in the Gross Domestic Product (G.D.P.) is a matter of serious concern in India." Support the statement with any five reasons.  **5**

25. What is bio-diversity? Why is bio-diversity important for human lives? Analyse.**  **5**

26. Why has federalism succeeded in India? Which three policies adopted by India have ensured this success?  **5**

27. Mention any five socio-economic changes responsible for breaking down the old notion of caste hierarchy in India  **5**

28. Show two ways in which industrial pollution degrades the environment? Suggest three measures to control environment degradation.  **5**

29. Explain any five features of the Tertiary sector.  **5**

## SECTION - D
### (Map Based Questions)

$(3 \times 1 = 3)$

30. (a) One feature A is shown in the given political outline map of India. Identify this feature with the help of the following information and write its correct name on the line marked on the map:  **3**

(A) A soil type  **1**

(b) On the same political outline map of India, locate and label the following features with appropriate symbols:

(B) Bhakra Nangal Dam  **1**

(C) A State which is the major producer of Cotton.  **1**

---

## Solutions

1. (a) Printing press was invented by Johannes Gutenberg in the year 1930

**OR**

(b) Kissa goi is known as the style of storytelling that was popular during the era of Munshi Premchand. It was also popular in Urdu and became very popular among the nobles of Delhi in the medieval period.

**Note**

*Other contributions of Johannes Gutenberg to printing include the invention of a process for mass-producing movable type; the use of oil-based ink for printing books; adjustable molds; mechanical movable type; and the use of a wooden printing press similar to the agricultural screw presses of the period.*

2. The position of India is second in the world, in terms of sugarcane production.

**Note**

*Brazil is the largest producer of sugarcane in the world. The second-largest producer of sugarcane is India. By 2030, these two nations will produce roughly 21% and 18% of the world's total sugar production, respectively.*

3. (**)

4. Another popular name of Rural local government in India is Panchayati Raj system.

5. The belief that the majority community should be able to rule a country in whatever way they want, by disregarding the wishes of the minority, this is called Majoritarianism.

6. $\text{Average} = \dfrac{\text{Total Income}}{\text{No. of members}}$

$= \dfrac{20,000}{4} = ₹5,000$

Average income of each person will be ₹5,000.

7. Tertiary sector helps in the development of the primary and secondary sector.

8. Also, known as manufacturing sector in which people are engaged in the activities where raw products are changed into other manufacturing products with the help of industrial activities.

9. (a) The multinational companies (MNC's) choose China as an alternative location for investment because:

(i) Since the revolution in 1949, China gradually came in the field of World economy. It attracted the foreign MNC's because of its lowest economic structure.

(ii) Apart from labour, China had the greatest population. They developed a sizeable customer base as well.

(iii) Wages in China were comparatively low. So, it was great attraction for the MNCs.

**OR**

(b) Three benefits of Industrialization on the society are as follows:

(i) The growth of industries leads to an increase in the production of goods and services that are available to people at cheaper rates.

(ii) It reduces dependence on other countries and improves the economy, which results in a higher standard of living.

(iii) It creates new job opportunities, helping to lower unemployment.

**10.** (a) The silk routes are a good examples of trade and cultural link between distant parts of the world, due to the following reasons:

(i) Several silk routes had identified over land and sea, knitting together vast regions of Asia and linking Asia with Europe and Northern Africa.

(ii) Buddhism emerged from India and spread in several directions with the help of silk route.

(iii) Precious metals like gold and silver flowed from Europe to Asia.

(iv) Chinese pottery travelled the same route, as did textile and spices from India.

**OR**

(b) Clashes between the weavers and the Gomasthas can be explained as follows:

(i) Earlier merchants had often lived within the weaving village, and had a close relationship with the weavers, looking after their needs but the new Gomasthas were outsiders with no long term social link with the village, they acted arrogantly, marched into villages with sepoys and peons, and punished weavers for delay in supply.

(ii) The weavers lost the bargaining power for prices and sell to different buyers; the price they received from the company was miserably low.

*Buddhism is one of the world's largest religions and originated 2,500 years ago in India. Buddhists believe that the human life is one of suffering, and that meditation, spiritual and physical labour, and good behaviour are the ways to achieve enlightenment, or nirvana.*

**11.** (a) The reasons for the enhancement of literacy in the 17th and 18th century in most of the parts of Europe were:

(i) Churches of different denominations were set up, and schools in villages began for peasants, artisans etc.

(ii) By the end of the 18th century in some parts of Europe literacy rates were as high as 60 to 80%.

(iii) As literacy and schools spread in European countries, there was a virtual reading mania. Now people wanted to read and printers produced books in ever increasing numbers.

**12.** (a) The British government curbed the freedom of the Indian press after the revolt of 1857 because :

(i) The attitude to freedom of the press changed. Enraged Englishmen demanded a clamp down on the 'native' press.

(ii) As vernacular newspapers became assertively nationalist, the colonial government began debating measures for stringent control.

(iii) The Indian press proved to be a crucial weapon in awakening nationalist feelings among the masses.

*The first printing press in India was established at the Jesuit St. Paul's College in Old Goa in 1556.*

**13.** (i) The improper use of forest land has degraded the available land area and has made conservation of forests difficult. Human activities such as deforestation, mining and quarrying have contributed to the slow growth rate of forests. Thus, land under forest has increased by only about 4% since 1960-61.

(ii) Technological development has led to industrialization which has increased the use of natural resources.

(iii) Technological development has converted the subsistence agriculture to commercial agriculture and this has led to the over utilization of soil.

(iv) Economic development has led to increasing urbanization and modernization which demands more resources.

*India's total forest and tree cover was 80.9 million hectares, which accounted for 24.62% of the geographical area of the country.*

**14.** (**)

**15.** The roof top rainwater harvesting is the most common practice in Shillong inspite of the fact that Cherrapunjee and Mawsynram receiving the highest rainfall in the world are situated only at a distance of 55 kms from there. Because Shillong faces acute shortage of water. Nearly every household in the city has a rooftop rainwater harvesting structure. Nearly 15-25% of the total water requirement of the household comes from rooftop water harvesting.

*Mawsynram receives the highest rainfall in India. It receives over 10,000 millimetres, or 390 inches, of rain in an average year, and the vast majority of the rain it gets falls during the monsoon months.*

**16.** The features I like the most are:

(i) About 1/3 seats are reserved for women in the rural local bodies.

(ii) Reservation of seats for SC and ST at all three tiers in accordance with their population percentage.

(iii) A uniform five-year term and elections to constitute new bodies must be completed before the expiration of the term.

**17.** Social differences emerge in a society when people belonging to different social groups share differences and similarities cutting across the boundaries of their groups.

No, every social difference does not lead to social division. Social differences may divide similar people but can also unite very different people such as Carlos and Smith who came together to fight social evils practiced in the society.

**18.** Forms of power sharing are:

(i) Horizontal form of power sharing e.g., Legislative, Executive and Judiciary.

(ii) Vertical form of power sharing e.g., Union government and State government.

(iii) Power sharing between political parties and pressure groups and movements e.g. colonial government.

**19.** (i) **Common goals:** There are some requirements which are common to all such as income, freedom, equality, security, respect etc.

(ii) **Different goals:** Development and progress does not means the same for every individual. Each individual has its own idea of development.

For example: Schools for students, irrigation for farmers and employment for unemployed youth.

(iii) **Conflicting goals:** It might be possible that development for some may become destructive for others.

For Example: Industrialists may want dams for electricity but it may displace the natives of that region due to land submergence.

**20.** (i) There are thousands of casual workers in the service sector who search for daily employment. For example:

petty workers, painters, street vendors, rickshaw pullers, etc.

(ii) Many workers do not find work every day. While many, like street vendors, spend the whole day working but earn very little.

(iii) Workers do not have better work opportunities.

**21.** (i) Goals of each person or group are determined according to their aspirations. Everyone seeks to achieve the goal that are most important to them and which can fulfill their desires and aspirations.

(ii) The goals of landless labourers and rich farmers, or the goal of a man or a woman are bound to be different.

(iii) The social, cultural, and economic position of the people varies, which results in different developmental goals.

(iv) The goals of development of a person or group may be disastrous for others: For example, industrialists may want more dams to generate electricity, but the same dam may submerge the land, disrupting the life of people whose habitat has been submerged.

**22.** (a) Factors that led to the Great Depression of 1929 were:

(i) Over production in crops and a fall in the prices of the crops.

(ii) As prices fall heavily and agricultural income declined, farmers tried to expand production and bring a larger volume of production to the market but it pushed down the prices.

(iii) In the mid of 1920's many countries financed their investments through loans from the US. Because it was extremely easy to raise loans in the US.

(iv) The countries that depended crucially on US for loans faced an acute crisis in 1928.

(v) The withdrawal of US loans affected the rest of the world in different ways in Europe, it led to the failure of small major banks and the collapse of currencies and in Latin America, it identified the slump in agricultural and raw material prices.

(vii) The US double its import duties in order to protect its economy during depression but dealt another severe blow to the world trade.

(b) Cotton factories become an intimate part of the English landscape in the early 19th century due to the following reasons:

(i) Inventions in the 18th century increased the efficiency of carding, twisting, spinning, etc.

(ii) Centralised and integrated process.

(iii) Creation of cotton mill by Richard Arkwright.

(iv) Proper supervision and control.

(v) New mills and new technologies.

*India is the largest producer of cotton in the world, accounting for about 22% of the world's cotton production. India has the largest area under cotton cultivation, which is about 37% of the world's area under cotton cultivation*

**23.** (a)

(i) They feared that if there was no control over the printed material, then rebellion and irrational thoughts might spread.

(ii) Religious authorities felt that free print material could make the people rebel against their cherished religions.

(iii) Many monarchs felt that if no control was applied, then printed books could lead to rebellions against the state authorities.

(iv) Many writers and artists began to fear that if no control was extended on the printed materials, the authorities of the valuable publications would be destroyed.

(b) (**)

**24.** The declining share of agriculture in the gross domestic product (G.D.P.) is a matter of serious concern in India. Following are the five reasons:

(i) Government is reducing investment in agricultural sectors, especially in the irrigation sector.

(ii) Subsidy on fertilizers has decreased, leading to a rise in cost of production.

(iii) Farmers are facing challenge from international competition.

(iv) Reduction of import duties on agricultural products.

(v) Farmers are withdrawing their investments from agriculture causing a downfall in the employment in agricultural and results into disguised unemployment.

**25.** (**)

**26.** Federalism is the system of government in which power is shared among the different levels of government not withing the single constitutional body.

In India, we have governments at the state level and at the centre. Panchayati Raj is the third tier of government.

The policies that ensures success are:

(i) **Linguistic states:** States are divided on the basis of the language spoken in the state or region.

Eg. Gujarati is the language of Gujarat, Assamese is the language of Assam.

(ii) **Language policy:** All languages have equal status. There is not state or national language.

(iii) **Centre state relations:** Powers are distributed among the states and centre.

**27.** Socio-economic changes are responsible for breaking down the old notion of caste hierarchy in India are:

(i) Efforts of social reformers like Phule, Mahatma Gandhi, Dr. B.R. Ambedkar have worked against the evil of caste system in India.

(ii) Occupational mobility and making of the position as landlords has been also a reason for this socio-economic change in India.

(iii) Impact of Western culture, introduction of new education system has also contributed in decreasing the stringency of casteism.

(iv) Increase of literacy rate has declined the effects of discrimination and caste prejudices.

(v) Availability of opportunities and economic development has also changed the perspective of Indian citizens.

**28.** Industrial pollution degrades environment in the following ways:

(ii) Air is polluted by gases like-carbon dioxide, carbon monoxide etc., which are harmful for humans.

Effluents from industries pollute rivers. Paper pulp, textile, chemicals industries pollute land and soil due to their toxic materials.

Steps to control industrial pollution can be explained as follows:

(i) Smoke can be reduced by using oil or gas instead of coal in factories.

(ii) Treating effluents before releasing them in rivers and ponds.

(iii) Minimizing use of water for processing by reusing and recycling.

**29.** Tertiary sectors also known as service sectors. The main features of tertiary sectors are:

(i) It involves activities that help in the development of the primary and secondary sector.

(ii) It does not produce any kind of goods but they aid and support in the production process.

(iii) It Tertiary sector helps to transport goods, produced in primary or secondary sector or arrange for wholesale and retail sale.

(iv) Helps in providing banking service.

(v) These activities generate service other than goods, it is called service sector. It also includes teachers, doctors and other professionals who are not connected with production of goods.

30.

# All India 2015

# CBSE Board Solved Paper Term-II

## SECTION - A

### (Very Short Answer Questions)

(8 × 1 = 8)

1. What was the main aim of the French revolutionaries? **1**

   **OR**

   What is the meaning of concentration camps?***

2. How do minerals occur in sedimentary rocks? **1**

3. What was the main aim of the popular movement of April 2006, in Nepal? ** **1**

4. How can you say that democracies are based on political equality?

5. Why do political parties involve partisan-ship?

6. What is meant by Double Coincidence of wants? **1**

7. Suppose your parents want to purchase Gold jewellery along with you; then which logo will you look for on the jewellery?** **1**

8. How does money act as a medium of exchange? **1**

## SECTION - B

### (Short Answer Questions)

(12 × 3 = 36)

9. How did nationalism develop through culture in Europe? Explain. **3**

   **OR**

   How did Paul Bernard argue in favour of economic development of Vietnam Explain.**

10. Describe the main features of 'Poona Pact'. **3**

11. How did 'Salt March' become an effective tool of resistance against colonialism? Explain? **3**

12. Explain the importance of railways as the principal mode of transportation for freight and passengers in India. **3**

13. Why has the 'Chhota Nagpur Plateau Region' the maximum concentration of iron and steel industries? Analyse the reasons.** **3**

14. How can solar energy solve the energy problem to some extent in India? Give your opinion. **3**

15. "Dynastic succession is one of the most serious challenges before -the political parties." Analyse the statement:** **3**

16. How is democracy accountable and responsive to the need and expectations of the citizens? Analyse. **3**

17. "A challenge is an opportunity for progress." Support the statement with your arguments**. **3**

18. Why is modern currency accepted as a medium of exchange without any use of its own? Find out the reason. **3**

19. "Foreign trade integrates the markets in different countries." Support the statement with arguments. **3**

20. Explain with as example how you can use the right to seek redressal.** **3**

## SECTION - C

### (Long Answer Questions)

(7 × 5 = 35)

21. Describe any five steps taken by the French Revolutionaries to create a sense of collective identity among the French people. **5**

    **OR**

    Describe any five steps taken by the French for the development of the' 'Mekong Delta Region'.**

22. What is the manufacturing sector? Why is it considered the backbone of development? Interpret the reason. **5**

23. Which is the most abundantly available fossil fuel in India? Assess the importance of its different forms. **5**

24. What is meant by a political party? Describe the three components of a political party. **5**

25. Suggest are five effective measures to reform political parties. **5**

26. How do banks play an important role in the economy of India? Explain. **5**

27. "Globalization and greater competition among producers has been advantageous to consumers. Support the statement with examples. **5**

*Note: (**) Marked questions are out of syllabus so these are not explained or answered.*

# SECTION - D
## (Map Based Questions)

(3 × 2 = 6)

28. Three features A, B and C are marked on the given political outline map of India. Identify these features with the help of the following information and write their correct name on the lines marked in the map:                  3

A.  The place where the Indian National Congress Session was held in 1927.

B.  The place associated with the Peasant's Satyagraha.

C.  The place relate to calling off the Non-Cooperation Movement.

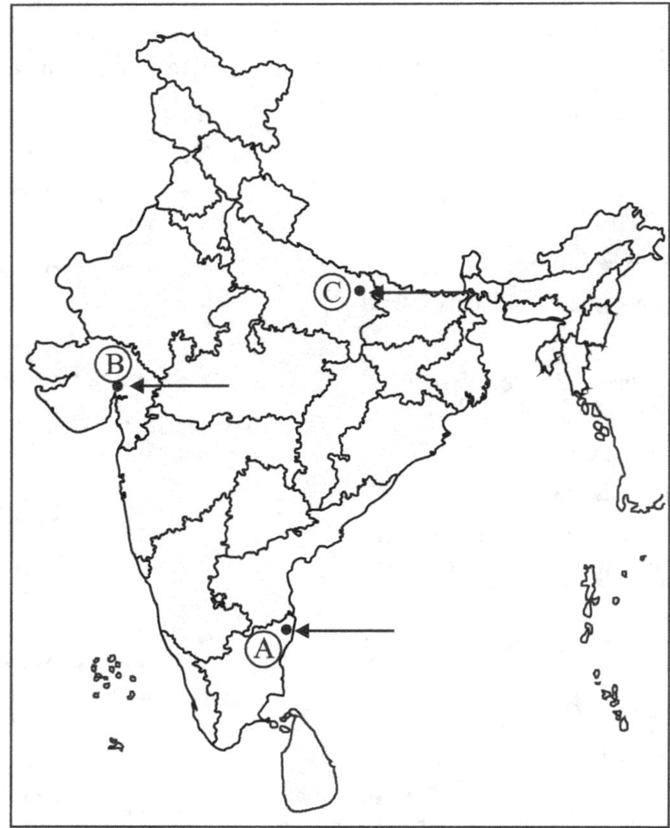

29. Two features A and B are marked on the given political outline map of India. Identify these features with the help of the following information and write their correct names of the lines marked in the map:                  3

A.  Iron-ore mine

B.  Terminal Station of East-West Corridor**.

On the same political outline map of India, locate and label the following:

Vishakhapatnam-Software Technology Park.**

## Solutions

**1.** The aim of French revolutionaries is abolition of monarchy, foundation of a secular and democratic republic, liberation of the people of Europe from dictatorship, drafting of a formal constitution etc.

*Note*

*Monarchy is a political system in which supreme authority is vested in the monarch, an individual ruler who functions as the head of state. Dictatorship is a form of government in which one person or a small group possesses absolute power without effective constitutional limitations.*

**2.** Minerals are formed in the sedimentary rocks due to deposition, accumulation and concentration in horizontal strata over long periods under great heat and pressure or coal.

**3.** (**)

**4.** Democracies are based on political equality as individuals have equal weight in electing representatives.

**5.** Parties are a part of the society and thus they involve partisanship.

**6.** Double Coincidence of wants refers to situation when both the parties agrees to sell and buy each other's commodities.

**7.** (**)

**8.** Money acts as a medium of exchange because it acts as an efficient link between the exchange of commodities.

**9.** Nationalism developed through culture in Europe as:

(i) The Culture played an important role. The idea of the nation, art and poetry, stories and music helped to express and shape nationalist felling.

(ii) Romanticism was a cultural movement which sought to develop a particular form of nationalist sentiment.

(iii) Romantic artists and poets generally criticized the glorification of reason and science and focused instead on emotions, intuition and mystical feeling Johann Gottfried Herder a, german philosopher claimed that true German culture was to be discovered among the common people through folk songs, folk poetry and folk dances that the true spirit of the nation was popularised.

**10.** The Poona Pact was the agreement between Mahatma Gandhi and Dr. B.R. Ambedkar signed on 24 September, 1932. The major points in this pact were as follows:

(i) Certain percentage of the seats allotted to the general Non-Muslim electorate would be reserved for the depressed classes.

(ii) 148 seats were to be allotted to the depressed classes in the provincial legislatures. This was more than double from the 71 seats as promised in the Communal Award.

(iii) Adequate representation would be given to the depressed classes in the civil services.

(iv) A certain sum of money from the educational grant would be allotted for the education of the Depressed Classes in all provinces.

*Note*

*The Communal Award was created by British Prime Minister Ramsay MacDonald on August 16, 1932. Also known as the MacDonald Award, it extended the separate electorate to depressed classes (now known as the Scheduled Caste) and other minorities.*

**11.** Mahatma Gandhi found salt a powerful symbol that could unite the nation. Salt was the most essential item of food and was consumed by rich and poor alike. On 6th April Gandhiji reached Dandi, violated law, and made salt. This march developed the feeling of nationalism, people in different parts of the country broke the salt law and manufactured salt and demonstrated in front of government salt factories.

**12.** The railways is the lifeline of the country because of the reasons mentioned below.

(i) Railway are useful in conducting business, sightseeing, pilgrimage along with transportation of goods over longer distances.

(ii) The Indian Railway have a Vast network of 7,031 stations, 7,817 locomotives, 5,321 passenger service vehicles, 4,904 other coach vehicles and 2,28,170 wagons as on 31st March, 2004.

(iii) It is the largest public undertaking in the country. Thus, the railway is playing an important role in our economy.

*Note*

*Lord Dalhousie is regarded as the father of Indian railways. The first railway on the Indian subcontinent ran over a stretch of 21 miles from Bombay to Thane.*

**13.** (**)

**14.** Following are the reasons why solar energy solves the energy problem:

(i) It will reduce the dependence of rural households on firewood.

(ii) Use of Solar Energy will reduce the pressure on conventional sources of energy.

(iii) Since the sun shines across the globe, it makes every country a potential energy producer, thus allowing for greater energy independence and security.

(iv) As India has been blessed with abundance of sunlight, water, wind and biomass, we must use these to overcome present day energy crisis.

 **Note**

*To bring about a green revolution in the country, the government has set an ambitious target of having 500 GW of installed renewable energy by 2030, which includes the installation of 280 GW of solar power and 140 GW of wind power.*

**15.** (**)

**16.** Democracy is people's own government.

(i) In a democracy, people have the right to choose their representatives and they control over them.

(ii) Government fulfill the needs and expectations of the people.

(iii) The democratic government develops mechanisms of citizens to held the government accountable.

**17.** (**)

**18.** The modern currency i.e. rupee, does not have any value of it's own because it is not as precious as gold and silver, it is made up of paper. However it is used for transaction in exchange for some good and services. But it is still considered as a medium of exchange, as it is authorized by the Government of India.

**19.** (i) Foreign trade provides opportunities for both producers and buyers to reach beyond the domestic market of their own countries good travel from one country to another.

(ii) For the buyers, import of goods produced in another country provides opportunity to extent their choice of goods beyond what is domestically produced.

(iii) Competition among producers of various countries prevail as they can sell their products not only in the domestic market but also compete in the market, of other countries.

(iv) Foreign trade has bee the main channel connecting countries. For example. Silk route connects Indian and South Asia to the markets in both the East and West.

**20.** (**)

**21.** The French revolutionaries, created a sense of collective identity amongst the French people through the following ways:

(i) A central administrative system made uniform laws for the entire nation.

(ii) New hymns, oaths and martyrs were commemorated in the name of the nation.

(iii) They gave financial assistance and refused to buy or sell imported goods.

(iv) They formed the Indian Industrial and Commercial Congress in 1920 and the Federation of Indian Chamber of Commerce and Industries, FICCI in 1927 to organism business intereset.

(v) Ideas of la patrie (the fatherland) and le citoyen (the citizen) emphasising the notion of a united community enjoying equal rights under a constitution.

**22.** The industries which are involved in the production of good in large quantities after processing raw materials to more valueable products are called manufacturing industries. For example-Iron and Steel industries.

Manufacturing sector is considered the backbone of development in general and economic development because:

(i) Manufacturing industries help in modernising agriculture and reduces the heavy dependence of people on agricultural income by providing them jobs in secondary and tertiary sectors.

(ii) Export of manufactured goods expands trade and commerce, and brings in much needed foreign exchange.

(iii) Industrial development is necessary for eradication of unemployment and poverty from our country. It was also aimed at bringing down regional disparities by establishing in tribal and backward areas.

(iv) Countries get higher values for their products when they transform their raw materials into a wide variety of furnished good.

**Note**

*The Indian manufacturing sector currently contributes 16–17% to GDP and gives employment to around 12% (2014) of the country's workforce. It is extremely low when compared to East Asian nations, where it ranges from 25% to 35%.*

**23.** Coal is the most abundantly available fossil fuel in India. The quality depend on the degrees of compression and the depth and time of burial.

(i) Decaying plants in swamps produces Peat. It has a low carbon and high moisture contents and low heating capacity.

(ii) Lignite is a low grade brown coal, which is soft with high moisture content. The principal lignite reserves are in Neyveli in Tamil Nadu and are used for generation electricity.

(iii) Coal that has been buried deep and subjected to increased temperatures in Bituminous coal. It is the most popular coal grade bituminous coal which has a special value for smelting iron in blast furnaces.

(iv) Anthracite is the highest quality hard coal which carries 80-90% carbon content.

**24.** A political party is a group of people who come together to contest election and hold power in the government. They agree on some policies and programmes for the society with a view to promote the collective good.

A political party has three components: the leaders, the active members and the followers.

(i) **The leaders :** Every Political party has come prominent leaders who formulate policies and programmes for the party and choose candidates for contesting elections.

(ii) **The active members:** They are involved in different committees of the party and participate directly in their activity. They are the ones, who climb a ladder from being the follower and become the assistant of the leaders to gain knowledge about the politics.

(iii) **The followers :** They believe in the party's ideology and support the party by casting their votes in favour of the party at the time of election. They are simply the follower of the leaders and work under the able guidance of the active members.

**25.** Political parties can be reformed in the following ways:

(i) According to anti-defection law of Constitution, any MLA or MP changing political party will loose their seat in the Legislature. It help in bringing defection down and elected MP and MLA have to abide by party's rule regulations.

(ii) Election Commission of India makes it necessary for political parties to hold their organization elections and file their income tax returns.

(iii) Supreme Court passed an order that made mandatory for every candidate who contests election to file Affidavit disclosing details of his property and criminal cases pending against him.

(iv) A law should be made to regulate the internal affairs of political parties. It should be made compulsory for political parties to maintain a register of it's members, to follow it's own constitution, to have an independent authority, to act as a judge in case of party disputes, to hold open elections to the highest posts.

**Note**

*The Lok Sabha comprises a total of 545 seats for Members of Parliament (MPs). The Election Commission will hold elections to fill 543 of these seats. The President nominates two members to the Lok Sabha from the Anglo-Indian Community seats.*

**26.** (i) Banks provides a safe foundation for individuals and businesses to invest or deposit their money, which allows the bank to use the money in its possession for loans.

(ii) The ability for the public to receive these loans enables them to make purchases, which drives the economy at higher level.

(iii) The bank take the deposits, and turn them into assets. This is accomplished by the banks investing the money that is deposited in a way that gains them higher returns that what is being paid to the depositor's account when they receive interest.

(iv) Banks mediate between people having surplus cash and those in need of it.

(v) They give interest to the depositors, and they charge interest on those taking loans from the banks.

**27.** Globalization and greater competition among producers-both local and foreign, has been of advantage to consumers in the following ways

(i) Consumer can enjoy improved quality at lower prices for several products. This has led to higher standard of living.

(ii) Companies have invested in new technologies to raise their production quality to compete with the MNCs thus, ensuring that consumers get better quality products get satisfied.

(iii) Indian companies has collaborated with MNCs to produce more functional and advanced products, thus, benefitting the consumers.

(iv) There is great choice available to the consumers in goods.

(v) The quality of goods has been improved and due to the competition the prices of various products has decreased.

**28.**

Chauri Chaura
C
B
Kheda or
Ahmedabad
A
Madras
(Chennai)

**29.**

B
A
Chhattisgarh,
Durg
Porbandar
30.2 Vishakhapatnam
(Software Technology Park)

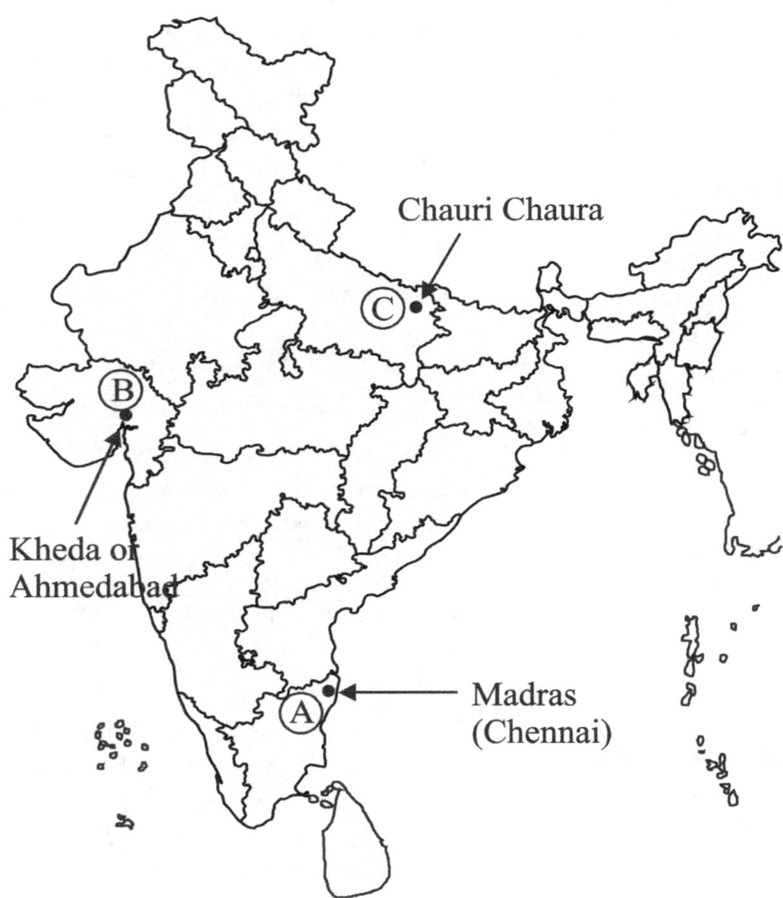

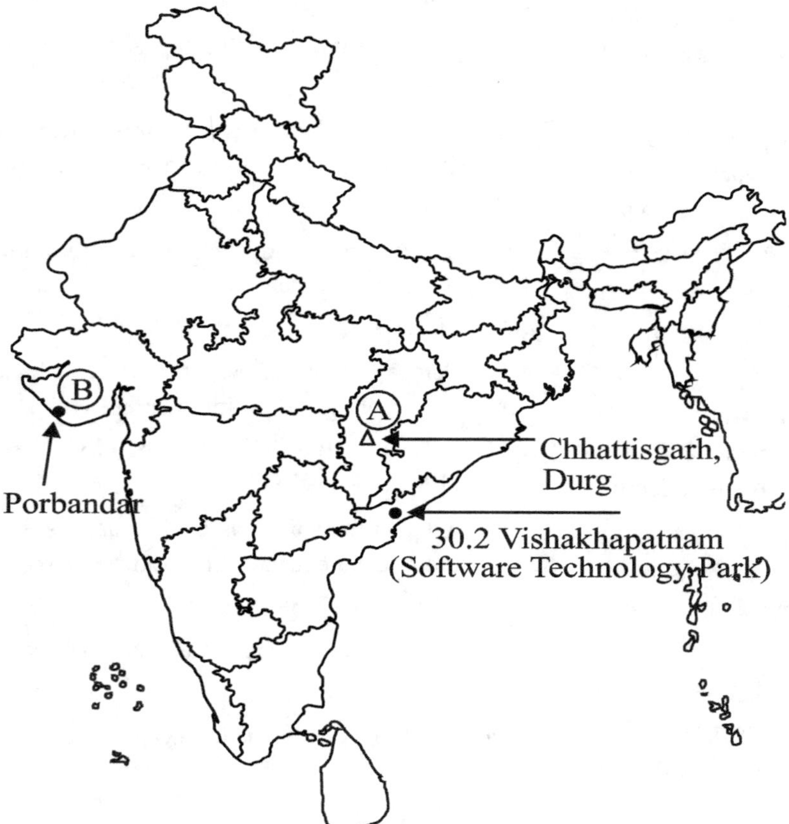

# CBSE Board Solved Paper Term-I

## SECTION - A

### (Very Short Answer Questions)

$(8 \times 1 = 8)$

1. Which brothers of Germany contributed in compiling the text for children?     **1**

   **OR**

   By whom was the novel 'Pride and Prejudice' written?**

2. Which factor is mainly responsible for maximum land degradation in India?     **1**

3. Name the two athletes who raised the issue of Civil Rights in the Mexico Olympics (1968).**     **1**

4. What other factors besides politics keep the federations united?     **1**

5. What is meant by the system of 'checks and balances'?     **1**

6. Give any two examples of non-renewable resources.     **1**

7. Suggest anyone way to create employment opportunity in the rural areas.     **1**

8. In which sector does government own most of the assets and provides the basic services?     **1**

## SECTION - B

### (Short Answer Questions)

$(12 \times 3 = 36)$

9. What attracted the Europeans to Africa? Give any three reasons.     **3**

   **OR**

   Why was getting jobs in the British mills always difficult for the workers in the 19th century? Give reasons.

   **OR**

   Examine the living conditions of different sections of society in Bombay prior to reclamation.**

10. Why did the developing countries organize the G-77? Give three reasons.     **3**

    **OR**

    How was foreign trade from India conducted before the age of machine industries? Explain.

**OR**

Which three features of the big modern city of Calcutta fascinated the Gods as described in the novel written by Durgacharan Roy? Explain.**

11. What was Protestant Reformation?     **3**

    **OR**

    Who translated the novel "Henrietta Temple" in Malayalam? Why did the translator give up the idea of translating English novels?**

12. Explain how print helped the poor people to express their ideas on various issues.     **3**

    **OR**

    Explain how novel reading became a popular source of pleasure in India.**

13. What is the importance of pulses in our economy? Why are pulses grown as a rotation crop?     **3**

14. Explain any three causes of water scarcity.     **3**

15. Explain how communities have conserved and protected forest and wildlife in India.     **3**

16. How does religion influence the political set up in our country?     **3**

17. Explain the three major provisions of the Constitutional Amendment of 1992 which really strengthened the third tier of democracy in India?     **3**

18. " In an democracy, political expression of social division in very normal and can be healthy". Justify this statement with suitable arguments.**     **3**

19. Why do people look at a mix of goals for development? Explain.     **3**

20. With the example of sugarcane, explain the interdependence of all the three sectors of the economy.     **3**

## SECTION - C

### (Long Answer Questions)

$(9 \times 5 = 45)$

21. What is the main criterion used by the World Bank in classifying different countries as rich and poor countries? What are the limitations of this criterion?     **5**

*Note: (**) Marked questions are out of syllabus so these are not explained or answered.*

**22.** Explain the effects of the Great Depression of 1929 on the Indian economy.                                                      **5**

**OR**

How did cotton factories become an intimate part of the English landscape in the early century? Explain.

**OR**

Describe the role of industrialisation in shaping of the modern cities in England.**

**23.** 'The shift from hand printing to mechanical printing led to the print revolution in Europe. Explain the statement with examples.                                                    **5**

**OR**

How did the novels fulfil the task of nation building during the British period? Explain.**

**24.** What is the need for conservation of water resources? Suggest three measure to conserve water resources.      **5**

**25.** What is meant by 'resources'? Mention the four basis to classify the resources.                                          **5**

**26.** How far is it correct to say that it is not politics that gets caste ridden but it is the caste that gets politicised? Explain.

**27.** Highlight the reasons for the increase in the feeling of alienation among the Sri Lankan Tamils after independence.

**28.** What does HDI stand for? Explain the main criteria of measuring HDI according to UNDP Report of 1990.      **5**

**29.** State any five features each of public sector and private sector.**

## SECTION - D

### (Map Based Questions)

(3 × 1 = 3)

**30.** (a) One feature A is shown in the given political outline map of India. Identify this feature with the help of following information and write its correct name on the line marked on the map:

(A) A soil type.                                                                                 **1**

(b) On the same political outline map of India, locate and label the following features with appropriate symbols:

(B) Corbett National Park**                                                         **1**

(C) Tungabhadra Dam                                                               **1**

## Solutions

**1.** Grimm brothers of Germany contributed in compiling the text for children in the form of folk tales.

**OR**

(**)

**2.** Overgrazing is one of the main reason for land degradation. States, where overgrazing has resulted in land degradation are, Gujarat, Rajasthan, Madhya Pradesh and Maharashtra.

*Note*

*Other reasons for land degradation are deforestation, excessive use of fertilisers and pesticides, overgrazing, salination, waterlogging, desertification, soil erosion, wasteland, etc.*

**3.** (**)

**4.** Culture, cooperation, mutual respect, history and ideology are some other factors which keep the federations united.

**5.** The distribution of power among the legislature, executive and judiciary in the government is called a system of 'checks and balances' which is mainly used to restrict their powers.

**6.** Coal and minerals are the two examples of non-renewable resources.

**7.** Opening of cold storage in rural areas creates employment opportunity as they can store their products in it.

*Note*

*Agriculture is the main occupation in rural areas. The percentage of the rural population in India is 65.13%, which is why agriculture is so important to the country's economy.*

**8.** In service sector or public sector or tertiary sector, the government own most of the assets and provides the basic services.

**9.** Europeans were attracted towards Africa due to following reasons:

(i) Poor and backward military resistance power of Africa, made it easy for Europeans to conquer.

(ii) Crop production and plantation prospects attracted them.

(iii) They were attracted towards Africa due to it's vast mineral and land resources.

**OR**

It was very difficult to get jobs in the British mills. In the 19th century even after the number of mills had multiplied because:

(i) There were always less jobs than the demand.

(ii) In the 19th century, agricultural sector was suffering loss. So, the unemployed villages started to move into the cities in search of employment. Which created disguised employment.

(iii) Industrialists provide the right to recruit workers to the jobbers. Jobbers were the trusted workers or employees for them. Jobbers recruited their known people to work in industries. So, it was very difficult for the new worker to get job opportunities in British mills.

**OR**

(**)

**10.** The G-77 is the largest intergovernmental organization of developing countries in the United Nations. India is a member of this group. The developing countries of the world organise the G-77 because:

(i) Developing countries are getting nothing from the growth and development of western economy along with the World bank and International Monetary Fund (IMF). So, they need to organize them as G-77 group.

(ii) Another organization New International Economic Order (NIEO) provides developing countries a right to control their own resources, helps in the development and the fair pricing of their raw materials and develops market to access the manufacturing goods.

(iii) G-77 wanted a change in the international financial system which was proposed by Bretton Woods conference. There was no work done for the eradication of poverty and there was no development in their colonies.

OR

Before the age of machine industries, the foreign trade from India was conducted as follows:

(i) Camels were used to transport bales of silk and cotton through the roads, the mountain passes and the deserts.

(ii) India was dominant over the international market in textile products like silk and cotton goods. They were the best in the world. India had the trade relations with Persia, Armenia, Afghanistan and Central Asia.

(iii) India was famous for trade by sea ways Surat was very famous port city for sea trade with the different regions like the Gulf and Europe. Another trade centres were Coromandel coast and Hoogly river in Bengal to the South east Asian countries.

*The G-77 (Group of 77) was founded on June 15, 1964, by 77 developing nations signatories to the "Joint Declaration of the Seventy-Seven Developing Countries" issued at the end of the first session of the United Nations Conference on Trade and Development (UNCTAD) in Geneva.*

**OR**

(**)

**11.** What was Protestant Reformation?      **[3]**

**OR**

Who translated the novel "Henrietta Temple" in Malayalam? Why did the translator give up the idea of translating English novels?**

(i) In the 16th Century the Catholic church was dominated by the Rome. There exists many deformities that came in the path of church which needed to improve.

(ii) For improving Catholic church, the movements took place in the 16th century which was called Protestant Reformation.

(iii) Martin Luther was a very popular social reformer of 16th century, he wrote a well famous book 'Ninety five theses'. This book totally criticised many malpractices and rituals of the church.

(iv) After the movement several traditions against catholic church were developed.

**12.** (i) Public libraries were set up for the poor people. In the late 19th century, issue of casteism began to be written in presses.

(ii) Jyotiba Phule wrote 'Gulamgiri' which exposed the ill-treatment of the lower castes.

(iii) Dr. B. R. Ambedkar and Ramaswamy Naicker wrote about the untouchability, the evils of society.

(iv) People could buy cheap books where they could read the thoughts of philosophers and writers. They could also write their own books in their languages to express their feelings and emotions.

**OR**

(**)

**13.** (i) Protein is the main source of energy and pulses are the main source of protein. Pulses are the leguminous crops, they are helpful to restore the fertility of the soil.

(ii) Leguminous crops have the feature of nitrogen fixation naturally it gets nitrogen from the atmosphere directly. So, it is helpful in maintaining the quality of the soil.

(iii) Pulses need less water and can survive in dry conditions. Since India is the largest producer of the pulses in the world so, it helps in the development of economy of the country.

(iv) In the Rabi season Arhar, Urad and Moong and in the Kharif season Masur, Peas and Grains are grown.

(v) According to UN-Water 2.3 billion people live in water-stressed countries.

*India is the largest producer of pulses in the world. The top 10 pulse-producing states in India are Rajasthan, Madhya Pradesh, Maharashtra, Uttar Pradesh, Karnataka, Andhra Pradesh, Gujarat, Jharkhand, Tamil Nadu, and Telangana.*

**14.** The causes of water scarcity are:

(i) Since, India is the most populated country in the world and for more population, it need more water to produce crops or other domestic use.

(ii) Excessive use of water in the industries.

(iii) Production of hydro electricity.

(iv) Over exploitation of water in urban areas.

(v) According to UN-Water 2.3 billion people live in water-stressed countries.

Global warming is one of the major reasons behind water scarcity. It is a condition where average air temperatures become warmer and water from rivers and lakes evaporates faster, which may lead to the drying up of water bodies.

*India has 18 percent of the world's population, but only 4 percent of its water resources, making it among the most water-stressed countries in the world.*

**15.** Role of communities in the conservation of forest and wildlife can be explained as follows:

(i) The Chipko movement was started to stop the felling of trees for commercial purposes. The movement was non-violent, and the villagers of the Himalayas hugged trees to stop them from being felled.

(ii) In Alwar, Rajasthan, the people of five villages have declared 1200 hectare of forest as the "Bhairodev Dakav Sonchuri". They set their own rules and regulations which do not allow hunting etc.

(iii) In 'Sariska Tiger Reserve Rajasthan, people of nearby villages have fought against mining activities and protecting the natural habitat of wildlife.

**16.** (i) Mahatma Gandhi said, "Religion can never be separated from politics" in India. India is a vast country having lots of differences. People are divided on the basis of religion too. Religion influences the political setup in our country.

(ii) Religion based politics is not always dangerous as they look like. The values of religions can play a vital role in politics.

(iii) India is democratic country having the followers of each religions who have equal rights and prevents discrimination and oppression for celebrating practice of religion.

**17.** 73rd Amendment of 1992 added part IX to the constitution of Indian entitled as "panchayats." The major provisions of this amendment are:

(i) The tennure of Panchayati Raj institution fixed at five years and creation of three tier Panchayati Raj structure at zila, block and village level.

(ii) To review the financial position of the Panchayati Raj institution, each state to setup a State Finance Commission for five years.

(iii) Creation of State Election Commission of conduct elections to Panchayati Raj institutions.

(iv) One-third of the total number of seats to be reserved for women.

**18.** (**)

**19.** People of all groups look at a mixed goals for development. There are so many goals to which all the people look at for development and these are:

(i) Students need better education and job opportunities.

(ii) Women need safe and secure society and surroundings at home, job place etc.

(iii) Pollution is the most severe problem of today's environment, so people seek a pollution free environment.

(iv) We are living in a democracy, so we need things like equal treatment, freedom right, security and respect etc.

**20.** Economy is divided into three sectors.

(i) Primary sector-Directly dependent on nature.

(ii) Secondary sector- Conversion of natural resources into products.

(iii) Tertiary sector-Service sector.

Sugarcane is a natural product which we grow naturally, that makes it the part of primary sector. "When it is converted into sugar or jaggery, it needs machines to perform task, like sugar mills that ultimately makes it a part of secondary sector and use of transport, banking service or other service sector to export sugar to the markets and sugarcane to the factories becomes a part of tertiary sector. This shows that most of the time every three sectors work together to perform various task.

**21.** The World Bank was created in 1944 and is dedicated to providing financing, advice, and research to developing nations to aid their economic advancement. World Bank classifies the whole globe as a rich or poor country.

(i) World bank works on the basis of average income or per capita income of the particular country to be declared as poor or rich.

(ii) Any country having more than or equal to 45,3000 per annum in the year 2004 is classified as a rich country and less than or equal to 3700 per annum is called a low-income country or a poor country.

Limitations are as follows:

(i) It is based on income criterian but more income can not always ensure a good quality of life. Freedom, equality and equal opportunities are necessary for the same.

(ii) They use per capita income to classify but it hides disparities like two country may have equitable distribution. In other country, it may be possible that most of citizens are poor while very few of them are extremely rich.

*It was created in 1944 as the International Bank for Reconstruction and Development (IBRD) along with the IMF. The IBRD later became the World Bank. It has 189 member countries. Its aim is to reduce poverty and build shared prosperity in developing countries.*

**22.** The Great Depression of 1929 was a world wide economic depression that lasted, for 10 years.

It was triple of the usual amount garnered over the next four days. The stock prices fell 23 percent due to the effects of the Great depression. The effects can be explained as:

(i) The Great Depression of 1929 devasted also the US economy. Since half of the banks failed.

(ii) As international prices crashed, prices in India also jumped quickly.

(iii) Between 1928 and 1934, wheat prices in India fell by 50 percent.

(iv) Peasants' indebtedness increased across India. They had to sell whatever valuables they possessed.

**OR**

In 19th century, a series of inventions took place which increased the efficiency of production at every step of the production process, particularly in the field of cotton textiles.

(i) Cotton mills were created by the Richard Arkwright. It increased the cloth production all over the world.

(ii) Because of industrialisation, production output per worker increased and also the quality of thread and yarn improved.

(iii) New machines were purchased by the factory owners and they setup these machines under one roof. The process became more centralised and was managed well.

(iv) More supervision was needed then in the field of quality, regulation of labour etc.

(v) New mills and factories with advanced technology became visible in the early 19th century.

**OR**

(**)

23. The shift from hand printing to mechanical printing known as print revolution.

(i) The Print Revolution influenced people's conceptions and opened new ways of looking at things. It transformed the lives of people by opening the door of knowledge to a vastly literate population.

(ii) Handwriting became more stylish after the invention of mechanical printing. Letters were made up of metals in this type of printing style.

(iii) Paper borders were made and some other patterns were used in the printing to make it more attractive.

(iv) In the books printed, the rich space for decoration was kept blank on the printed page for the purchaser to choose the design and the painting school that would do the illustration.

(v) The second half of the fifteenth century saw 20 million copies of printed books flooding the markets in Europe. The number went up in the sixteenth century to about 200 million copies.

**OR**

(**)

24. Water is the basic need of the people. 0.5% of earth's water is available fresh water. It is a natural resource needed by every living being on the globe. Reasons to conserve water:

(i) The pollution in water resources are increasing polluted day by day, especially in the urban areas and are not suitable for drinking purpose.

(ii) The availability of water is uneven, so it is necessary to make it available to all.

(iii) Water resources are limited and our population is increasing day by day so the water requirement is also increasing day by day.

(iv) It is necessary to conserve water to make it available to all for the continuation of our livelihood and to save our ecosystem as well as human beings.

Measure to Conserve Water Resources:

(i) Use drip irrigation and sprinklers methods to irrigate the fields.

(ii) Avoid water wastage in domestic as well as at all other levels.

(iii) Recharge ground water by using rain water harvesting etc.

25. Everything that is available in our environment which can be used to satisfy our needs is called a Resource. Resources are technological accessible, economically feasible and culturally acceptable. Examples are coal, minerals, forest, land, water, fossil fuels etc. Resources are classified as follows:

(i) On the basis of origin.

(a) Biotic : living resources like plants etc.

(b) Abiotic: Non living resources like solar energy, land etc.

(ii) On the basis of exhaustibility.

(a) Renewable : Which can be recreated like solar energy etc.

(b) Non-Renewable: Which cannot be recreate like fossil fuels.

(iii) On the basis of ownership.

(a) Individual (Personal) : Owned by an individual person

(b) Community : Owned by the whole community.

(c) National: Owned by a country.

(d) International : Accessed by all nations.

(iv) On the basis of status of development.

(a) Potential : Resources which are found in a region, but have not been utilized.

(b) Developed : Which are surveyed and quality and quantity shows the utilization.

(c) Reserve: Which can be used for meeting future requirements.

(d) Stock: Which can not be used due to the lack of appropriate technology to used these resource.

**26.** Politics also influences the caste system and at the same 26 caste identifies by bringing them into the polities. We can explain it as follows:

(i) Caste groups like backward and forward came together to get benefit in the politics.

(ii) Every caste group tries to become bigger by incorporating with other similar castes or sub castes.

(iii) Caste groups demands the power sharing in politics and become in a position of decision making.

(iv) Political parties are using the castes and their separatism to gain power, they are not even trying to end this evil practice of caste discrimination.

(v) Negotiation are done by the coalition of different caste groups to make impact on the politics.

**27.** Sri Lanka got freedom in 1948 are followed the democratic rule over the country. They adopted a policy of majoritarianism. They established Sinhala supremacy and neglected the Sri Lankan Tamils after independence.

(i) The government provides preference to Sinhala community in all kinds of job.

(ii) Sinhala became the official language of Sri Lanka in 1956 after passing an act.

(iii) Buddhism became the state religion Sri Lankan Tamils felt that all political parties led by Buddhist Sinhala leaders were sensitive to their religion and language.

(iv) They denied equal political rights to Tamils. So, they launched parties and struggled against them for regional autonomy and equality of opportunity.

**28.** HDI stands for Human Development Index. The main criteria of measuring HDI according to UNDP can be explained as follows:

(i) UNDP published HOI to compare different countries based on education, health and per capital income of the country.

(ii) HDI Determines the rank of a country in three areas i.e., life expectancy, education all level and per capital income.

(iii) India ranks at 132nd position out of 191, according to the latest Human Development Report 2022.

The four primary indicators of HDI are life expectancy in terms of health, predicted years of schooling in terms of education, mean years of schooling in terms of education, and Gross National Income per capita in terms of standard of living.

**Note**

*The highest life expectancy in the world is found in Japan, where the average lifespan is 84 years, whereas the current life expectancy for India in 2023 is 70.42 years.*

**29.** Public sector: It is a service sector, providing service to the people:

(i) It is owned by the government.

(ii) Motive of this public sector is the welfare of the masses and all the activities are guided by the interest of nation.

(iii) Most of the services provided by the government itself.

(iv) Employees feel free secured disciplined and punctual.

(v) Government earns money by different taxes etc.

For example : Railways, Postal services, Banking etc.

**Private Sector:**

(i) It is governed by the private individuals or private companies.

(ii) Jobs in this sector is to earn profit.

(iii) Services are provided in the hands of individuals.

(iv) Jobs in this sector are less secured.

(v) This sector charges high rates for the use of services.

Examples are: TISCO, Reliance Industries etc.

30.

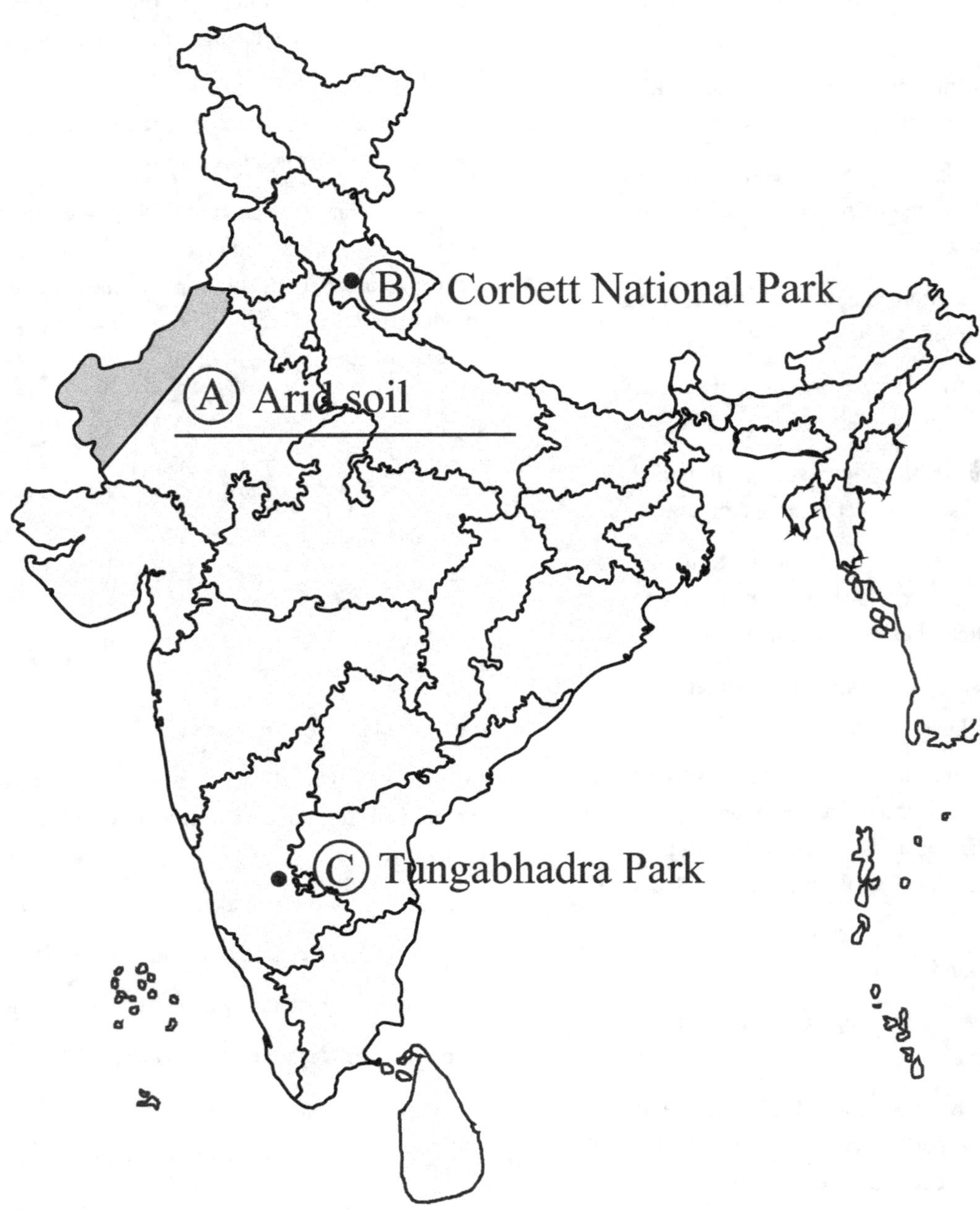

# CBSE Board Solved Paper Term-I

## SECTION - A

### (Very Short Answer Type Questions)

**(8 × 1 = 8)**

1. Which method of hand-printing was developed in China?

   **OR**

   Who wrote the novel 'Oliver Twist'?**

2. What is the most common indicator for measuring economic development of a country? **1**

3. What measure was adopted by the democratically elected government of Sri Lanka to establish Sinhala Supremacy? **1**

4. Much of the official work in Indian States is done in which language? **1**

5. Who are represented by the term 'African American'?**1**

6. What is the advantage of per capita income? Mention any one. **1**

7. Name the sector which continued to be the largest employer even in the year 2000. **1**

8. What do final goods and services mean? **1**

## SECTION - B

### (Short Answer Type Questions)

**(13 × 3 = 39)**

9. "The silk routes are a good example of vibrant pre-modern trade and cultural links between distant parts of the world." Explain how. **3**

   **OR**

   Describe any three main reasons for the decline of textile exports from India in the 19th century.

   **OR**

   How did the development or expansion of Bombay (Mumbai) differ from London? State any three points of difference between the two. **

10. What attracted the Europeans to Africa? Give any three reasons. **3**

    **OR**

    Explain the role played by advertisements in creating new consumers for the British products.

    **OR**

    How did air pollution become a nuisance for the Londoners? What steps were taken to solve the problem?**

11. Highlight any three circumstances that led to the intermingling of the hearing culture and the reading culture. **3**

    **OR**

    How did the historical novels in India try to create a sense of Pan-Indian belonging?**

12. Highlight any three innovations which have improved the printing technology from nineteenth century onwards. **3**

    **OR**

    Describe the growth of Hindi novels from their origin to the period of excellence.**

13. Mention any three features of arid soils. **3**

14. Assess the need for the conservation of forests and wildlife in India. **3**

15. Describe any three traditional method of rainwater harvesting adopted in different parts of India. **3**

16. "The Government of India gives holidays for the festivals of most of the religions." Why is it so? Give your viewpoint. **3**

17. Explain the status of women's representation in India's legislative bodies. **3**

18. Why do some people think that it's not correct to politicize social divisions? Give three reasons.** **3**

19. Classify the economic sectors on the basis of nature of activities. Mention the main feature of each. **3**

20. Why is NREGA also called the Right to Work? Explain.

    The Central Government in India has passed an act called the National Rural Employment Guarantee Act, 2005. **3**

21. Apart from income, which other six things people look for growth and development? **3**

## SECTION - C

### (Long Answer Type Questions)

**(8 × 5 = 40)**

22. Explain the effects of the Great Depression of 1929 on the Indian economy. **5**

    **OR**

    Explain the process of industrialization in Britain during the 19th century.

*Note: (**) Marked questions are out of syllabus so these are not explained or answered.*

**OR**

Describe the features of the big modern city of Calcutta (Kolkata) as viewed by the gods in the novel written by Durgacharan Ray.**

23. How far is it right to say that the print culture was responsible for the French revolution? Explain.     **5**

**OR**

Analyse the role and involvement of women in the readership and authorship of novels in India.**

24. Suggest any five measures to control land degradation in India.     **5**

25. Provide a suitable classification for resources on the basis of ownership. Mention main features of any three types of such resources.     **5**

26. Identify the determinants of the outcomes of the politics of social division and explain them.**     **5**

27. Explain the factors that have led to the weakening of the caste system in India.     **5**

28. Describe any five conditions or aspects that you would consider before accepting a job.     **5**

29. Explain with examples that there are other important development goals also besides income.     **5**

## SECTION - D

### (Map Based Questions)

**(1 + 1 + 1 = 3)**

30. **(i)** One item A is shown in the given political outline map of India. Identify this item with the help of following information and write its correct name on the line marked on the map.

    **(A)** A Type of Soil

    **(ii)** On the same political outline map of India, locate and label the following items with appropriate symbols.

    **(B)** Sariska Wildlife Sanctuary**

    **(C)** Salal Dam     **3**

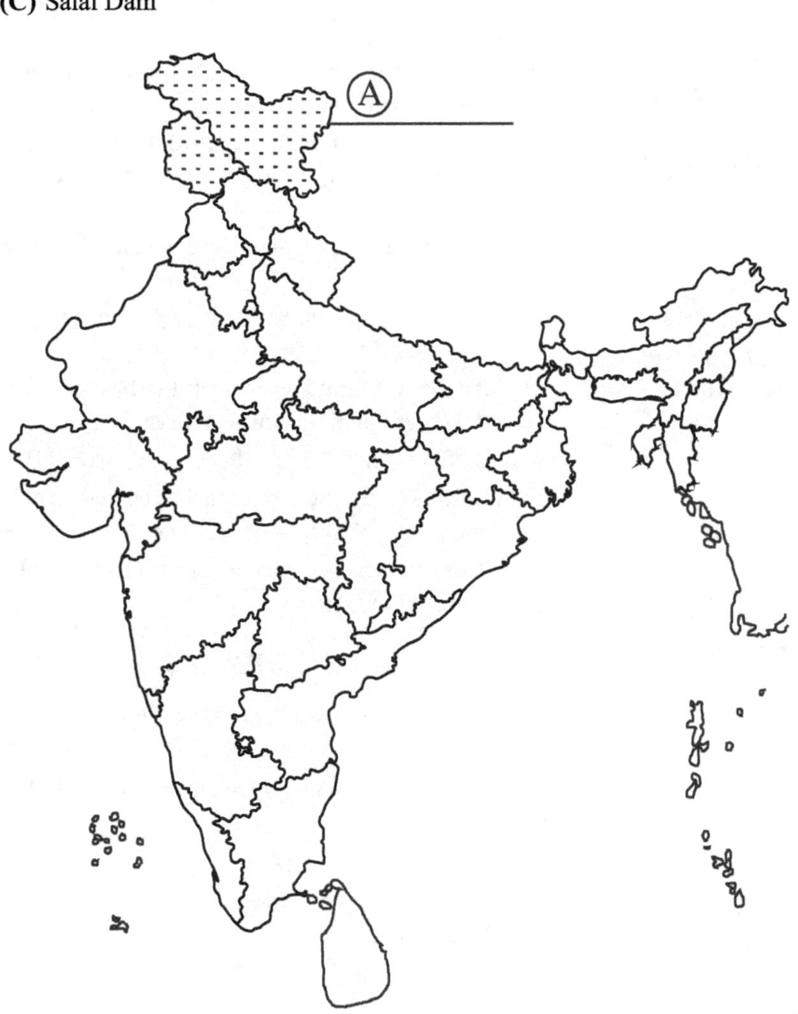

## Solutions

1. From AD 594 books in China were printed by rubbing paper against the inked surface of woodblocks.

2. Income per capita is the most common indicator.

3. An Act was passed to make Sinhala the official language of Sri Lanka in 1956. The government followed preferential policies favouring Sinhala applicants for University positions and government jobs.

4. Much of the official work in Indian States is done in the official language of the concerned state.

**Note**

*Assamese, Bengali, Gujarati, Hindi, Kannada, Kashmiri, Konkani, Malayalam, Manipuri, Marathi, Nepali, Odia, Punjabi, Sanskrit, Sindhi, Tamil, Telugu, Urdu, Bodo, Santhali, Maithili, and Dogri are the 22 languages presently in the eighth schedule to the Constitution.*

5. (**)

6. Per capital income helps to compare the development of countries as it tells us whether people in one country are better off than others in a different country.

**Note**

*According to the per capita GDP of countries in 2023, Luxembourg, one of the smallest countries in the European Union, has a population of 634,000 and is the richest country in this ranking with a per capita GDP of nearly \$130,000.*

7. The primary sector continued to be the largest employer even in the year 2000.

8. The various production activities in the primary, secondary and tertiary sector produce large number of goods and services for consumption and investment are final goods and services.

9. "The silk routes are a good example of vibrant pre-modern trade and cultural links between distant parts of the world." This can be justified through the following points:

   **(i)** Buddhism emerged from Eastern India and spread in several directions through the silk route.

   **(ii)** The routes on which cargoes carried Chinese silk to the west were known as, Silk routes. Historians have discovered several silk routes over land and by sea, covering vast regions of Asia and connecting Asia with Europe and Nothern Africa.

   **(iii)** Pottery from China, textile and spices from India and South Asia also travelled the same route. In return, precious metals like gold and silver flowed from Europe to Asia.

**OR**

Three main reasons for the decline of textile exports from India in the 19th century are :

   **(i)** As cotton industries developed in England, industrial groups began to pressurise the Government to impose import duties on cotton textiles so that Manchester goods could sell in Britain without facing any competition from outside.

   **(ii)** Industrialists persuaded the East India Company to sell British manufactures in Indian market as well. Exports of British cotton goods increased dramatically in the early 19th century.

   **(iii)** The export market for the Indian cotton weavers collapsed and the local market shrank, being glutted with Manchester imports. The imported cotton goods were cheap and Indian weavers could not compete with them.

10. The reason Europeans were attracted to Africa are:

    **(i)** Europeans were attracted to Africa because of valuable minerals like gold, coal and silver etc.

    **(ii)** In the late 19th century, Europeans were attracted to Africa due to its vast resource of land and minerals.

    **(iii)** Europeans came to Africa hoping to establish plantations and mines to produce crops and minerals for export to Europe.

**OR**

Role played by advertisements in creating new consumers for the British products:

    **(i)** When Manchester industrialists began selling cloth in India, they put labels on the cloth bundles to make the place of manufacture and the name of the company familiar to the buyer.

    **(ii)** When buyers saw 'Made in Manchester', written in bold on the label they felt confident to buy the cloth.

    **(iii)** But labels did not carry words and texts. They carried images and were beautifully illustrated with images of Indian gods and goddesses.

    **(iv)** The printed image of Krishna or Saraswati was also intended to make the manufacture from a foreign land, appear familiar to Indian.

11. Circumstances that led to the intermingling of the hearing culture and the reading culture:

    **(i)** With the printing press, a new reading public emerged. Printing reduced the cost of books. Access to books created a new culture of reading. Earlier reading was restricted to the elite class.

    **(ii)** Common people lived in a world of oral culture. They heard sacred texts read out, ballads recited and folk tales narrated. Hence Knowledge was transferred orally.

    **(iii)** Printers began publishing popular ballads and folk tales, illustrated with pictures. These were sung and recited at gatherings. Oral culture thus entered print and printed material was orally transmitted.

12. Three innovations which have improved the printing technology from nineteenth century onwards are as follows:

(i) The quality of printing plates became better and methods of feeding paper improved.

(ii) Automatic paper reels and photoelectric controls of the colour register were introduced.

(iii) The accumulation of several individual mechanical improvements transformed the appearance of printed texts.

13. Features of arid soils:

(i) Arid soil are saline in nature. Due to presence to dry climate and high temperature, evaporation occurs at a faster rate. Hence, this soil lacks humus and moisture.

(ii) Contains a considerable amount of soluble salts and owing to dry climate and lack of vegetation, contains a low percentage of organic matter too.

(iii) Arid soils range from red to brown in colour and have a sandy texture.

14. There is a need to conserve the forests and wildlife in India because:

(i) Conservation of biodiversity is necessary because it preserves the ecological diversity and preserves our life support systems i.e., water, air and soil. For example, the plants, animals and micro-organisms recreate the quality of the air we breathe, the water we drink and the soil that produces our food without which we cannot survive.

(ii) To preserves the genetic diversity of plants and animals for better growth and breeding of species. For example, in agriculture we are still dependent on traditional crop varieties. Fisheries too are heavily dependent on the maintenance of aquatic biodiversity.

(iii) Forest are primary producers on which all other living beings depend not only for food but indirectly for many other forest produces which are used for different purposes.

*India has a great variety of fauna, numbering 92,037 species, of which insects alone include 61,375 species. It is estimated that about two times that number of species remain to be discovered in India alone.*

15. Different rainwater harvesting systems practised in India are:

(i) In arid and semi-arid regions agricultural fields were converted into rain fed storage structures. Rainwater was allowed to stand and moisten the soil. These structures are called 'Khadins' and 'Johads'.

(ii) In the western Himalaya's diversion channels called 'guls' or 'kuls' are built to utilize rainwater for agriculture.

(iii) In the semi-arid and arid regions of Rajasthan, all houses had underground tanks or tankas for storing drinking water. The tanks were connected to the roofs of the houses through a pipe. Rain falling on the rooftops would travel down the pipe and was stored in these underground tankas.

16. The Government of India gives all religious holidays because India is a secular state. Many provisions were adopted in the Constitution to make India a secular state and these are:

(i) There is no official religion for the Indian State.

(ii) Constitution allows the State to intervene in the matters of religion in order to ensure equality within religious communities for example Article 17 Which bans untouchability.

(iii) The constitution provides to all individuals and communications freedom to profess, practice and propagate any religion and prohibits discrimination on the grounds of religion.

*Articles 25 and 26 make India a secular state and give the citizens the right and freedom to profess their respective religions and faiths. Further, Article 26 says that all denominations can manage their own affairs in matters of religion.*

17. The way to ensure that women related problems gets adequate attention is to have more women as elected representatives. To achieve this, it is legally binding to have a fair proportion of women in the elected bodies.

(i) Panchayati Raj in India has reserved one-third seats in Local government bodies for women.

(ii) In India, the proportion of women in legislature has been very low. The percentage of elected women members in Lok Sabha is not even 15 per cent and in State Assemblies less than 10 per cent. India is lagging behind several developing countries of Africa and Latin America. Women organisations have been demanding reservations of at least one-third seats in Lok Sabha and State Assemblies for Women.

(iii) And only recently, in March 2010, the women's reservation bill was passed in the Rajya Sabha ensuring 33% reservation to women in parliament and State Legislative bodies though it was never voted in Lok Sabha.

*As of December 2022, women constituted 61.3 percent of the Rwandan parliament (lower or single house). This makes it the country with the highest share of women in parliament worldwide, followed by Cuba.*

18. (**)

19. On the basis of nature of activities, economic sectors are classified into:

(i) Primary sector : It forms the base for all other goods that we subsequently make. Since most of the natural products we get, are from agriculture, dairy, fishing, forestry, this sector is also called sector for agriculture and related activities.

**(ii) Secondary Sector** It is also called the industrial sector. It covers activities in which natural products are changed into other forms through various ways of manufacturing. It can take place in a factory, workshop or at home.

For Example: Making sugar from sugarcane.

**(iii) Tertiary sector:** It is also called the service sector. This sector produces services that act as aid and support to the primary and secondary sectors. Services like police, transport, hospitals, educational institutions, post and telegraph, courts, storage, trade and communication and banking are some of the examples of activities of the tertiary sector.

**20.** The main objectives of the NREGA 2005 are:

**(i)** To implement the Right to Work in around 625 district of India.

**(ii)** To guarantee 100 days of employment per household in a year by the government. In case the government fails to give employment within 15 days it offers unemployment allowance.

**(iii)** Equal payment for men and women, wages to be paid within a fortnight, 1/3 beneficiaries should be women, and facilities such as creche, drinking water, and shade have to be provided at the workplace.

**21.** High per capita income is not the only attribute to good equality life. It cannot buy all the essential things required for a good buy all the essential things required for a good life.

Pollution-free atmosphere to ensure good health, protection from infectious diseases, lowering of mortality rate, promotion of literacy, job security, good working conditions etc., are essential for a good standard of living and for growth and development.

**22.** Effects of the Great Depression on the Indian Economy:

**(i)** India had become an exporter of agricultural goods and importer of manufactured goods. This situation continued well into the 20th century during the British rule. The depression had immediate effect on Indian trade. India's exports and imports halved between 1928 and 1934.

**(ii)** The prices fell in India as a result of the international price crash. Wheat prices fell by 50 per cent between 1928 and 1934. Peasants and farmers suffered due to the fall of prices. Their income lowered but the colonial government refused to reduce the revenue they collected.

**(iii)** With the collapse of gunny bag export, jute prices crashed. Peasants, who had borrowed in the hope to increase their production fell deep into debts due to the crash of jute prices by 60 per cent.

**(iv)** To meet their expenses peasants used up their savings, mortgaged lands and sold whatever jewellery and precious metals they had.

**(v)** Town dwelling landowners, who received rents, people with fixed income or salaried class became better off

with the falling of prices of the foodgrains and other commodities. Industrial investments were not much affected as the Government extended tariff protection to industries.

**OR**

The most dynamic industries in Britian were cotton and metals. Cotton was the leading sector in the first phase of industrialization up to the 1840s. Later iron and steel industry led the way. With the expansion of railways in England from the 1840s and in the colonies from 1860s, the demand for iron and steel increased. The new industries could not displace traditional industries. At the end of the 19th century, less than 20 per cent of the total workforce was employed in technologically advanced industrial sectors.

The pace of change in the 'traditional' industries was not set by steam-powered cotton or metal industries. Ordinary and small innovations were the basis of growth in many non-mechanised sectors such as food processing building, pottery, glass work, tanning, furniture making and production of implements. Though the technological changes occurred slowly. New technology was expensive and merchants and industrialists were cautious about using it. 'The machine often broke down and their cost of repair was costly.

**23. (i)** The existing values, norms and institutions, which were never questioned earlier, were revalued through debates and discussions by the public in print.

**(ii)** There was an outpour of literature that mocked royalty and criticised their morality. The existing social order was criticised.

**(iii)** Through cartoons and caricatures, they made people aware that while common people were going through tremendous hardship, the monarchy remained absorbed in merry-making and did not care about sufferings of common people.

**(iv)** Print culture created a new environment of debate and dialogue. New ideas of social revolution were born.

**(v)** The writing spread the view that everything should be judge through the application of reason and rationality.

**24.** Measures to control land degradation in India are:

**(i)** Construction of terraces for farming and building of dams in hilly area to check soil erosion

**(ii)** Proper discharge and disposal of industrial wastes after treatment.

**(iii)** Management of grazing by animals.

**(iv)** Planned management of forests, planting of shelter belts of plants and more plants can be planted to check soil erosion.

**(v)** Control on mining activities.

**25.** On the basis of ownership, there are four types of resources:

**(i) Individual resources:** Resources, which are owned privately by individuals, e.g., farmers own pieces of land or houses. Plantation, pasture lands and water in wells are some resources owned by individuals.

**(ii) Community owned resources :** These resources are accessible to all the members of the community, e.g., public parks, and playgrounds, ponds etc.

**(iii) National resources :** All the resources within the political boundary of a nation including the territorial water (oceanic area up to 12 nautical miles from the coast) extending into the ocean and resources therein belong to the nation, e.g., minerals, forests, wildlife, land, etc.

**(iv) International resources :** There are international institutions which own and regulate some resources, e.g., the oceanic resources beyond 200 km of the Exclusive Economic. Zone belong to the open ocean. No individual country can utilise these without the concurrence of international institutions.

### Note

*An "exclusive economic zone," or "EEZ," is an area of the ocean, generally extending 200 nautical miles (230 miles) beyond a nation's territorial sea, within which a coastal nation has jurisdiction over both living and nonliving resources.*

**26.** (**)

**27.** Reasons which have contributed to weakening caste system were:

**(i)** Efforts of Gandhiji and B. R. Ambedkar who advocated and worked to establish a society in which caste inequalities are absent.

**(ii)** Socio-economic changes such as : Urbanisation, Growth of literacy and education, Occupational mobility, Weakening of landlord's position in the village, Breaking down of caste hierarchy.

**(iii)** The Constitution of India prohibited any caste-based discrimination and laid the foundations of policies to reverse the injustices of the caste system.

**(iv)** Fundamental right has played a major role since they are provided to all citizens without any discrimination.

For example : Articles 17 ban on untouchibility.

**28.** Before accepting a job many factors need to be considered such as:

**(i)** Facilities for families, working conditions or opportunity to learn.

**(ii)** Job may give less wages but may offer regular employment that enhances sense of security. Another job however, may offer high wages but no job security and also leave no personal time.

**(iii)** The terms of employment are as per government rules and regulations.

**(iv)** Several other benefits like paid leave, provident fund, gratuity, etc., are available or not.

**(v)** Provisions for medical benefits and safe working environment. A safe and secure environment may allow more women to take up a variety of jobs.

**29.** Other aspects such as equal treatment, freedom, security, opportunity to learn, good working conditions, pollution-free atmosphere, job security and good social life are very important for a good quality life.

Money or material things that one can buy with it, is one factor on which our life depends. But quality of our life also depends on non-material things, for example, the role of our friends in our life. Another example, if we get a job in a far off place, before accepting it we would try consider many factors apart from income such as facilities for our family, working atmosphere or opportunity to learn. Similarly, for development, people look at a mix of goals. It is true that if women are engaged in paid work, their dignity increases. However, it is also the case that if there is respect for women there would be more sharing of house work and greater acceptance of women.

**30.**

# CBSE Board Solved Paper Term-II

## SECTION - A
### (Multiple Choice Questions)

(9 × 1 = 9)

1. What type of conservative regimes were set up in 1815 in Europe ? **1**
Choose the appropriate answer from the following :
(a) Autocractic     (b) Democratic
(c) Aristocratic     (d) Dictatorial

**OR**

Who, among the following, was the head of the Revolutionary Society formed by Phan Boi Chau ? **1**
(a) Prince Cuong De     (b) Phan Boi Chau
(c) Phan Chu Trinh     (d) Liang Qichao

2. In which one of the following Indian National Congress Sessions was the demand of 'Purna Swaraj' formalised in December 1929 ? **1**
(a) Madras Session     (b) Lahore Session
(c) Calcutta Session     (d) Nagpur Session

3. National Waterway No. 1 is navigable between which of the following places ? **1**
(a) Sadiya and Dhubri
(b) Allahabad and Haldia
(c) Udyogamandal and Champakkara
(d) Kottapuram and Komman

4. Which one of the following political parties came to power in Bolivia in 2006 ? **1**
(a) The Communist Party
(b) The Republican Party
(c) The Socialist Party
(d) The Conservative Party

5. Which one of the following is the most popular form of government in the contemporary world ? **1**
(a) Dictatorship     (b) Monarchy
(c) Military Rule     (d) Democracy

6. Which one of the following is a 'National Political Party'? **1**
(a) Samajwadi Party     (b) Rashtriya Janata Dal
(c) Rashtriya Lok Dal     (d) Bahujan Samaj Party

7. Which one of the following days is being observed as 'National Consumers' Day' in India ? **1**

(a) 24 December     (b) 25 December
(c) 10 December     (d) 31 December

8. Which one of the following laws was enacted by the Government of India in October 2005 ? **1**
(a) The Right to Property Act
(b) The Right to Education Act
(c) The Consumer Protection Act
(d) The Right to Information Act

9. Which one of the following refers to investment ? **1**
(a) The money spent on religious ceremonies
(b) The money spent on social customs
(c) The money spent to buy assets such as land
(d) The money spent on household goods

## SECTION - B
### (Short Answer Questions)

(3 × 12 = 36)

10. Explain the conditions that were viewed as obstacles to the economic exchange and growth by the new commercial classes during the nineteenth century in Europe. **3**

**OR**

How did students in Vietnam fight against the colonial government's efforts to prevent Vietnamese from qualifying for 'white collar jobs' ? Explain.

11. Why did Gandhiji decide to launch a nationwide Satyagraha against the proposed Rowlatt Act, 1919 ? Explain. **3**

12. Describe the main features of the 'Salt March'. **3**

13. What are the two main ways of generating electricity? How are they different from each other ? Explain. **3**

14. Name the non-metallic mineral which can split easily into thin sheets. Mention its uses. **3**

15. Why are efficient means of transport pre-requisites for the fast development of the country ? Explain. **3**

16. Name the six 'National Political Parties' in India in a chronological order. **3**

17. What inspiration do we get from Bolivia's popular struggle ? Explain any three values that we can learn from it. **3**

18. How is democractic government known as responsive government ? Explain with examples. **3**

19. How have markets been transformed in recent years? Explain with examples. **3**

**20.** Explain any three factors which gave birth to the 'Consumer Movement' in India. **3**

**21.** Explain with an example, how credit plays a vital and positive role for development. **3**

## SECTION - C

### (Long Answer Questions)

**(5 × 8 = 40)**

**22.** How had revolutionaries spread their ideas in many European States after 1815 ? Explain with examples. **5**

**OR**

Explain, with examples, how religious groups played an important role in the development of anti-colonial feelings in Vietnam. **5**

**23.** How did different social groups conceive the idea of 'Non-Cooperation' ? Explain with examples. **5**

**24.** Why is there a pressing need for using renewable energy sources in India ? Explain any five reasons. **5**

**25.** "Advancement of international trade of a country is an index to its prosperity." Support the statement with suitable examples. **5**

**26.** "About hundred years ago there were few countries that had hardly any political party. Now there are few countries that do not have political parties." Examine this statement. **5**

**27.** Compare the popular struggles of Nepal and Bolivia. **5**

**28.** "Globalisation has been advantageous to consumers as well as to producers." Support the statement with suitable examples. **5**

**29.** Why are rules and regulations required in the market-place ? Explain. **5**

## SECTION - D

### (Map Based Questions)

**(2 + 3 = 5)**

**30.** (I) Two features A and B are marked in the political outline map of B. Identify these features with the help of the following information and write their correct names on the lines marked in the map.

**2**

A. The place where the Indian National Congress Session was held in 1927.

B. The place which is associated with the movement of Indigo Planters.

(II) On the same political outline map of India, locate and label the following with appropriate symbols. **3**

(i) Narora — a nuclear power plant

(ii) Rourkela — an iron and steel plant

(iii) Kandla — a major sea port

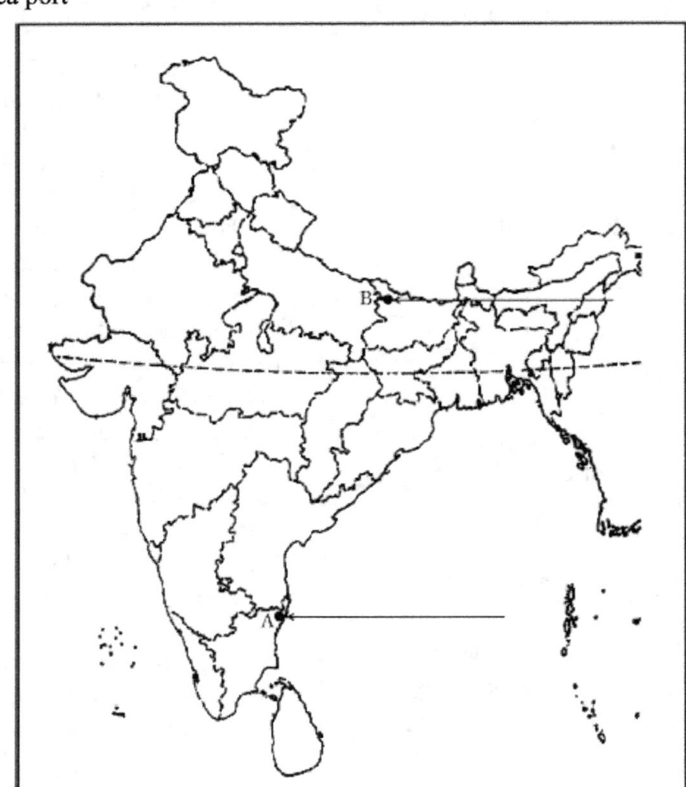

## Solutions

**1. (a)** Autocratic conservative regimes were set up in 1815 in Europe. They did not tolerate criticism and dissent, and attacked the activities that questioned the legitimacy of autocratic governments.

**OR**

**(c)** Scholar's Revolt of 1868 was mainly against imposition of Christianity in Vietnam. The Scholars Revolt of 1868 was an early revolt against French control and spread of Christianity. It was led by angry officials at the imperial court. They organized an uprising in Ngu An and Ha Tien provinces and killed nearly a thousand Catholics.

**Features:**

- It was a movement which was led by officials at the imperial court in 1868.
- The revolt was against the spread of Catholicism and French power in Vietnam.
- More than 1000 Catholics were killed in the revolt.
- The French crushed the movement, but this uprising served to inspire other patriots to rise up against them.

**2. (b)** Indian National Congress became the symbol of Nationalist feelings and Indian Independence. The masses started associating themselves with the Congress as their representatives and believed in the leaders of the Congress. The Congress also had popular leaders who were very effective and great and they demanded full independence of India. The Indian National Congress demanded full Independence or Purna Swaraj on 19th December 1929 at the Lahore session.

 *Note*

*The Declaration of Purna Swaraj was a resolution which was passed in 1930 because of the dissatisfaction among the Indian masses regarding the British offer of Dominion status to India. Swaraj means 'Self-rule or Sovereignty', or Declaration of the Independence of India, it was promulgated by the Indian National Congress, resolving the Congress and Indian nationalists to fight for Purna Swaraj, or complete self-rule/total independence from the British rule. The flag of India was hoisted by Jawaharlal Nehru on 31 December 1929 on the banks of Ravi river, in Lahore. The Congress asked the people of India to observe 26 January as Independence Day . The flag of India was hoisted publicly across India by Congress volunteers and the general public who aspired for self-governance and wanted to achieve independence.*

**3. (b)** The Allahabad-Haldia National waterway stretches on the Ganga River and connects Allahabad (Prayagraj), in Uttar Pradesh, with Haldia in West Bengal.

**4. (c)** The Socialist party, a political party of Bolivia, which emerged on January 28th 1921. The members of this party are known as "Saaverdristas". In 2006, this party came to power in Bolivia.

 *Note*

*The United Socialist Party was associated with the revolutionary governments of Colonels José David Toro Ruilova and Germán Busch Becerra, between 1936 and 1939. For the 1938 elections, the United Socialist Party was the component of the pro-military Socialist Single Front. The United Socialist Party elected some deputies of National Congress in 1940, and during the first 2 years of Enrique Peñarand's administration they were among the government's opponents in parliament. However, in his third year in office, Enrique Peñaranda formed a so-called cabinet of concentration which the United Socialist Party joined. It was in office when the Peñaranda government was overthrown on 20 December 1943. With the coup d'état of 1943 and the coming to power of Major Gualberto Villarroel, the United Socialist Party split, with a dissident group forming the Independent Socialist Party, which for some time cooperated with the Villarroel regime.*

**5. (d)** Democracy is considered as the best form of government because of the following reasons:

In democracy, people have the right to choose their rulers. If rulers do not work well, people will not elect him in the next election. Democracy has more freedom of speech than any other forms of government.

**6. (d)** The Bahujan Samaj Party (BSP) is the third largest national political party in India. It was formed mainly to represent Bahujans (literally meaning 'People in majority'), referring to people from the Scheduled Castes, Scheduled Tribes and Other Backward Castes (OBC), as well as religious minorities that together consist of 85 percent of India's population but still divided into 6000 different castes. The party claims to be inspired by the philosophy of B. R. Ambedkar, Mahatma Jyotiba Phule, Narayana Guru, Periyar E. V. Ramasamy and Chhatrapati Shahuji Maharaj. It was founded by Kanshi Ram in 1984, who named his protégée Mayawati as his successor in 2001. The BSP was the third most voted-for party in the 2014 general election but still failed to win any seats in the 16th Lok Sabha.

7. **(a)** National Consumer Rights Day in India falls on 24th December every year because on this day in 1986, India's Consumer Protection Act came into effect. So, the day is observed to make people aware of their rights as consumers to avoid getting exploited.

*In India, the rights of consumers were taken seriously when the Consumer Protection Act of 1986 was enacted. The aim of this bill was to safeguard the consumer against exploitation like the selling of defective goods, unfair trade, fraudulence, and deficiency in services. Over the years, India's economy has undergone a transformation, significantly altering how many Indians shop and travel. This was a result of the rising market competition, innovations, and increasing presence of e-commerce services, which expanded the options available to consumers. So the tried-and-trusted habits of the consumer have been disrupted, which created a need for the Consumer Protection Act to be revised and revamped. Taking this dynamic and advanced marketplace into perspective, India's parliament passed the updated Consumer Protection Bill on August 6, 2019.*

8. **(d)** The RTI Bill was passed by Parliament of India on 15 June 2005 and came into force with effect from 12 October 2005. This law empowers Indian citizens to seek any accessible information from a Public Authority and makes the Government and its functionaries more accountable and responsible.

9. **(c)** Land can be bought as an investment or sold off later at a high price as a business opportunity. Land is a great asset for investors because of its price stability, its flexible nature, and zero maintenance cost.

10. Customs duties were viewed as an obstacle to economic change and growth by new commercial classes because they hindered international trade, limited the growth of domestic industries, and reduced consumer choice and purchasing power. As a result, these classes advocated for the removal or reduction of customs duties to foster free trade and promote economic growth.

**OR**

The Tonkin Free Schools were started in 1907. Their main aim was to provide western-style education. This education included classes in science, hygiene and French. It was not enough to acquire knowledge in science and western ideas but was also important to learn to look 'modern'.

11. The Anarchical and Revolutionary Crimes Act of 1919, popularly known as the Rowlatt Act, was a law that applied in British India. It was a legislative council act passed by the Imperial Legislative Council in Delhi on 18 March 1919, indefinitely extending the emergency measures of preventive indefinite detention, imprisonment without trial and judicial review enacted in the Defence of India Act 1915 during the First World War. Mahatma Gandhi, among other Indian leaders, was extremely critical of the Act and argued that not everyone should be punished in response to isolated political crimes.

*The act was prepared on the recommendation of the Rowlatt Commission (1918) replacing the old Defense of India Act (1915), which was enacted during the First World War, with a permanent statute that granted the British government additional control over Indians. Mahatma Gandhi called the Rowlatt Act a "Black Act" which sparked the horrific Jallianwala Bagh Massacre in April 1919, as a reaction to which the Non-Cooperation Movement was launched by INC. British Government on March 1922, abolished the Rowlatt Act, the Press Act, and twenty-two other laws after adopting the recommendations of the Repressive Laws Committee.*

12. Mahatma Gandhi found in salt a powerful symbol that could unite the Indian nation. Gandhi presented the British government with many demands. When Gandhi reached the port town of Dandi, he broke the salt law ceremoniously by making salt from sea water. Salt March was an effective symbol of resistance against colonialism because -

(i) All classes could identify with salt as it was a cheap and essential food item.

(ii) Tax on salt and the monopoly over its manufacturing was a sign of the oppression of British Rule.

(iii) It would affect the British Economy.

The choice of salt as a symbol of protest against the colonial rule was a remarkable indicative of Gandhi's tactical wisdom. By making the salt as his target he wanted to garner the maximum participation of the masses in the National Movement.

13. Electricity is generated by hydropower and thermal power. Hydro electricity is generated by running water while thermal power is generated by burning coal, petroleum and natural gas. Electricity is most often generated at a power plant by electromechanical generators, primarily driven by heat engines fuelled by combustion or nuclear fission but also by other means such as the kinetic energy of flowing water

and wind. Other energy sources include solar photovoltaic and geothermal power.

### Note

*A thermal power station is a type of power station in which heat energy is converted to electrical energy. In a steam-generating cycle heat is used to boil water in a large pressure vessel to produce high-pressure steam, which drives a steam turbine connected to an electrical generator. The low-pressure exhaust from the turbine enters a steam condenser where it is cooled to produce hot condensate which is recycled to the heating process to generate more high pressure steam. This is known as a Rankine cycle. The design of thermal power stations depends on the intended energy source: fossil fuel, nuclear and geothermal power, solar energy, bio fuels, and waste incineration are all used. Certain thermal power stations are also designed to produce heat for industrial purposes; for district heating; or desalination of water, in addition to generating electrical power.*

**14.** Mica is a non metallic mineral. Mica is a mineral made up of a series of plates or leaves. It splits easily into thin sheets. These sheets can be so thin that a thousand can be layered into a mica sheet of a few centimeters high. Non-metallic minerals are minerals that do not contain any metals. Some examples of non-metallic minerals are limestone, mica, gypsum, coal, dolomite, phosphate, salt, and granite. Mineral fuels like coal and petroleum are also non-metallic minerals.

### Note

*Mica, any of a group of hydrous potassium, aluminum silicate minerals. It is a type of phyllosilicate, exhibiting a two-dimensional sheet or layer structure. Among the principal rock-forming minerals, micas are found in all three major rock varieties—igneous, sedimentary, and metamorphic. The major uses of sheet and block mica are as electrical insulators in electronic equipment, thermal insulation, gauge "glass", windows in stove and kerosene heaters, dielectrics in capacitors, decorative panels in lamps and windows, insulation in electric motors and generator armatures, field coil insulation.*

**15.** Efficient means of transport are pre-requisites for fast development. Goods and services do not move from supply locales to demand locales on their own. The movement of these goods and services from their supply locations to demand locations necessitates the need for transport. The pace of a country depends upon the production of goods and services as well as their movement over space. Therefore efficient means of transport and communication are prerequisites for fast development.

**16.** Six National Political Parties on the basis of their foundation are:

(i) Indian National Congress (1885)

(ii) Communist Party of India (1925)

(iii) Communist Party of India-Marxist (1964)

(iv) Bharatiya Janata Party (1980)

(v) Bahujan Samaj Party (1984)

(vi) National Congress Party (1999)

**17.** The inspirations we get from Bolivia's popular struggle are: collectiveness, power of the common people and the role played by political organisation. Three values we can learn from it are: Unity, Mass mobilisation, Public demonstration.

**18.** Any individual can question the decisions made by a ruler or government and check whether it is beneficial for the country or not. The democratic government is a responsive government as it is responsive to the needs of the needs and expectations of the citizens. It is the most basic outcome of democracy. Democracy is accountable and responsive to the needs and expectations of the citizens because:

(i) In a democracy people have the right to choose their representatives and the people will have control over them.

(ii) Citizens have the right to participate in decision making that affects them all.

**19.** In a matter of last few years, our markets have been transformed. As consumers in today's world, some of us have a wide choice of goods and services before us. The latest models of digital cameras, mobile phones and televisions made by the leading manufacturers of the world are within our reach. Every season, new models of automobiles can be seen on Indian roads. Today, Indians are buying cars produced by nearly all the top companies in the world. A similar explosion of brands can be seen for many other goods: from shirts to televisions to processed fruit juices.

**20.** The factors that gave birth to the consumer movement in India are manifold. It started as a "social force" with the need to protect and promote consumer interests against unfair and unethical trade practices. Extreme food shortages, hoarding, black marketing and adulteration of food led to the consumer movement becoming an organised arena in the 1960s. Till the 1970s, consumer organisations were mostly busy writing articles and holding exhibitions.

**21.** Credit plays a crucial role in a country's development. By sanctioning loans to developing industries and trade, banks provide them with the necessary aid for improvement. This leads to increase in the production, profits and employment. However, caution must be exercised in the case of loans from the informal sector which include high interest rates that may be more harmful than good. For this reason, it is important that the formal sector gives out more loans so that borrowers are not duped by moneylenders, and can ultimately contribute to national development.

22. The reasons for the rise of revolutionary movements are as follows:

    (i)   Mass discontent leading to popular uprisings.

    (ii)  Dissident political movements with élite participation.

    (iii) Strong and unifying motivations across major parts of the society.

Giuseppe Mazzini put together various programs for a unitary Italian republic. He subsequently founded underground societies like Young Italy in Marseilles and Young Europe in Berne. So in this way Mazzini spread revolutionary ideas in Europe by the contribution that he done in Italy to unify it.

**OR**

In the first decade of the twentieth century a 'go east movement' became popular. Go East Movement was movement which was launched in the first decade of the twentieth century in Vietnam. The movement becomes popular because early Vietnamese nationalists had a close relationship with Japan and China. They provided models for those looking to change, a refuge for those who were escaping French police, and a location where a wider Asian network of revolutionaries could be established

- Go east movement it was started in 19th century by Vietnamese.

- Around 300 Vietnamese students were sent to Japan to acquire modern education.

- They wanted to overthrow French from Vietnam.

- They wanted to establish Nguyen dynasty.

23. In the rural areas, the idea of Non-cooperation was interpreted as a fight against the landlords and talukdars who levied very high rents and other cesses on the peasants. In pursuance of self-rule, the peasants demanded reduction in revenue, abolition of the system of begar and boycotted exploitative landlords. People were asked to withdraw their children from government-controlled or aided schools and colleges. People were asked to boycott foreign goods and use only Indian-made goods. People were asked to boycott the elections to the legislative councils. People were asked not to serve in the British army.

*Begar- forced labour- a form of social labour without payment. Its origin goes back to the pre-money era when labour was viewed as an important item of exchange. The land of the king and his men and priests were cultivated by peasants in exchange of some tenurial rights in land granted by the king. When the state became a more elaborate and complex affair in later period, the demesne lands of the ruling classes, particularly of the landlords, were worked by their prajas or subjects gratis. This was considered to be a pious act to give free labour to the priestly classes. Village people always gave free labour in working temple lands also. Such a free labour system is not to be confused with the use of slave and bonded labours. Free labour was given either in exchange of some rights obtained in land or some invisible merit obtained from rulers or from priests. It was a social arrangement made possible under the pre-monetised modes of production and social relations.*

24. One of the threats the world is facing today is the possible near end of non-renewable energy sources. Uncontrolled use of these sources, initiated by the industrial revolution, is growing at a faster rate as the machineries and other aspects of modern technology use them as fuel. Even though some nations are taking alternate choices to preserve whatever resources are left in the world by choosing renewable energy as sources, highly populated countries like India are yet to fulfil this mission. As the rate of consequences like global warming is clearly visible and is affecting the world, it is a necessity for India to take wise and long-term actions to prevent this.

25. International Trade is considered an economic barometer for a country. The exchange of goods between people, groupings of states, and nations is known as trade. An indicator of a nation's economic prosperity is the growth of its international trade. As a result, it is regarded as a nation's economic barometer. Advancement of international trade of a country is an index to its prosperity.

26. A political party is an organization that coordinates candidates to compete in a particular country's elections. It is common for the members of a party to hold similar ideas about politics, and parties may

promote specific ideological or policy goals. Political parties have become a major part of the politics of almost every country, as modern party organizations developed and spread around the world over the last few centuries. It is extremely rare for a country to have no political parties. Some countries have only one political party while others have several. Parties are important in the politics of autocracies as well as democracies, though usually democracies have more political parties than autocracies. Autocracies often have a single party that governs the country, and some political scientists consider competition between two or more parties to be an essential part of democracy.

**27.** These two stories are from very different contexts. The movement in Nepal was to establish democracy, while the struggle in Bolivia involved claims on an elected, democratic government. The popular struggle in Bolivia was about one specific policy, while the struggle in Nepal was about the foundations of the country's politics. Both these struggles were successful but their impact was at different levels.

Nepal was under the rule of kings until 2006. The protest against kings' rule and the Restoration of democracy in Nepal is considered one of the most popular struggles and movements in the world. Nepal won democracy in 1990, King Birendra remained head of state and real power was exercised by popularly elected representatives. Unfortunately, King Birendra was killed in a mysterious massacre of the royal family in 2001. Soon after his death King Gyanendra became the new king of Nepal. He took the advantage of weakness and unpopularity of the democratically elected Government and started exploiting the people of Nepal. In the month of February 2005, the king dismissed the prime minister who was in power then, dissolving the popularly elected parliament. The movement for democracy began in the month of April of 2006 and was aimed at regaining control over the government from the king.

Bolivia is a poor country in Latin America. Earlier the government was supplying municipality water. Due to the pressure from World Bank, the government sold the rights of water supply for the city of Cochabamba multinational company. On gaining control the MNC immediately increased the price of water by four times which came up to the bill of Rs 1000 for water alone for a month. Bolivia is a poor country where the average family income is around Rs 5000 for a month. Paying 20% of their income for water alone made their life difficult to survive. This raises a protest. Labours, human rights, and community leaders formed an alliance.

**28.** Globalization allows companies to find lower-cost ways to produce their products. It also increases global competition, which drives prices down and creates a larger variety of choices for consumers. Lowered costs help people in both developing and already-developed countries live better on less money. They have greater choice. Better quality of products is available for consumption due to competition. It has reduced the cost of goods and services considerably. Producers now have access to international markets for their products.

**29.** Rules and regulations are required in the marketplace to protect consumers. Sellers often abdicate responsibility for a low-quality product, cheat in weighing out goods, add extra charges over the retail price, and sell adulterated/ defective goods.

Rules are the regulations that the people under a government need to follow. They guarantee the smooth run of community life. They also ensure the safety of the citizens by giving instructions that help to reduce accidents.

**30. (I) (a)** In 1927, the Indian National Congress Session was held in---- Madras.

**(b)** Champaran--- is the place where the movement of Indigo Planters was started.

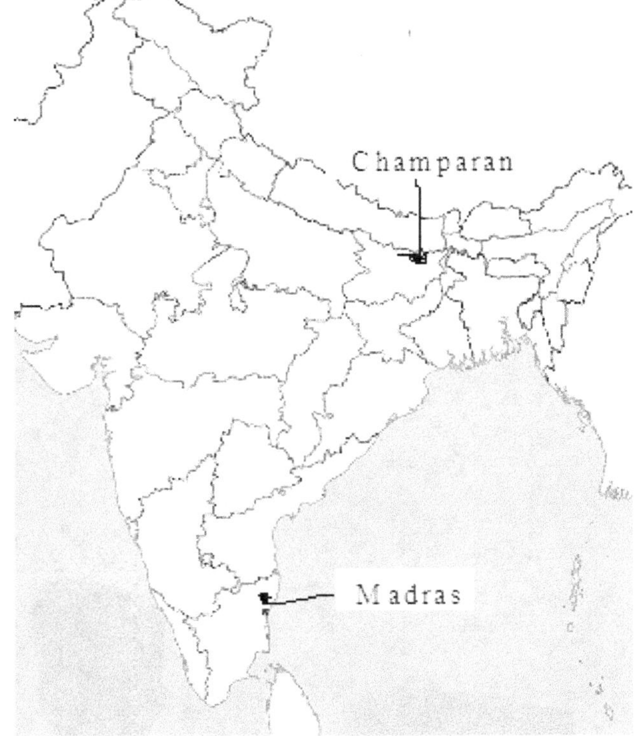

*Note*

*Gandhi was unaware of this until an agriculturist from Bihar, Rajkumar Shukla, met him and told him of the woes of the people of Champaran. He requested Gandhi to go to the place and see for himself the state of affairs there. Gandhi was them attending the Congress meeting at Lucknow and he did not have time to go there. Rajkumar Shukla followed him about, begging him to come and help the suffering villagers in Champaran. Gandhi at last promised to visit the place after he had visited Calcutta. When Gandhi was in Calcutta, Rajkumar was there too, to take him to Bihar. Gandhi went to Champaran with Rajkumar early in 1917. On his arrival the District Magistrate served him with a notice saying that he was not to remain in the district of Champaran but must leave the place by the first available train.*

*Gandhi disobeyed this order. He was summoned to appear before the court.*

*The Government withdrew the case against Gandhi and allowed him to remain in the district. Gandhi stayed there to study the grievances of the peasants.*

**(II)** Narora-    Nuclear Power Plant

(i)   Rourkela –   An Iron And Steel Plant

(ii)  Kandla -    A Major Sea Port

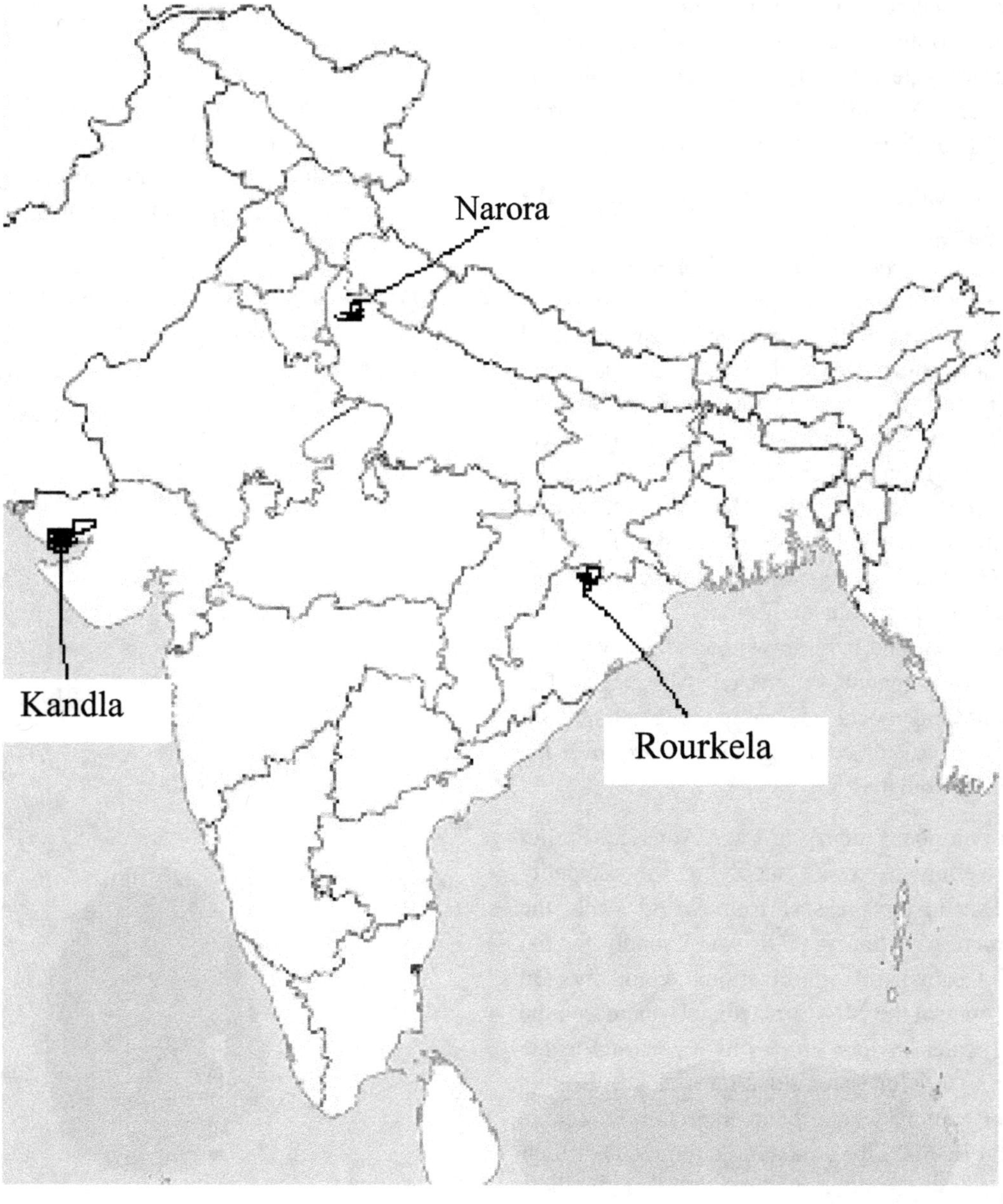

# All India 2013

# CBSE Board Solved Paper Term-II

## SECTION - A

### (Multiple Choice Questions)

(1 × 9 = 9)

1. The artisans, industrial workers and peasants revolted against which one of the following in 1848? **1**
   (a) Economic Hardship  (b) Political Instability
   (c) Monarchy  (d) Revolutionary War

   **OR**

   Who, among the following, led the Scholars Revolt of 1868, in Vietnam?
   (a) Teachers and Students
   (b) Professionals
   (c) Officials of Imperial Court
   (d) The Elites

2. Which one of the following was the main reason to withdraw Non-cooperation Movement? **1**
   (a) Movement turning violent
   (b) Leaders were tired
   (c) Satyagrahis needed to be trained
   (d) All of the above

3. India is referred to as a 'Super Power' in the world in which one of the following non- Conventional sources of energy? **1**
   (a) Solar Energy  (b) Wind Power
   (c) Bio Gas  (d) Tidal Energy

4. Which one of the following is a public interest group? **1**
   (a) BAMCEF
   (b) Railway Employees Union of India
   (c) Sarafa Bazar Union
   (d) Merchant's Union

5. Which one among the following countries has a two-party system? **1**
   (a) United Kingdom  (b) China
   (c) Indo-China  (d) Japan

6. Democracies are different from one another in terms of which one of the following? **1**
   (a) Culture  (b) Social situations
   (c) Economic activities  (d) All the above

7. Which one of the following is the main source of credit for rich urban households? **1**

   (a) Moneylenders  (b) Businessmen
   (c) Banks  (d) Self-help groups

8. Which one of the following was the main aim to form 'World Trade Organisation'? **1**
   (a) To liberalise international trade
   (b) To promote trade of rich countries
   (c) To promote trade of poor countries
   (d) To promote bilateral trade

9. Hallmark is the certification maintained for standardisation for which one of the following? **1**
   (a) Jewellery  (b) Electrical goods
   (c) Edible oil  (d) Refrigeration

## SECTION - B

### (Short Answer Questions)

(3 × 11 = 33)

10. Why was the decade of 1830s known as great economic hardship in Europe? Explain any three reasons. **3**

    **OR**

    Why was the 'Tonkin School' started in Vietnam? Explain any three reasons?

11. Explain any three measures taken by the British government to repress the movement started against the Rowlatt Act. **3**

12. Which were the two types of demands mentioned by Gandhi in his letter to Viceroy Irwin on 31 January 1930? Why was the abolition of 'salt tax' the most stirring demand? Explain. **3**

13. Explain any three objectives of the 'National Jute Policy, 2005'. **3**

14. Why is India not able to perform to her full potential in iron and steel production? Explain any three reasons. **3**

15. How are means of transport and communication complementary to each other? Explain with three examples. **3**

16. What are pressure groups? How are they different from political parties? Explain. **3**

17. How do you feel that democracy is better than any other form of government? Explain. **3**

18. Explain with examples how some countries face foundational challenge of democracy. **3**

*Note: (**) Market questions are out of syllabus so these are not explained or answered.*

**19.** How are local companies benefitted by collaborating with multinational corporations? Explain with examples.
**3**

**20.** 'Cheap and affordable credit is essential for poor households both in rural and urban areas.' In the light of the above statement, explain the social and economic values attached to it.
**3**

## SECTION - C

### (Long Answer Questions)

**(5 × 9 = 45)**

**21.** Explain the 'Right to Seek Redressal' with an example.
**5**

**22.** Describe the role of culture in shaping the feelings of nationalism in Europe from 1830 to the end of the 19th century.
**5**

**OR**

Describe any five features of the 'Go East Movement'.

**23.** Why did Gandhi start the 'Civil Disobedience Movement'? Explain any four features of the movement.
**5**

**24.** Why is it necessary to conserve mineral resources? Suggest any four ways to conserve mineral resources.
**5**

**25.** 'Advancement of the international trade of a country is an index of its economic prosperity.' Justify the statement with five arguments.
**5**

**26.** 'No party system is ideal for all countries and in all situations.' Justify the statement with five arguments.   **5**

**27.** 'Democracies do not appear to be very successful in reducing economic inequalities'. Examine the statement with examples.
**5**

**28.** What are the two categories of sources of credit? Mention four features of each.
**5**

**29.** How has improvement in technology stimulated the globalisation process? Explain with five examples.   **5**

## SECTION - D

### (Map Based Questions)

**(2 + 3 = 5)**

**30. (I)** Two features, A and B, are marked in the political outline map of India. Identify these features with the help of the following information and write their correct names on the lines marked in the map:
**2**

**(A)** The place where the Indian National Congress Session was held in 1927.

**(B)** The place where the Non-cooperation Movement was called off.

**(II)** On the same given political map of India, locate and label the following features with appropriate symbols:
**3**

**i.** Kaiga – Nuclear Power Plant
**ii.** Bhilai – Iron and Steel Centre
**iii.** Kandla – Major Sea Port

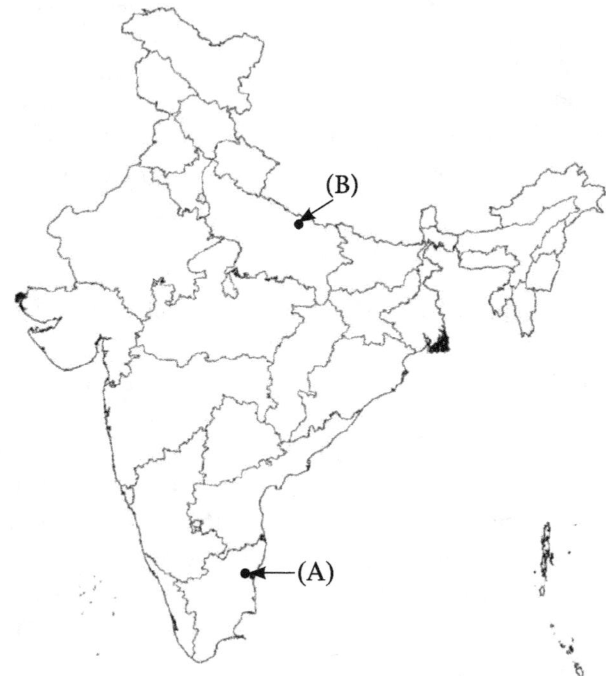

**Solutions**

**1.** **(a)** The artisans, industrial workers and peasants revolted against the economic hardships in 1848. The revolutionary war was initiated by delegates from 13 American colonies in congress against Great Britain over the objection to parliament taxation.

**OR**

**(c)** Scholar's Revolt of 1868 was mainly against imposition of Christianity in Vietnam. The Scholars Revolt of 1868 was an early revolt against French control and spread of Christianity. It was led by angry officials at the imperial court. They organized an uprising in Ngu An and Ha Tien provinces and killed nearly a thousand Catholics.

**Features:**

- It was a movement which was led by officials at the imperial court in 1868.

- The revolt was against the spread of Catholicism and French power in Vietnam.

- More than 1000 Catholics were killed in the revolt.

- The French crushed the movement, but this uprising served to inspire other patriots to rise up against them.

**2.** **(a)** Gandhi decided to withdraw the Non-Cooperation Movement due to various incidents of violence perpetrated by the masses, especially the Chauri Chaura incident in 1922 where the people clashed with the police, setting a police-station on fire.

 *Note*

*The Non-cooperation movement was a political campaign launched on 5 September 1920, by Mahatma Gandhi to have Indians revoke their cooperation from the British government, with the aim of persuading them to grant self-governance. This came as result of the Indian National Congress (INC) withdrawing its support for British reforms following the Rowlatt Act of 18 March 1919, which suspended the rights of political prisoners in sedition trials, and was seen as a "political awakening" by Indians and as a "threat" by the British, which led to the Jallianwala Bagh massacre of 13 April 1919.*

**3.** **(b)** India is referred to as a super power in wind power. The largest wind farm cluster is located in Tamil Nadu, starting from Nagarcoil and all the way to Madurai.

 *Note*

*A wind turbine turns wind energy into electricity using the aerodynamic force from the rotor blades, which work like an airplane wing or helicopter rotor blade. When wind flows across the blade, the air pressure on one side of the blade decreases. The difference in air pressure across the two sides of the blade creates both lift and drag. The force of the lift is stronger than the drag and this causes the rotor to spin. The rotor connects to the generator, either directly (if it's a direct drive turbine) or through a shaft and a series of gears (a gearbox) that speed up the rotation and allow for a physically smaller generator. This translation of aerodynamic force to rotation of a generator creates electricity.*

**4.** **(a)** BAMCEF is made up of government employees. It works towards social justice in society. It also aims for social equality in society. Human rights organisation is also an example of public interest group.

**5.** **(a)** The United Kingdom has a bi-party system. Bi-party system means that, in some countries, there are only two main parties and the power changes between the two parties only. Several other parties may exist in such countries; they might take part in the elections and secure a few seats in the national legislature. However, the majority to form the government could be secured only by one of the two main contending parties. The two major parties in the UK are the Labour Party and the Conservative Party, and in the USA, the Democratic Party and the Republican Party are the two main parties.

**6.** **(d)** Democracies are different from others in terms of culture, social situations, and economic activities. Democracies vary from one another in terms of their cultural practices, social trends, and economic pursuits. Because of this, their problems and the necessary reforms also differ. Every democratic nation is in a unique condition from every other one, and they all have pretty distinctive cultures. The social requirements, standards, and practices, as well as the kind of economic activity they engage in, differ from thosea in other democracies. However, the spirit of democracy is still about access to democratic rights and a fair system of power distribution.

**7.** **(c)** The rich urban households are usually more educated, and are thus aware of the fact that the banks give loans on a lower rate of interest. They also have better access to banks, and are not deterred by paperwork unlike the poorer sections of society.

8. **(a)** The World Trade Organization (WTO) is an intergovernmental organization that regulates and facilitates international trade. With effective cooperation in the United Nations System, governments use the organization to establish, revise, and enforce the rules that govern international trade. It officially commenced operations on 1 January 1995, pursuant to the 1994 Marrakesh Agreement, thus replacing the General Agreement on Tariffs and Trade (GATT) that had been established in 1948. The WTO is the world's largest international economic organization, with 164 member states representing over 98% of global trade and global GDP.

9. **(a)** Hallmark is a system for gold as well as silver jewellery sold in India, certifying the purity of the metal. It certifies that the piece of jewellery conforms to a set of standards laid by the Bureau of Indian Standards, the national standards organization of India. India is the second biggest market for gold and its jewellery.

10. The 1830s were the years of great economic hardship in Europe due to the following reasons-

   - There was enormous increase in population all over Europe.

   - There were more seekers of jobs than employment.

   - People migrated from rural areas to the cities to live in overcrowded slums.

OR

The Tonkin Free Schools were started in 1907. Their main aim was to provide western-style education. This education included classes in science, hygiene and French. It was not enough to acquire knowledge in science and western ideas but was also important to learn to look 'modern'.

11. Measures by British to repress Rowlatt Satyagraha:

   - British decided to stop the nationalists. Local leaders of Amritsar were arrested.

   - Mahatma Gandhi was ordered not to enter Delhi.

   - Martial law was imposed after protests in Amritsar. On 13 April, the Jallianwalla Bagh massacre happened on the orders of General Dyer.

*Rowlatt Act was passed on the recommendations of Sedition Committee chaired by Sir Sidney Rowlatt. This act had been hurriedly passed in the Imperial Legislative Council despite the united opposition of the Indian members. It gave the government enormous powers to repress political activities and allowed detention of political prisoners without trial for two years.*

12. The two types of demands mentioned by Gandhi in his letter to Viceroy Irwin on 31 January 1930 were:

   - The reduction of land revenue.

   - The abolition of the salt tax.

   But abolition of salt tax was most stirring demand because Gandhi knew that salt-tax affected all sections of society especially the poor.

13. In 2005, National Jute Policy was formulated with the objective of increasing productivity, improving quality, ensuring good prices to the jute farmers and enhancing the yield per hectare.

14. India is an important iron and steel producing country in the world yet we are not able to perform to our full potential largely due to:

   - High costs and limited availability of coking coal.

   - Lower productivity of labour.

   - Irregular supply of energy and

   - Poor Infrastructure.

15. Science and technology have radically improved communication between distant areas facilitating transport between both. For example, a person in Delhi can know the transport facilities in Odisha through communication. Transport, communication and trade are indeed complementary to each other as: transportation has allowed movement of ideas, people and technology from one country to other which helps in development. This helps in establishment of good relations with other countries.

16. Pressure groups are guided by issues which affect a certain group of people, for example, Narmada Bachao Andolan was working against construction of a dam on Narmada River which later on became a movement against dams; whereas political parties focus on almost all the matters that concern the state or nation.

*A pressure group is a group of people who are organised actively for promoting and defending their common interest. It is called so, as it attempts to bring a change in public policy by exerting pressure on the government. It acts as a liaison between the government and its members. The pressure groups are also called interest groups or vested groups. They are different from the political parties, as they neither contest elections nor try to capture political power. They are concerned with specific programmes and issues and their activities are confined to the protection and promotion of the interests of their members by influencing the government.*

**17.** A democratic government is a better government because it is an accountable form of government. Democracy improves the quality of decision making. Democracy provides a method to deal with differences and conflicts. Democracy enhances the dignity of citizens.

**18.** Certain mindsets and systems will take years to change as they have taken years to develop. Nepal is a very good example of foundational challenge of democracy. India faced this problem after the independence and Pakistan is still facing this problem due to military interference in the government.

**19.** Many MNCs collaborate with local companies of the host country to invest and expand their businesses. In such collaborations, MNCs get entry into a new market. On the other hand, the local companies gain additional investments and access to the latest technology.

**20.** Cheap and affordable credit is essential for Poor households in rural areas because it helps the poor farmers or poor people living there to get loans and then they can invest in either farming or nonfarm activities. The cheap word tells that the interest rate would be low so at the end they have to pay less money.

**21.** Right to seek redressal means the right to demand redress in the event of unfair trade practices or market manipulation. It also requires the right to a just resolution of a consumer's genuine grievances. Consumers must file a lawsuit whether they have legitimate complaints. For example, a consumer has bought a pressure cooker with a faulty safety valve. This has caused him severe damage. He has the right to seek redressal from the company that has manufactured this pressure cooker.

**22.** Culture played an important role in creating the idea of the nation, art and poetry, stories and music helped to express and shape nationalist feelings. Romanticism a cultural movement which sought to develop a particular form of nationalist sentiment. Romantic artists and poets generally criticized the glorification of reason and science and focused instead on emotions, intuition and mystical feelings. German philosopher Johann Gottfried Herder claimed that true German culture was to be discovered among the common people. It was through folk songs, folk poetry and folk dances that the true spirit of a nation was popularized.

**OR**

In the first decade of the twentieth century a 'go east movement' became popular. Go East Movement was movement which was launched in the first decade of the twentieth century in Vietnam. The movement becomes popular because early Vietnamese nationalists had a close relationship with Japan and China. They provided models for those looking to change, a refuge for those who were escaping French police, and a location where a wider Asian network of revolutionaries could be established

*Culture encompasses the social behavior, institutions, and norms found in human societies, as well as the knowledge, beliefs, arts, laws, customs, capabilities, and habits of the individuals in these groups. Culture is often originated from or attributed to a specific region or location. Humans acquire culture through the learning processes of enculturation and socialization, which is shown by the diversity of cultures across societies. A cultural norm codifies acceptable conduct in society; it serves as a guideline for behavior, dress, language, and demeanor in a situation, which serves as a template for expectations in a social group. Accepting only a monoculture in a social group can bear risks, just as a single species can wither in the face of environmental change, for lack of functional responses to the change.*

**23.** This was the first nationwide movement while all others were restricted to urban areas. People among rural areas also had an opportunity to register their participation. The participation of women was in large numbers. Four features of the civil disobedience movement-

- Defiance of salt laws,

- Boycott of liquor,

- Boycott of foreign cloth and British goods of all kinds,

- Non-payment of taxes and revenues.

**24.** Mineral resources should be conserved because the geological process of mineral formation is quite slow due to which the rate of replenishment is infinitely small whereas the rate of consumption is quite high. Mineral resources found on the earth surface are limited in number and are exhaustible. Minerals are a non-renewable resource and finite. The geological processes of mineral formation are so slow that the rates of replenishment are infinitely small in comparison to the present rates of consumption.

*Note*

*A Mineral Resource is a concentration or occurrence of solid material of economic interest in or on the Earth's crust in such form, grade or quality and quantity that there are reasonable prospects for eventual economic extraction. Mineral Resources are subdivided, in order of increasing geological confidence, into Inferred, Indicated and Measured Mineral Resources, as indicated in Figure below. A Mineral Reserve is the economically mineable part of a Measured and/or Indicated Mineral Resource. It includes diluting materials and allowances for losses, which may occur when the material is mined or extracted and is defined by studies at Pre-Feasibility or Feasibility level as appropriate that include application of Modifying Factors. Such studies demonstrate that, at the time of reporting, extraction could reasonably be justified.*

**25.** International trade allows countries to expand their markets and access goods and services that otherwise may not have been available domestically. As a result of international trade, the market is more competitive. This ultimately results in more competitive pricing and brings a cheaper product home to the consumer. Advancement of international trade of a country is an index to its economic prosperity. Foreign trade or international trade is the exchange of goods and services between countries. It is an important component of the economy.

**26.** No party system is ideal for all countries and all situations. It is because no country chooses its party system; it evolves over a long time depending on the nature of the society. A party system relies on a country's social and regional division, its history of policies, and its system of elections. The absence of political parties would mean that there would be no formal representation of different interest groups in the government. This would make it difficult for the government to understand and address the concerns of different sections of society. Party system

is not something any country can choose. It evolves depending on the nature of society, its social and regional divisions, its history of politics and system of elections. Each country develops a party system that is conditioned by its special circumstances.

**27.** Democracies do not appear to be very successful in reducing economic inequality. The economic imbalance between the rich and the poor is increasing in democratic countries. Governments can intervene to promote equity, and reduce inequality and poverty, through the tax and benefits system. This means employing a progressive tax and benefits system which takes proportionately more tax from those on higher levels of income, and redistributes welfare benefits to those on lower incomes. The poor constitute a large proportion of our voters and no party likes to lose their votes, yet democratically elected governments have not addressed the question of poverty as one would have expected them to. The people in several poor countries are now dependent on the rich countries even for food supplies.

*Note*

*Democracy is broadly understood to mean 'rule by the people'. In practice, it is often defined as people choosing their leaders in free and fair elections. Other definitions go beyond this. For example, some of them see democracy as people having additional individual rights and being protected from the state. Democracy gives citizens the right to influence important decisions over their own lives and allows them to hold their leaders accountable. But it can have other benefits too: democratic countries seem better governed than autocracies, seem to grow faster, and foster more peaceful conduct within and between them.*

**28.** The two sources of credit are formal sources and informal sources: Formal sources of credit: Banks and cooperative societies fall under the formal sector. One can obtain loans from banks or cooperative societies. The informal sector credit includes all those credit sources that do not have any organization to supervise them. Local landlords and friends are examples of informal sources of credit.

**29.** Technical equipment as cell phone, internet, telephone and microchip have contributed to globalization by exchanging ideas, capital and people to make convenient to move from one place to another as a fast pace to stimulate the process of globalization. With the help of internet we can find anything on single click. Transportation technology has stimulated the globalization process in the following ways: Faster trains connecting every nook and corner of a country and faster planes that cover the distance within a few hours have enabled the faster delivery of goods. Globalization is defined as the set of processes (economic, social, cultural, technological, and institutional) that contribute to the relationship between societies and individuals around the world.

**30.** (1) A – Indian national congress session was held in 127 at - Madras (Chennai)

*Note*

*The Indian National Congress was founded at Bombay in December 1885. The early leadership – Dadabhai Naoroji, Pherozeshah Mehta, Badruddin Tyabji, W.C. Bonnerji, Surendranath Banerji, Romesh Chandra Dutt, S. Subramania Iyer, among others – was largely from Bombay and Calcutta. A retired British official, A.O. Hume, also played a part in bringing Indians from the various regions together. Formation of Indian National Congress was an effort in the direction of promoting the process of nation building. In an effort to reach all regions, it was decided to rotate the Congress session among different parts of the country.*

B – Non cooperation movement was called off at -  Chauri Chaura in Uttar Pradesh

(2)

- Kaiga – Nuclear Power Plant
- Bhilai- Iron and Steel Centre
- Kandla – Major Sea Port

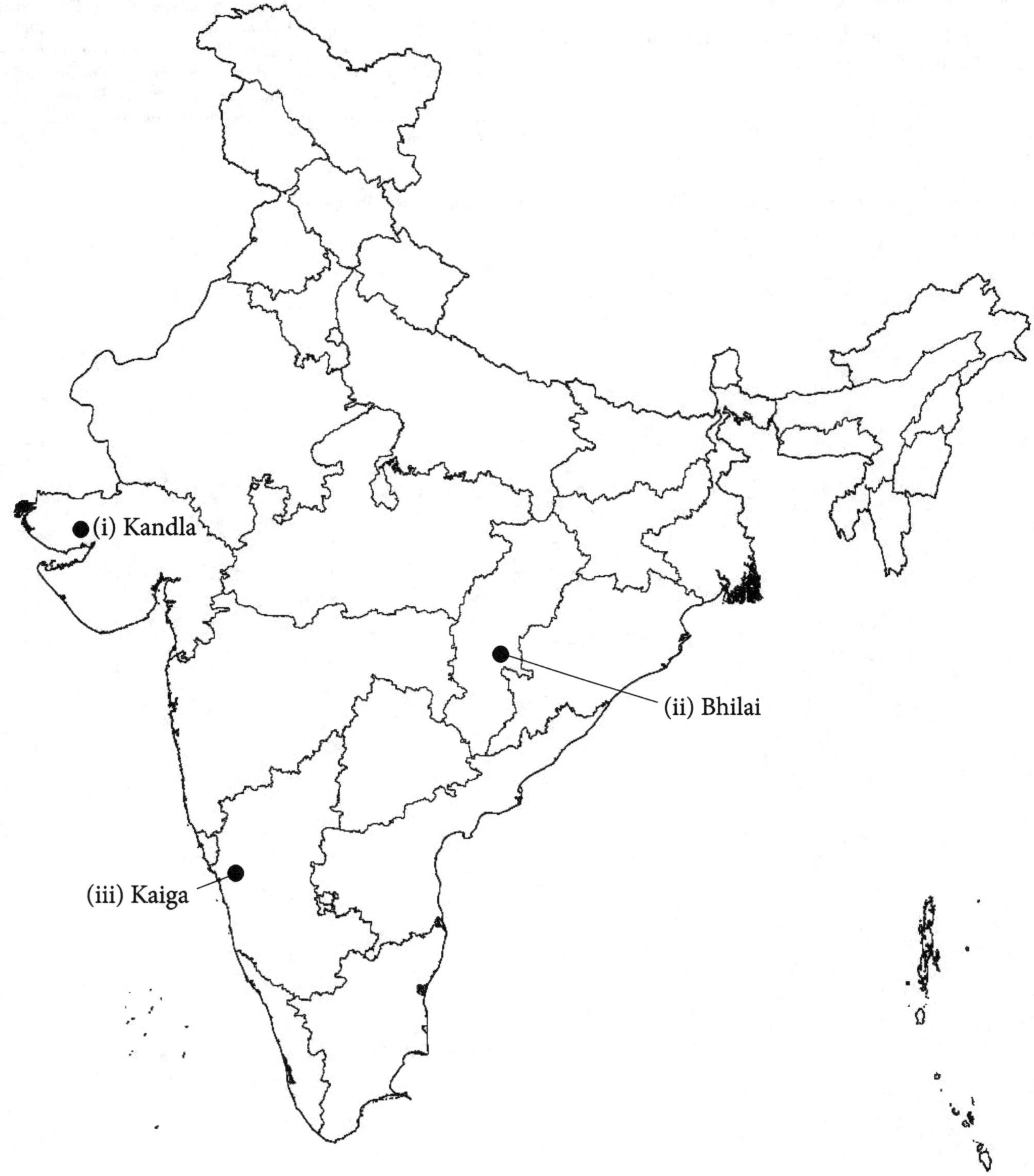